'This is a unique and important book, and one of the most comp~~~~~~ ~r conducting replicated single-case experiments t~ ~ ~ l curious clinicians and scientist practitioners who v evidence-based way. It provides not only the the~ trial", but also elegantly provides building blocks person-focused single-case experimental designs in

Johan W.S. Vlaeyen, *Professor of Be* , ~~~~~gy
Research, University of Leuven, Be~ ~~~~~~ University, Netherlands

'This impressive textbook distils Professor Morley's lifetime expertise into a single, easily accessible resource – an essential read for trainees and professionals in clinical psychology and related fields.'

Chris Barker, *Professor of Clinical Psychology, University College London*

'This superb book is a must-read for all applied psychologists and students. In it, Stephen Morley successfully integrates methodology and purpose in Single Case Design (SCD) with deceptive ease. Its clarity and focus makes this book the definitive work for single case studies and single case experimental design. It clearly captures the essence and value of SCD in both clinical and research contexts in a highly readable way, and will be the definitive text in the field. This book successfully re-invigorates our understanding of a crucial research tool in psychology.'

Paul Salkovskis, *Professor of Clinical Psychology and Applied Science, University of Bath*

'This highly accessible book starts with classic concepts in experimental design from the 60's and finishes with current debates on research synthesis. In between it covers key issues in measurement, design and analysis so that readers can make informed decisions and actually conduct high quality single case research. There are examples, "how to" sections, and a wealth of practical advice from a lifelong champion of applied clinical research. Next time a student or colleague asks me about a tricky issue in design or analysis, I will simply send them to Stephen Morley's book.'

Mark H. Freeston, *Ph.D., Head of Research and Development,*
Newcastle Cognitive and Behavioural Therapies Centre

Single-Case Methods in Clinical Psychology

Single-Case Methods in Clinical Psychology: A Practical Guide provides a concise and easily accessible introduction to single-case research. This is a timely response to the increasing awareness of the need to look beyond randomised controlled trials for evidence to support best practice in applied psychology. The book covers the issues of design, the reliability and validity of measurement, and provides guidance on how to analyse single-case data using both visual and statistical methods.

Single-case designs can be used to investigate an individual's response to psychological intervention, as well as to contribute to larger-scale research projects. This book illuminates the common principles behind these uses. It describes how standardised measures can be used to evaluate change in an individual and how to develop idiographic measures that are tailored to the needs of an individual. The issues of replication and generalising beyond an individual are examined, and the book also includes a section on the meta-analysis of single-case data. The critical evaluation of single-case research is examined, from both the perspective of developing quality standards to evaluate research and maintaining a critical distance in reviewing one's own work.

Single-Case Methods in Clinical Psychology will provide invaluable guidance to postgraduate psychologists training to enter the professions of clinical, health and counselling psychology and is likely to become a core text on many courses. It will also appeal to clinicians seeking to answer questions about the effectiveness of therapy in individual cases and who wish to use the method to further the evidence base for specific psychological interventions.

Stephen Morley (1950–2017) was Professor of Clinical Psychology and former director of the clinical psychology training programme at the University of Leeds. He was best known for his research work on pain, for which he was awarded honorary membership of the International Association for the Study of Pain in 2016. He taught generations of trainee clinical psychologists, delivered many workshops and wrote several book chapters on the topic of single-case methods.

Ciara Masterson is a Lecturer in Clinical Psychology at the University of Leeds.

Chris J. Main is an Emeritus Professor of Clinical Psychology at Keele University.

Single-Case Methods in Clinical Psychology

A Practical Guide

Stephen Morley

Edited by
Ciara Masterson and Chris J. Main

Routledge
Taylor & Francis Group

LONDON AND NEW YORK

First published 2018
by Routledge
2 Park Square, Milton Park, Abingdon, Oxon OX14 4RN

and by Routledge
711 Third Avenue, New York, NY 10017

Routledge is an imprint of the Taylor & Francis Group, an informa business

British Library Cataloguing in Publication Data
A catalogue record for this book is available from the British Library

Library of Congress Cataloging in Publication Data
Names: Morley, Stephen, author. | Masterson, Ciara, editor. | Main, Chris J., editor.
Title: Single-case methods in clinical psychology : a practical guide / Stephen Morley ; edited by Ciara Masterson and Chris J. Main.
Description: Abingdon, Oxon ; New York, NY : Routledge, 2018. | Includes bibliographical references.
Identifiers: LCCN 2017035717 | ISBN 9781138211490 (hardback) | ISBN 9781138211506 (pbk.) | ISBN 9781315412917 (e-pub) | ISBN 9781315412900 (mobipocket)
Subjects: | MESH: Psychology, Clinical – methods | Case Management – standards
Classification: LCC RC467 | NLM WM 105 | DDC 616.89 – dc23
LC record available at https://lccn.loc.gov/2017035717

ISBN: 978-1-138-21149-0 (hbk)
ISBN: 978-1-138-21150-6 (pbk)
ISBN: 978-1-315-41293-1 (ebk)

Typeset in Frutiger and Joanna
by Florence Production Ltd, Stoodleigh, Devon, UK
Printed and bound by CPI Group (UK) Ltd, Croydon, CR0 4YY

Contents

Tables

Figures

Preface

Studying individuals has been the bedrock of clinical psychology for as long as it has existed as a discipline. Narratives about individuals, their problems and how pioneering therapists helped them are plentiful, and these narratives provide useful ways of learning about therapy. Accounts of single cases can go beyond descriptive narrative accounts, and the development of psychometric methods allowed quantitative elements to be incorporated (Payne & Jones, 1957). Shapiro (1961, 1966) describes the development of single-case research within clinical psychology, but it remained for the advent of applied behaviour analysis in the 1960s to provide a set of research designs (Baer, Wolf & Risley, 1968) that remain the basis of experimental single-case research today. The combination of careful measurement on repeated occasions and systematic manipulation of treatment conditions enables clinician-researchers to make inferences about causality: such inferences are not possible from purely narrative accounts. One of the attractions of single-case research is its explicit recognition of the individual; the person who is essentially lost in the aggregation of data that occurs in randomised controlled trials.

Single-Case Methods in Clinical Psychology: A Practical Guide is written primarily for postgraduate psychologists training to enter the professions of clinical, health and counselling psychology, although I hope it will be of interest to anyone with an interest in single-case methods. Many trainees want to do outcome research and they are naturally curious about the effectiveness of psychological treatments. Developments in the methodology and design of randomised control trials now mean that high-quality trials (including feasibility studies) cannot be realistically done by an individual as part of a dissertation or thesis. Single-case research methods provide a usable alternative for those students interested in exploring the effects of treatments. Students are frequently required to submit case reports for examination and adopt quantitative methods, and single-case designs can facilitate judgements about causal processes in treatment.

Single-Case Methods in Clinical Psychology is not designed to be the definitive text – it is a short introduction to single-case research. I hope it will enable those new to the field to grasp the basic methods and issues in the field. More expansive texts are those by Barlow, Nock and Hersen (2009) and Kazdin (2010). The notable feature of both of these texts is that they devote separate chapters to each of the basic single-case designs discussed in Chapter 4 of *Single-Case Methods in Clinical Psychology*. Both Kazdin and Barlow *et al.* include many examples exploring the nuances of a particular design, and any student seriously intending to pursue single-case research should consult these. There are several other places where the current text differs from previous texts. First, it considers a rather broader range of measures. Most texts on single-case methodology focus on measures (obtained by direct observation of behaviour, which reflects the origins of single-case designs in applied behaviour analysis). *Single-Case Methods in Clinical Psychology* considers measures of subjective states via self-report in more depth. Second, the chapters on analysis are divided into separate sections on visual and statistical analysis and they place an emphasis on how to do it – albeit with a limited set of applications. *Single-Case Methods in Clinical Psychology* also includes material on the developing field of meta-analysis in single-case research. The final chapter in the book examines the evaluation of single-case studies so that the student can learn to critically appraise published research and their own studies.

After several years in the doldrums, single-case research shows evidence of a revival. This may be because the method has been included in recent evidence-based guidelines (Kratochwill *et al.*, 2013; Tate *et al.*, 2016; Vohra *et al.*, 2015), and there has been a notable upsurge of publications exploring new methods for the statistical analysis of single-case data.

A PERSONAL NOTE

My introduction to single-case methods happened early in my career as a psychologist. As an undergraduate and postgraduate I was lucky enough to have some inspired teachers. Tim Shallice was not the most fluent of lecturers but he could transmit a sense of intellectual curiosity. The second-year course on cognitive psychology could have been as dull as ditchwater, but Shallice made it thrilling as he gave us progress reports on an experimental neuropsychological study of a man with no apparent short-term memory (Shallice & Warrington, 1970). A few years later I began training as a clinical psychologist at the Institute of Psychiatry, London (now the Institute of Psychiatry, Psychology & Neuroscience) and was introduced to single-case methodology in two forms. First, I was allocated to Monte Shapiro as his clinical tutee. He supervised my early faltering attempts as a clinician and introduced me to the idea of idiographic measures and thinking about clients as exemplars of general psychological principles. Shapiro also encouraged a sense of enquiry. I learned that ignorance was OK, but not doing something about it was unacceptable. He frequently said he didn't know the answer to a particular question and packed me off to the library to find out. My enquiries became the focus of our next supervision session. I read Sidman's *Psychological Bulletin* critique of group data (Sidman, 1952) and then his classic text on methodology, 'Tactics of scientific research: evaluating experimental data in psychology' (Sidman, 1960). At the same time that I was being mentored by Shapiro, Bill Yule returned from a visit to the USA where he had been to study applied behaviour analysis. He introduced me to the writings of Baer and his colleagues (Baer *et al.*, 1968) that defined the set of 'simple' single-case designs that form the bedrock of Chapter 4. I also explored the developing statistical methods for time-series analysis (Jones, Vaught & Weinrott, 1977). They seemed to promise a great deal at the time but ultimately I think this proved to be limited (Chapter 6).

ACKNOWLEDGEMENTS

I have taught single-case methods to trainee clinical psychologists over many years, and this small book is the result of these endeavours. So my first thanks go to the many students at the University of Leeds who have patiently humoured me by engaging in teaching sessions with good grace and open minds. Also many thanks to my colleagues, past and present, on the University of Leeds clinical psychology training programme. They have been a wonderful source of support and fun over the years. In particular I must thank Gary Latchford, Dean McMillan and Stephen Barton.

My good friend Johan Vlaeyen has given me an opportunity to present material on single-case methods to the Dutch postgraduate school on a couple of occasions, and we have had many discussions about the role of single-case methods since then. He and his colleagues (especially Jeroen de Jong) have produced a superb set of single-case series on the fear-avoidance model for chronic pain, and generously allowed me access to their data. Aspects of this are discussed in Chapter 7.

While I was planning this book I was saddened to hear that my friend Malcolm Adams had died unexpectedly a few months before he planned to retire. Malcolm was an exceptional person; his organisational and diplomatic skills made him a natural leader for clinical psychologists involved in postgraduate training in the UK. He was also a good friend, with methodological and statistical nous that I unashamedly plundered on numerous occasions, and we collaborated on a couple of occasions to write papers on the analysis of single-case data.

My colleague Clare Dowzer is a fount of knowledge on all things related to Excel, and her help in developing the Leeds Reliable Change Calculator (Chapter 2) was invaluable. Dave Green, a long-time colleague, allowed me to ramble on about measurement issues and many other things over the years. I value his wisdom, joie de vivre, companionship and friendship. Patrick Onghena provided encouragement in writing the chapter on statistical analysis. A special note of thanks must go to people who kindly read and commented on the manuscript. Chris Main and Ciara Masterson gave invaluable advice and guidance, Matt Price kindly read it from the point of view of a clinical psychology student and Jenny Limond kindly gave me encouragement by commenting on the manuscript. Finally, I owe a huge debt of thanks to Alison, who has had to put up with 'the book' for more time than either she or I would wish: thank you.

Stephen Morley, April 2017, Leeds

REFERENCES

Baer, D. M., Wolf, M. M. & Risley, T. R. (1968). Some current dimensions of applied behavior analysis. *Journal of Applied Behavior Analysis*, 1(1), 91–7.

✳ Barlow, D. H., Nock, M. K. & Hersen, M. (2009). *Single Case Experimental Designs* (3rd edn). Boston: Pearson.

Jones, R. R., Vaught, R. S. & Weinrott, M. R. (1977). Time-series analysis on operant research. *Journal of Applied Behavior Analysis*, 10, 151–66.

✳ Kazdin, A. E. (2010). *Single-Case Research Designs: Methods for Clinical and Applied Settings* (2nd edn). Oxford: Oxford University Press.

Kratochwill, T. R., Hitchcock, J. H., Horner, R. H., Levin, J. R., Odom, S. L., Rindskopf, D. M. & Shadish, W. R. (2013). Single-Case Intervention Research Design Standards. *Remedial and Special Education*, 34(1), 26–38.

Payne, R. W. & Jones, H. G. (1957). Statistics for the investigation of individual cases. *Journal of Clinical Psychology*, 13(2), 115–21.

Shallice, T. & Warrington, E. K. (1970). Independent functioning of verbal memory stores: a neuropsychological study. *Quarterly Journal of Experimental Psychology*, 22(2), 261–73.

Shapiro, M. B. (1961). The single case in fundamental clinical psychological research. *British Journal of Medical Psychology*, 34, 255–62.

Shapiro, M. B. (1966). The single case in clinical psychological research. *Journal of General Psychology*, 74, 3–23.

Sidman, M. (1952). A note on functional relations obtained from group data. *Psychological Bulletin*, 49(3), 263–9.

Sidman, M. (1960). *Tactics of Scientific Research: Evaluating Experimental Data in Psychology*. New York: Basic Books.

Tate, R. L., Perdices, M., Rosenkoetter, U., Shadish, W., Vohra, S., Barlow, D. H. & Wilson, B. (2016). The Single-Case Reporting Guideline In BEhavioural Interventions (SCRIBE) 2016 statement. *Archives of Scientific Psychology*, 4(1), 1–9.

Vohra, S., Shamseer, L., Sampson, M., Bukutu, C., Schmid, C. H., Tate, R. & Moher, D. (2015). CONSORT extension for reporting N-of-1 trials (CENT) 2015 Statement. *BMJ*, 350, h1738.

Foreword

Sadly, Stephen Morley passed away before this book was quite finished. At his request we saw the book through to production, and in the final editorial polishing we have attempted to finish the book in the way Stephen would have wished. We should like to thank Carolyn Main for help with proofreading; Matt Price for his comments on Chapter 8; Clare Dowzer for her help with tables and figures and Ben Mitchell for proofreading, equation-checking and particularly helpful contributions to Chapter 6. Inevitably there will be slip-ups for which we have to take responsibility. We have added a short afterword in an attempt to capture the essence of the discussions we had with Stephen over his last few months regarding his intent in writing the book. We share his aspiration for a revival of interest in single-case methodology and its use in research and clinical practice.

Chris Main and Ciara Masterson

Chapter 1

Why single-case research?

We live in an era of 'big data' (Mayer-Schönberger & Cukier, 2013). The technology to acquire information on almost any aspect of our lives and to aggregate and analyse the data permeates our daily experience. Supermarkets collect information on our consumer preferences, Amazon recommends objects of desire to us, and our medical records are collated and analysed. Anonymised big data sets are freely available and provide a narrative on our society (Rogers, 2013). In clinical research improved statistical methods, data management and willingness on the part of research funders to pay for randomised controlled trials (RCTs) have resulted in a proliferation of large, multi-centre trials in almost every area of health care. The results of these trials are then aggregated with ever more sophisticated meta-analytic techniques and meta-regression to determine the impact of stratification or confounding factors. Governmental expert working groups convene to pore over the data to produce national guidelines, which may or may not be contentious. Although people vary in their response to treatment, these processes produce guidelines for the average case.

The evidence base derived from trials is almost certainly better than the evidence of expert opinion or clinical anecdote, and our understanding of what constitutes biased evidence is undoubtedly more sophisticated than it was a generation ago. Why is this important? Because we are able to exercise greater critical appreciation and scepticism and to consider what factors, other than the ones that we favour (e.g. the specific effects of a drug or a psychological intervention), account for the results. There are benefits to this; treatments with likely harmful consequences can be eliminated, health services can proscribe ineffective treatments, whether it is a drug or a psychological intervention, and cheap generic drug formulations can replace expensive proprietorial ones.

In the field of psychology the yardstick used to judge many of these effects is the average and, by implication, a significant proportion of the people treated will do worse than the average. Not a great selling point. The gerontologist John Grimley Evans (Grimley Evans, 1995) put the position more elegantly, 'Managers and trialists may be happy for treatments to work on average; patients expect doctors to do better than that'. The advantages of randomised controlled clinical trials are well known. They control many potential biases and exclude significant plausible competing hypotheses for the observed effects, but their limitations are also worthy of consideration (Westen, Novotny & Thompson-Brenner, 2004). For example, the selection criteria for enrolment in a trial often exclude a considerable number of potential participants (Schulz, Altman & Moher, 2010). As a consequence, many of the trials which form the basis for generic guidelines may be based on clinical samples that are highly selected, although large pragmatic trials partly overcome this constraint. In the field of psychological treatments the double-blind protocol, where neither the recipients of treatment nor the therapists are informed of the treatment being given, is impossible to implement in any meaningful way. Moreover it is neither feasible nor ethical to implement such a protocol in day-to-day clinical practice.

Double-Blind with therapy research not ethical or practical

Nevertheless RCTs, systematic reviews and meta-analyses are invaluable. The output from research using these methods provides replicable evidence for determining health policy but the immense power of these methods, combined with government-sanctioned guidelines, carries the danger of reducing the clinician to a passive consumer of 'health technology' rather than a professional actively engaged in the application and production of knowledge. Clinicians need tools both to deliver good health care and to generate robust practice-based evidence (Barkham, Hardy & Mellor-Clark, 2010) and single-case methods offer one such suite of tools (McMillan & Morley, 2010).

Just prior to a visit from the external quality assurance agency to the hospital where I contributed clinical sessions, staff were sent a memo. We were reminded to make sure that we were familiar with the current National Institute for Health and Care Excellence (NICE) guidelines for a range of disorders. It was anticipated that the staff might be asked about these. The implication was that knowledge of the guidelines was the guarantee that we would deliver a quality service. I felt more than a little uneasy about this. The work of the psychologists in this hospital was primarily concerned with people of all ages with a wide range of physical illnesses and problems: cancers, diabetes, cystic fibrosis, nephrology, urology, head injury and neuro-rehabilitation, epilepsies, reconstructive and plastic surgery, cardiac diseases, trauma, reproductive health, HIV and sexual medicine, and almost anything else in the realm of physical illness. It seemed to me that the chance of each of these being served by meta-analytic evidence for every common psychological complaint was remote. So the presence of relevant guidelines based on specific evidence seemed unlikely. I suspected that I and my clinical colleagues rarely saw prototypical textbook cases. The range of psychological problems varies enormously across clients, but the psychological processes involved in adjusting to potentially severe long-term health threats may be very similar across individuals with different physical disorders.

It is in this context of variability of the psychological impact on illness and the person's response to it that we must place the content of this book. Single-case methodology does have a place in clinical practice and research and offers a way of addressing these concerns. Given the current *zeitgeist*, it is unlikely that single-case research will usurp the randomised controlled trial, but it should be more prominent in both the development and evaluation of treatment (Schork, 2015). Replication of a treatment protocol across several patients, therapists and clinical settings (Heyvaert, Maes, Van den Noortgate, Kuppens & Onghena, 2012; Vlaeyen, Morley, Linton, Boersma & de Jong, 2012; Wright et al., 2015) provides evidence that a treatment has potential and is generalisable across relevant settings. Indeed where basic behavioural science has established the parameters and mechanisms of a phenomenon, it may not even be necessary to run an RCT. For example, Johnson and Pennypacker (1980) documented the development of time-out from reinforcement (recently popularised as the 'naughty step') as an effective punishment protocol in several species, including humans, so that there appeared to be no need for an RCT. Since Johnson and Pennypacker's 1980 analysis, time-out protocols have been included as a component of parent management packages (e.g. Cartwright-Hatton *et al.*, 2011; Kazdin, 1997), but there does not appear to be a trial of time-out on its own. Similarly Barlow, Nock and Hersen (2009) document the effectiveness of differential attention as an effective reinforcer, especially in the context of children's behavioural difficulties. The evidence for this was accrued over many replications using single-case methodology. Curious clinicians cannot perform RCTs to answer their questions about the outcomes of individual clients or the processes occurring in therapy. Clinicians want to know whether an intervention will work with a particular client, and randomised controlled trials cannot provide the answer. Fortunately single-case methods offer a clinically practicable, scientifically valid and credible alternative to supplement mainstream methods, and replicated experimental case series may offer a credible alternative to randomised controlled trials in some settings.

WHY THIS BOOK?

This book is written primarily for postgraduate students in clinical, health and counselling psychology as an introduction to quantitative single-case methods. Many students starting this stage of their career will have learned about basic research and statistical methods, but usually this learning will have been restricted to group-based methods and few will have encountered single-case research methods. Despite this, most training programmes will require students to complete case studies, often with a quantitative element. Such case studies provide an excellent vehicle for learning about clinical problems, but they can also be a vehicle for learning about research methods and how to use single cases to ask big questions in the field of psychological treatments. Students are also required to complete a research thesis. Many students are interested in therapy and helping people change, but few of their research theses broach this area. Perhaps in an environment dominated by randomised controlled trials, options for treatment-related research are seen as limited, but single-case research methods give the interested student an opportunity to engage in treatment research with the limited resources at their disposal.

Although students may be superficially familiar with basic psychometric concepts such as reliability and validity, they will often not know how to apply these ideas, for example to determine the error around a single score. Most of their experience will be with nomothetic measurements in the form of questionnaires and tests and the concept of idiographic measurement, i.e. a measure uniquely tailored to the individual, common in single-case research, will be unfamiliar. The experimental designs, the sequencing of observational conditions and the logic of the designs used in single-case research to rule out alternative plausible explanations for the pattern results will also be unfamiliar. Analysing single-case data requires some technical knowledge of methods not normally taught at undergraduate level, although the basic principle of careful description, including visual display of the data, followed by appropriate analysis, is the same as in group-based studies.

This book aims to address each of the building blocks needed to plan, conduct and analyse single-case research and the text aims to provide examples of 'how to do it' rather than merely reporting them in the abstract, and this is especially apparent in the sections on standardised measures (Chapter 2), idiographic measures (Chapter 3) and visual and statistical analysis (Chapters 5 and 6).

PURPOSES OF CASE STUDIES AND CASE EXPERIMENTS

Case studies in applied psychology come in several forms and have a variety of purposes. Hilliard (1993) distinguished between three basic categories of single-case research: (a) case studies, (b) single-case quantitative analyses and (c) single-case experiments.

Case studies

Case studies are primarily narrative and contain qualitative data. On the whole, case studies do not provide quantitative data and are usually concerned with providing a descriptive and interpretative account of what has happened in therapy. There is no formal attempt to experimentally manipulate the treatment and the account is essentially one based on passive observations. Nevertheless, cases studies and case report series have often formed the launch pad for influential therapeutic schools. One only has to think of the impact of Breuer and Freud's *Studies in Hysteria*, or Wolpe's description of systematic desensitisation (Breuer & Freud, 1955; Wolpe, 1958). These classic studies vary in their derivation; Breuer and Freud relied on clinical observations whereas Wolpe was guided by a series of laboratory studies. Nevertheless in neither instance did, nor could, an RCT pioneer the therapy. While trials of therapies are undoubtedly important sources of information for most clinicians, they do not seem to be the usual way in which clinical knowledge is acquired and assimilated. When trials are discussed in journal clubs, the focus is on critical appraisal and often the shortfalls of the trial are given priority consideration. Clinicians are more likely to discuss the details of problematic cases than an RCT. We do not teach clinical skills by asking students to read and absorb clinical trial data where the emphasis is on the average response. We provide a range of clinical examples and case vignettes to illustrate clinical phenomena and specific therapeutic tactics and, possibly, assessments of effectiveness and outcomes.

   Cases studies are the clinician's natural narrative in supervision or informally over coffee with a colleague. It is the clinical content of a case that keeps one awake at night, not the flaws in the design or method of the latest RCT. Similarly in teaching therapy we do not narrate the protocol of the trial, or the 'on the average' effect of a complex treatment. We narrate and discuss procedures in the context of individual examples and variations. The downside of this is that we may be too willing to listen and read about the latest successes with a 'new' therapy, especially in hard-to-treat cases. We may suspend or fail to employ our critical powers in evaluating new treatments, whether they are from a meta-analytic review, a single RCT or a series of cases (Lilienfeld, Ritschel, Lynn, Cautin & Latzman, 2014). As noted by Lilienfeld *et al.*, it is easy to fool ourselves about the effectiveness of treatment. Thus one aim of this book is to guard against this by developing a critical understanding of case studies.

Case studies may also play a critical role in the assessment of professional competence. In training programmes students are frequently required to write a case study or present a portfolio of cases to demonstrate their competence. Leaving aside the question of whether this written presentation is the best form of establishing competence (direct observation and session transcripts would be superior), the presentation of a written account does offer some benefits. It allows the student to provide a more measured, off-line, critical reflection and appraisal of their work than they are able to in the heat of the moment. The inculcation of critical thinking in the choice of assessment, measurement, determining when to take observations, implementation of treatment, relevant data analytic skills and reflective evaluation is surely essential in producing thoughtful professionals: professionals who will be less easily swayed by the seemingly compelling narrative around the 'new' therapy, especially when it is based on few cases and poor-quality case studies.

Single-case quantitative analysis

Hilliard (1993) used the term *single-case quantitative analysis* to apply to cases where quantitative data had been collected and analysed but where there was no attempt to directly manipulate any of the variables concerned. Examples of this might be the tracking of aspects of the therapeutic alliance, monitoring sessional estimates of progress towards outcome goals across a course of therapy or determining how two measures of therapy process co-vary, e.g. a therapeutic motivational interviewing statement and subsequent statement of intent to change. Such data can be subjected to a range of relatively sophisticated statistical analyses to test or generate hypotheses. I would also add a very common occurrence to Hilliard's category of single-case quantitative analysis, and that is the evaluation of pre- to post-treatment change as assessed by standardised outcome measures, now required by many clinical services. Here the investigator simply wants to know whether the individual has changed after a period of treatment but there is no attempt to determine whether treatment is responsible for the change. It is a common feature in case studies and there is robust method for analysing such data, which is presented in Chapter 2.

Single-case experiments

In the third category, *single-case experiments*, Hilliard (1993) identified studies where there are quantitative data with direct manipulation of the intervention and where the combination of these two features in the form of an experimental design would enable one to draw a valid conclusion about the impact of treatment on the outcome of interest. Single-case experiments always involve multiple measurements of the outcome variable over time, and this distinguishes them from the simple pre-treatment–post-treatment measurement case in the single-case quantitative analysis. The focus of this book is primarily on case studies that are quantitative and include repeated measures, a formal approach to the design of data collection in an attempt to rule out plausible alternative explanations, and that use systematic visual and/or statistical analytic methods. Single-case experiments provide a set of methodologically acceptable tools for evaluating efficacy and effectiveness in the clinical context where RCTs cannot be implemented.

Quantitative single-case research has a long history in clinical and applied psychology, and Kazdin's (2010) and Barlow, Nock and Hersen's (2009) classic texts provide an overview of the history. The field has been dominated by methods derived from applied behaviour analysis that emerged in the 1960s. Applied behaviour analysis is typified by: (1) a focus on directly observable behaviour most frequently quantified as count data, i.e. the frequency of occurrence per unit of time; (2) an experimental approach that strives to control the environment as much as possible in order to exclude confounding variables; (3) an attempt to ensure that the baseline behaviour is stable before introducing the treatment, i.e. there is minimal fluctuation; (4) treatments that are based on reinforcement principles; and (5) a reliance on visual analysis (Gast, 2010). While the current text is influenced by applied behaviour analysis, I take a rather broader view on what single-case methods include. This view is captured in Figure 1.1.

In Figure 1.1 the single case is seen as a potentially rich record of material (Elliott, 2002) in which observations can be made at a number of levels over time. There are three main phases that generally correspond to: (1) a period of assessment and when baseline observations can be made; (2) a period in which an intervention (treatment) is applied; and (3) a period of follow-up when further assessments of the impact of treatment can be made.

The vertical axis differentiates standard, target and process measures.

Standard measures

The first level is that of standardised measures with normative data. These are the sorts of measures with which most people are familiar and they include many of the questionnaires and tests used in clinical and health care settings. Suffice it to note that most standardised

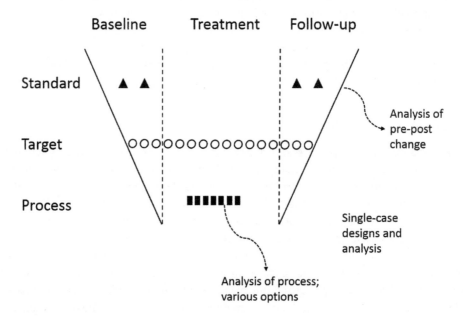

FIGURE 1.1 Schematic representation of different levels of measurement and study designs in single-case research

measures are not designed to be used on a very frequent basis. They are often too long and unwieldy to be used repeatedly in a short period of time. To this end they are most likely to be taken during the assessment/baseline period and at the end of treatment. The analysis of pre- and post-treatment differences in standardised measures can tell us whether a patient's score has changed in a meaningful way. Chapter 2 considers these measures and what one can achieve with them in more detail.

Target measures

The second level of measurement is that of target measures. One significant feature of single-case methods must be noted. Unlike randomised controlled trials, single-case methods often use measures that are specifically tailored to the individual. Whereas trials and other studies use standardised measures to capture information on constructs such as depression, anxiety, mood and disability, single-case methods generally measure aspects of a person's behaviour and experience that are uniquely problematic for them. The measures may include direct observation and counting the frequency of problem behaviour or self-report of experiences on scales tailored specifically for that individual.

Target measures represent the focus of treatment for the individual concerned. They represent the content of the person's complaint, e.g. 'I feel compelled to check the gas tap' rather than a construct such as obsessionality that is measured by a standardised measure (Chalkley, 2015). Target measures are often idiographic, i.e. tailored to the individual. The idiographic approach to assessment and measurement is markedly different from the standardised measures used in trials (Haynes, Mumma & Pinson, 2009). Idiographic measures can include direct observation or self-report of a particular behaviour, ratings of symptom or mood intensity, ratings of beliefs or anything that is deemed relevant to the particular individual. This marks a departure from the traditional single-case measures taken in applied behaviour analysis, where the focus is on observable behaviour and is more inclusive. Idiographic measures are designed to be taken more frequently than standardised measures, and Figure 1.1 represents this schematically with the observation being taken several times in the assessment/baseline, treatment and follow-up periods. Idiographic measures are discussed in more detail in Chapter 3, where issues concerning their validity and reliability are considered.

The repeated measurement of target problems is useful when we design experiments to answer questions such as whether the observed changes in a person are the result of treatment or the mere passage of time, an extra-treatment event or some other alternative explanation. These single-case experimental designs are considered in Chapter 4. Although they may be novel to many readers of this text, they are the standard designs established by researchers in applied behaviour analysis (Baer, Wolf & Risley, 1968) and are broadly applicable in clinical research. The analysis of data from single-case designs is covered in Chapters 5 and 6, and these chapters focus on how to conduct an analysis – topics that are not generally considered in the major texts on single-case research.

Process measures

The third level of measurement, process measures, can be taken at any point in a study. These are more variable in their scope and the type of measure taken, and may include both standardised and idiographic measures. In some psychotherapy research they will include the analysis of text that is then quantified (e.g. Field, Barkham, Shapiro & Stiles, 1994). Figure 1.1 depicts process measures taken on a number of occasions both across and within treatment sessions. Typical examples of process research include tracking the anxiety response during an exposure session, monitoring alliance across treatment sessions or experimentally testing whether a core therapeutic technique has the effect it is predicted to have. The level of process measures and their application are not dealt with in a specific chapter, but examples are scattered throughout the text. These are dealt with in a little more detail in Chapter 8, where the critical evaluation of single-case research is considered particularly in the context of Elliott's hermeneutic single-case efficacy design (Elliott, 2002).

VALIDITY IN SINGLE-CASE RESEARCH

More than 50 years ago, Campbell and his colleagues developed a systematic way of understanding the 'anatomy' of experiments that focused on identifying and understanding the ways in which an alternative hypothesis might account for the data (Campbell & Stanley, 1966; Cook & Campbell, 1979; Shadish, Cook & Campbell, 2002). Whilst their classification was primarily designed to characterise experimental and quasi-experimental designs for group-based research, it can be extended to experiments with single-cases. Campbell separated threats to the interpretation of experiments into several validity clusters, including internal validity, external validity, statistical conclusion validity and construct validity. A basic understanding of these provides a framework for designing and interpreting studies.

Internal validity

These are factors concerned with the design and execution of a particular study that may provide a plausible alternative account for the pattern of the results, i.e. they prevent one from concluding that the intervention was responsible for the change. Campbell identified several major threats to validity, some of which apply only to group-based studies, e.g. attrition, and these will not be discussed here. To understand each threat to validity we consider the simplest of quantitative case studies, the pre-treatment–post-treatment design where we have two measurement points, before and after treatment. If we observe a difference, the temptation is to conclude that the treatment was responsible for the change, but there are several other plausible alternatives to consider.

Maturation and history

Maturation refers to changes occurring within the individual over a given period that produce changes in the target variable irrespective of treatment. Studies that involve children's acquisition of language and other skills are obviously vulnerable to this effect. In the clinical context, maturation may appear in the guise of spontaneous remission. For example, depression is a self-limiting disorder in many cases and a proportion of people will improve after several weeks without treatment. This is a phenomenon called spontaneous remission. If treatment coincides with this period of spontaneous improvement, we are unable to detect whether treatment or spontaneous remission is the cause of the change.

In contrast, history refers to the possible impact of extra-treatment events mimicking a therapeutic effect on the target problem. For example, the closure of a contested divorce settlement, the resolution of an argument between friends or a change in medication may improve a client's anxiety independently of any therapeutic activity.

Testing

Testing is the name given to effects that can occur when a measurement is repeated. For many measures the mere repetition of the test may produce a difference in the scores. For example, intelligence and memory tests are likely to show practice effects, whereas people may learn to 'fake good or bad' on personality tests and symptom checklists. Measurement may also be reactive so that the very act of measurement provokes a significant change in the subject's behaviour. Reactivity usually, but not always, declines over time, so that changes between two occasions may not be due to a 'true' change but merely to a decrease in reactivity. Reactivity can be a significant feature when behavioural observation is used to measure a variable, but it can be countered by using unobtrusive recording measures.

Instrumentation

This refers to a change in the calibration of the instrument itself. For example, a steel ruler will give a different reading depending on its temperature. Contraction and expansion of the ruler will mean that an object measured with the 0° Celsius ruler will appear longer than when it is measured with the 25° Celsius one. In psychological measurement it is the observer who may change their calibration. One example of this is 'observer drift', which is found when observers change their criteria for detecting or recording behaviour during the study. Consistent scoring can be maintained by repeated checking of the observers by independent judges (Cone, 2001). Self-report measures of symptom intensity are also subject to instrumentation effects. For example, women frequently report that their scaling of pain changed markedly after the experience of childbirth. More generally, subjective ratings are sensitive to contextual effect, which may change over occasions of measurement. The differential sensitivity across the scale and the context in which ratings are made may lead to problems, including 'ceiling' or 'floor' effects (Poulton, 1989).

Statistical regression

All psychological measures have a degree of error associated with them, i.e. they have less than perfect reliability. Thus any score will only be an estimate of the true score. On repeating the test the person's score will probably change. If they initially scored at one extreme of the scale the second score will tend toward the middle of the scale, for purely statistical reasons. When standardised questionnaires are used in pre-treatment–post-treatment designs, unreliable measurement and therefore regression to the mean should be taken into account. An example of how to do this is given in Chapter 2.

Reactive intervention

Glass, Willson and Gottman (1975) identified a reactive intervention as a possible threat to validity in some circumstances. It is closely linked to the idea of statistical regression. When a person scores at the extreme of a scale it may be tempting to introduce an intervention because the perceived need seems great. But the extreme score may be an exception and we might reasonably expect the next observation to be less extreme (statistical regression). Alternatively the extreme score might have been produced by an adverse event that has a short-term impact, e.g. a row with one's partner. Implementing the intervention is a reaction to the circumstances and is problematic because we cannot separate the genuine effect of treatment from the likelihood that the change may simply be the result of a natural fluctuation.

Diffusion of treatment

Campbell originally identified diffusion of treatment as a threat to validity in group-based field experiments in which conditions of treatment vs non-treatment are being compared to each other. Members of the non-treatment group might get to hear about the treatment and take steps to implement it in some form. In single-case studies diffusion of treatment takes a different form, and in Chapter 4 we consider single-case designs where different conditions are implemented in different phases of the study. Diffusion of treatment will occur when a treatment element given in one phase is carried over to another phase. This may be a particular problem in the ABAB design (see Chapter 4) where a treatment period (B) is followed by a non-treatment phase (A): a period of treatment is followed by withdrawal of the treatment for a period of time. Some participants may be reluctant to follow this protocol and maintain treatment in the non-treatment phase. In alternating treatment designs where two or more treatments are each delivered briefly on several occasions, there may be carry-over effects so that the first treatment is still having an effect as the second treatment is introduced. For some types of treatment, e.g. cognitive behaviour therapy, where one is attempting to change a person's appraisal and beliefs, preventing carry-over presents a particular challenge.

Analytic validity

Campbell originally used the term statistical conclusion validity to indicate whether the statistical analysis and interpretation of the data had been carried out appropriately. We broaden the term to cover both statistical and visual analysis of single-case data. It might be more appropriate to call this threat to validity 'analytic validity', so that it covers all aspects of data analysis and inference. Analytic validity has been a source of some debate within single-case research where much of the data are technically difficult to analyse because of the small sample size and almost certain violation of important statistical assumptions about the structure of errors. Some authorities (Baer, 1977; Parsonson & Baer, 1992) eschew statistical analysis in favour of visual inspection of a data plot. While this is a valid method under some circumstances, there are occasions when visual analyst can draw the wrong conclusions (Fisher, Kelley & Lomas, 2003; Franklin, Gorman, Beasley & Allison, 1997).

Chapters 5 and 6 discuss basic methods for analysing single-case data using both visual and statistical methods.

Construct validity

Construct validity refers to the extent to which the theoretical interpretations may be placed on the data. In many group-based studies, researchers are interested in the relationship between two constructs, e.g. health status and exercise. These cannot normally be indexed by a single measure and it is usual to take multiple measures. In the majority of single-case studies, clinicians and researchers are interested in criterion variables such as the number of panic attacks or frequency of self-mutilation, and the 'causal' variables (treatment) are directly manipulated and measured. Nevertheless, unless we have a measure of therapy *per se*, e.g. the extent to which the therapist has adhered to a treatment protocol and delivered it competently (Waltz, Addis, Koerner & Jacobson, 1993), this can be problematic. Even if we satisfy ourselves that the therapist was competent, there may be other explanations for the effectiveness of therapy, e.g. non-specific and therapist alliance factors (Wampold & Imel, 2015). In conclusion, although issues of construct validity are not often discussed in single-case reports, careful conceptual analysis of the measures and intervention should always be made (Elliott, 2002) – see Chapter 8.

External validity

External validity is concerned with the extent to which the results obtained in the particular study may be extended to other participants, therapists, to different settings, i.e. different clinics, whether the findings will generalise to different measures of the problem and whether the finding will generalise across time, i.e. will the treatment remain effective beyond the period of study?

In this situation the first step to establishing external validity is to replicate the effect over a series of clients. Several authors (Barlow et al., 2009; Cook & Campbell, 1979; Kazdin, 2010; Kratochwill & Levin, 1992; Kratochwill et al., 2010) provide excellent discussions of external validity and the role of replication. It is useful to consider three domains to which one might wish to generalise the findings of a case study. (1) *Population validity*: for which members of which populations is this procedure useful or applicable? (2) *Ecological validity*: how far can the findings be replicated with different therapists, settings and measurement procedures? (Answering both of these questions is essentially a matter of replication by many investigators across different populations.) (3) *Manipulation validity*: will a conceptually similar intervention have the same effect? For example, it is tacitly assumed that many events will serve as punishment reinforcers, i.e. they reduce the frequency of behaviour, but these events may not be interchangeable. An example of this is the differential effectiveness of aversive stimulation and time-out in their capacity to suppress self-mutilation in the Lesch–Nyhan syndrome (Anderson, Dancis & Alpert, 1978). These investigators conducted a series of single-case studies demonstrating that aversive stimulation was not an effective punisher, whereas time out from social reinforcement was effective and did suppress self-mutilation that is typical in Lesch–Nyhan syndrome.

THE CURIOUS CLINICIAN: DOING RESEARCH IN THE CLINIC

Niko Tinbergen, a founding father of what is now the discipline of behavioural ecology, recounts in his autobiography, *Curious Naturalists*, how as a recent graduate he was wandering across heathland in the Netherlands wondering what to do with the rest of his life (Tinbergen, 1974). He observed a wasp entering a burrow and wondered how this tiny animal located its nest. There and then he began to experiment. Assuming that the wasp might use some aspect of the visual environment to navigate, Tinbergen set about modifying it by changing the location of pine cones, stones and twigs. His curiosity and inventiveness led to a successful and distinguished career, culminating in a Nobel Prize (Kruuk, 2003). Being a curious clinician may not lead to this level of success, but it will enrich practice and research. There is, after all, much to be curious about, even in everyday practice, and one of the aims of this book is to illustrate how quantitative methods applied to the single case can help answer a range of questions (Morley, 2007), as shown in Table 1.1 and discussed below.

Challenges in case formulation

Most schools of psychotherapy require that the individual should be understood in terms of their developmental history and the influence of the current social environment on their behaviour, and that a therapeutic intervention should be preceded by a clinical formulation of the case. Much of the relevant data is obtained through interviews with the client, their family and others involved with their well-being, carers and schoolteachers, by examining existing written records and through direct observation. Clinicians may make judgements about causal influences by assessing how similar a particular client is to others they have

TABLE 1.1 Questions for curious clinicians

- Questions about formulation
    - What contributes to the development and maintenance of a problem?
    - What are the controlling factors for the target variables?
- Simple outcome question
    - Has the client improved?
- Simple treatment question
    - Is the improvement a result of treatment?
- Complex treatment question
    - Does the treatment have a specific effect or do the non-specific components of the treatment account for change?
- Comparative treatment question
    - Is one treatment more effective than another?
- Questions about a theory or process
    - Does the therapy work for the reasons given in the theoretical rationale?

After Morley (2007)

seen with the same type of problem. They will try to identify the relationship between the occurrence of the problem and likely significant events. In addition to interviews and reviews of documentation, quantitative methods based on the single case may be used to determine the co-variation between current events and aspects of the problem behaviour. For example, during an initial interview a client (Clara) complained that she experienced intense panic attacks and that, because she thought these happened when she left home, she was beginning to restrict her activity. However, she had to leave home every day to take her two young children to school and reported that often she did not experience an attack while doing this. Clara agreed to keep a diary of when the panics occurred and to note where she was and any concurrent events. Table 1.2 shows a summary of her diary record that was analysed by partitioning it in a series of 2 × 2 tables in an attempt to reveal associations. In panel (a), panic attacks were tabulated against location. There is only a weak association between being outside and having a panic. A content analysis of her detailed diary showed that the important trigger event seemed to be certain types of assertive social interaction and the data were re-tabulated in panel (b), and it appears that when Clara felt she had to be assertive she was likely to panic. Finally, panel (c) indicates that assertive responses were as likely to be demanded at home and were not associated with being outside. An intervention to develop her skills in expression and assertion was effective.

Although mere observation does not constitute an experimental method as such, aspects of experimental method can be used to clarify the relationship between variables of interest. In some settings it may be possible to deliberately manipulate conditions that are

TABLE 1.2 Assessing co-variation between panic attacks and other events

Panel (a)	Location	
	At home	Outside
Panic attack	8	14
No panic attack	29	29
Panel (b)	**Social situation**	
	Assertion required	No assertion required
Panic attack	19	3
No panic attack	0	58
Panel (c)	**Location × Social situation**	
	Assertion required	Assertion not required
At home	8	0
Outside	11	3

Panel (a) shows the association (lack of) between location and the occurrence of panic attacks. Panel (b) shows the association between the demands of the social situation and the occurrence of panic attacks. In panel (c) the frequency of panic attacks is tallied by location and the demands of the social situation. It is clear that panics occur when assertion is demanded rather than when Clara was out of her home.

suspected of having functional significance. For example, a proportion of people with learning disabilities engage in self-harming behaviour, typically repetitive, rhythmic behaviour such as head-banging, biting part of their body, scratching or poking (Matson & Turygin, 2012). Understanding why this behaviour occurs is essential for development of effective treatments (Sturmey, Maffei-Almodovar, Madzharova & Cooper, 2012). There is considerable variability in self-harming, and several hypotheses about why it occurs have been advanced. These include negative reinforcement, such as escaping from task demands or other forms of aversive stimulation; positive reinforcement; obtaining attention from others; and automatic (sensory) reinforcement (Iwata et al., 1994). The standard way of determining the function of the behaviour for an individual is to observe the person under several conditions when only one of the contingencies is effective. It is then possible to compare the rate of self-harm under each condition. Due care must be taken to ensure the overall safety of the individual. This sort of data collection sequence is known as either a multi-element design or alternating treatment design, and is discussed further in Chapter 4.

Simple questions about the outcome of treatment

Has the client improved?

The minimal requirements for determining whether improvement has occurred are pre- and post-intervention measures. However, as discussed above, any change in the measure could be attributable to a number of factors other than genuine change. The standard way of determining the validity of a change is to use a between-group design, the randomised controlled trial. But this is not possible in routine clinical treatment or in many research settings where funding is limited. It is, however, possible to answer the general question of whether a client has improved if we have good psychometric information about the measures used to assess the individual. Knowledge of psychometrics can help us determine whether any observed change is genuine, i.e. not attributable to unreliability, and if normative data are available we can determine whether the change made is sufficiently large to be considered clinically important. These issues are discussed in Chapter 2.

Is the treatment effective?

The simple pre-treatment–post-treatment design does not enable us to infer that the change produced is due to therapy, even if we exploit the psychometric information to the full. It can only tell us that a reliable measurable change has occurred, not that it is attributable to the treatment per se. In order to draw conclusions about treatment effectiveness in an individual we need to take repeated measurements prior to the start of treatment and during treatment. Inferences about the effectiveness of treatment will be strengthened if we can show that change happens only when treatment is introduced and experimentally withdrawing or otherwise manipulating the treatment will enhance the validity of findings. There are several ways of achieving this, and experimental single-case designs are discussed and illustrated in Chapter 4. It is not possible to analyse data from single-case studies using conventional statistical tests. Analysis of these studies has often relied on the graphical presentation of data and interpretation of the data plots, but there are potential problems with this and several statistical methods for data analysis have been considered (see Chapters 5 and 6).

Why did the patient improve and what part of the treatment was responsible for the change?

Any experimental investigation of why a treatment works involves a comparison between two or more conditions, and an investigator usually assigns patients to different groups and uses 'dismantling' designs to compare various elements of the treatment. In some instances it is possible to investigate this question in single cases. There are a number of possible designs that can be used to do this, the most common being the alternating treatments design in which a single person receives both treatments in a carefully designated order. The alternating treatments design is discussed in Chapter 4.

Will this treatment be of any use to other clients and clinicians?

This question addresses the issue of the external validity and replicability of single-case studies. Replication is the essence of science and good clinical practice. It has been briefly considered above, and the importance of replication and external validity is considered in further detail in Chapter 7.

CONCLUSIONS

This text is written primarily for postgraduate clinical, health and counselling psychologists as an introduction to single-case research methods. Clinical psychologists in training invariably have to complete some form of written case study: the first purpose of this text therefore is to encourage, where possible, the adoption of quantitative methods and consideration of how to determine when and how often to take measures, an element of experimental design. If we do not want to draw erroneous conclusions about the efficacy of our work (Lilienfeld et al., 2014), then one way of combating this tendency is to apply some of the basic principles of single-case methods. The combination of attention to measurement issues, some basic principles of experimental design and careful analysis will contribute greatly to our ability to draw reasonable conclusions about a particular case.

The second purpose of the book is as an introduction to single-case methods as a viable research strategy in clinical settings. It is far more likely that a research-minded clinician or group of clinicians will be able to implement single-case experiments than an RCT. The research application of single-case methods requires replication over a number of cases and the possibility of being able to plan the study in greater detail. As a consequence of this there are additional design options, such as the introduction of multiple baseline designs across subjects and the application of randomisation procedures. Good quantitative case studies and single-case experiments require considerable thought and as in any field, repetition and critical evaluation of one's efforts will enhance one's competence.

There are signs of a resurgence of interest in single-case methods with recent reviews in mainstream journals (Smith, 2012), the establishment of best practice guidelines (Kratochwill et al., 2010, 2013), critical appraisal and reporting guidelines (Tate et al., 2013;

Tate, Perdices, Rosenkoetter, McDonald, *et al.*, 2016; Tate, Perdices, Rosenkoetter, Shadish, *et al.*, 2016) and considerable attention to developing statistical methods for the analysis of single-case data (Shadish, 2014). There are several excellent texts on experimental single-case methods that repay more advanced study (Barlow *et al.*, 2009; Kazdin, 2010). The primary purpose of the present book is to cover the basic principles of measurement, design and analysis of single-case data.

REFERENCES

Anderson, L., Dancis, J. & Alpert, M. (1978). Behavioral contingencies and self mutilation in Lesch–Nyhan disease. *Journal of Consulting and Clinical Psychology*, 46, 529–36.

Baer, D. M. (1977). Perhaps it would be better not to know everything. *Journal of Applied Behavior Analysis*, 10(1), 167–72.

Baer, D. M., Wolf, M. M. & Risley, T. R. (1968). Some current dimensions of applied behavior analysis. *Journal of Applied Behavior Analysis*, 1(1), 91–7.

Barkham, M., Hardy, G. E. & Mellor-Clark, J. (2010). *Developing and Delivering Practice-based Evidence: A Guide for Psychological Therapies* (1st edn). Chichester: Wiley-Blackwell.

Barlow, D. H., Nock, M. K. & Hersen, M. (2009). *Single Case Experimental Designs* (3rd edn). Boston: Pearson.

Breuer, J. & Freud, S. (1955). *Studies on Hysteria* (Vol. II). London: Hogarth.

Campbell, D. T. & Stanley, J. C. (1966). *Experimental and Quasi-experimental Designs for Research*. Chicago: Rand McNally.

Cartwright-Hatton, S., McNally, D., Field, A. P., Rust, S., Laskey, B., Dixon, C. et al. (2011). A New Parenting-Based Group Intervention for Young Anxious Children: Results of a randomized controlled trial. *Journal of the American Academy of Child and Adolescent Psychiatry*, 50(3), 242–51.

Chalkley, A. J. (2015). *The Content of Psychological Distress*. London: Palgrave.

Cone, J. D. (2001). *Evaluating Outcomes: Empirical Tools for Effective Practice* (1st edn). Washington, D.C.: American Psychological Association.

Cook, T. D. & Campbell, D. T. (1979). *Quasi-Experimentation: Design and Analysis Issues for Field Settings*. Chicago: Rand McNally.

Elliott, R. (2002). Hermeneutic single-case efficacy design. *Psychotherapy Research*, 12(1), 1–21.

Field, S. D., Barkham, M., Shapiro, D. A. & Stiles, W. B. (1994). Assessment of Assimilation in Psychotherapy – a quantitative case-study of problematic experiences with a significant other. *Journal of Counseling Psychology*, 41(3), 397–406.

Fisher, W. W., Kelley, M. E. & Lomas, J. E. (2003). Visual aids and structured criteria for improving visual inspection and interpretation of single-case designs. *Journal of Applied Behavior Analysis*, 36(3), 387–406.

Franklin, R. D., Gorman, B. S., Beasley, T. M. & Allison, D. B. (1997). Graphical display and visual analysis. In R. D. Franklin & D. B. Allison (eds), *Design and Analysis of Single-case Research* (pp. 119–58). Mahwah, NJ: Lawrence Erlbaum.

Gast, D. L. (2010). *Single Subject Research Methodology in Behavioral Sciences*. New York: Routledge.

Glass, G. V., Willson, V. L. & Gottman, J. M. (1975). *Design and Analysis of Time Series Experiments*. Boulder: Colorado University Press.

Grimley Evans, J. (1995). Evidence-based or evidence-biased medicine. *Age and Ageing*, 24(6), 461–3.

Haynes, S. N., Mumma, G. H. & Pinson, C. (2009). Idiographic assessment: conceptual and psychometric foundations of individualised behavioral assessment. *Clinical Psychology Review*, 29(2), 179–91.

Heyvaert, M., Maes, B., Van den Noortgate, W., Kuppens, S. & Onghena, P. (2012). A multilevel meta-analysis of single-case and small-n research on interventions for reducing challenging behavior in persons with intellectual disabilities. Research in Developmental Disabilities, 33(2), 766–80.

Hilliard, R. B. (1993). Single-case methodology in psychotherapy process and outcome research. Journal of Consulting and Clinical Psychology, 61(3), 373–80.

Iwata, B. A., Pace, G. M., Dorsey, M. F., Zarcone, J. R., Vollmer, T. R., Smith, R. G. et al. (1994). The functions of self-injurious behavior: an experimental-epidemiological analysis. Journal of Applied Behavior Analysis, 27(2), 215–40.

Johnson, J. M. & Pennypacker, H. S. (1980). Strategies and Tactics in Human Behavioural Research. Hillsdale: Lawrence Erlbaum.

Kazdin, A. E. (1997). Parent management training: Evidence, outcomes, and issues. Journal of the American Academy of Child and Adolescent Psychiatry, 36(10), 1349–56.

Kazdin, A. E. (2010). Single-Case Research Designs: Methods for Clinical and Applied Settings (2nd edn). Oxford: Oxford University Press.

Kratochwill, T. R., Hitchcock, J., Horner, R., Levin, J., Odom, S. L., Rindskopf, D. & Shadish, W. R. (2010). Single-case technical documentation. Retrieved from What Works Clearinghouse website: http://ies.ed.gov/ncee/wwc/pdf

Kratochwill, T. R., Hitchcock, J. H., Horner, R. H., Levin, J. R., Odom, S. L., Rindskopf, D. M. & Shadish, W. R. (2013). Single-case intervention research design standards. Remedial and Special Education, 34(1), 26–38.

Kratochwill, T. R. & Levin, J. R. (eds) (1992). Single-case Research Designs and Analysis. Hove: Lawrence Erlbaum.

Kruuk, H. (2003). Niko's Nature: The Life of Niko Tinbergen and his Science of Animal Behaviour. Oxford: Oxford University Press.

Lilienfeld, S. O., Ritschel, L. A., Lynn, S. J., Cautin, R. L. & Latzman, R. D. (2014). Why ineffective psychotherapies appear to work: A taxonomy of causes of spurious therapeutic effectiveness. Perspectives on Psychological Science, 9(4), 355–87.

Matson, J. L. & Turygin, N. C. (2012). How do researchers define self-injurious behavior? Research in Developmental Disabilities, 33(4), 1021–6.

Mayer-Schönberger, V. & Cukier, K. (2013). Big Data: A Revolution that will Transform how we Live, Work and Think. London: John Murray.

McMillan, D. & Morley, S. (2010). Single-case quantitative methods. In M. Barkham & G. E. Hardy (eds), A Core Approach to Delivering Practice-based Evidence. Chichester: Wiley.

Morley, S. (2007). Single case methodology in psychological therapy. In S. J. E. Lindsey & G. E. Powell (eds), The Handbook of Clinical Adult Psychology (3rd edn, pp. 821–43). London: Routledge.

Parsonson, B. S. & Baer, D. M. (1992). The visual analysis of data, and current research into the stimuli controlling it. In T. R. Kratochwill & J. R. Levin (eds), Single-case Research Design and Analysis: New Directions for Psychology and Education (pp. 15–40). Hillsdale, NJ: Lawrence Erlbaum.

Poulton, E. C. (1989). Bias in Quantifying Judgments. Hove: Erlbaum.

Rogers, S. (2013). Facts are Sacred: The Power of Big Data. London: Faber & Faber.

Schork, N. J. (2015). Personalized medicine: Time for one-person trials. Nature, 520(7549), 609–11.

Schulz, K. F., Altman, D. G. & Moher, D. (2010). CONSORT 2010 Statement: updated guidelines for reporting parallel group randomised trials. BMJ, 340.

Shadish, W. R. (ed.)(2014). Special issue: Analysis and meta-analysis of single-case designs. Journal of School Psychology, 52(2), 109–248.

Shadish, W. R., Cook, T. D. & Campbell, D. T. (2002). Experimental and Quasi-experimental Designs for Generalized Causal Inference. Boston, MA: Houghton Mifflin.

Smith, J. D. (2012). Single-case experimental designs: A systematic review of published research and current standards. *Psychological Methods*, 17(4), 510–50.

Sturmey, P., Maffei-Almodovar, L., Madzharova, M. S. & Cooper, J. (2012). *Self-Injurious Behavior: Handbook of Evidence-Based Practice in Clinical Psychology*. Chichester: John Wiley.

Tate, R. L., Perdices, M., Rosenkoetter, U., McDonald, S., Togher, L., Shadish, W. et al, . . . Vohra, S. (2016). The Single-Case Reporting Guideline In BEhavioural Interventions (SCRIBE) 2016: Explanation and elaboration. *Archives of Scientific Psychology*, 4(1), 10–31.

Tate, R. L., Perdices, M., Rosenkoetter, U., Shadish, W., Vohra, S., Barlow, D. H. et al, . . . Wilson, B. (2016). The Single-Case Reporting Guideline In BEhavioural Interventions (SCRIBE) 2016 statement. *Archives of Scientific Psychology*, 4(1), 1–9.

Tate, R. L., Perdices, M., Rosenkoetter, U., Wakim, D., Godbee, K., Togher, L. & McDonald, S. (2013). Revision of a method quality rating scale for single-case experimental designs and n-of-1 trials: the 15-item Risk of Bias in N-of-1 Trials (RoBiNT) Scale. *Neuropsychol Rehabil*, 23(5), 619–38.

Tinbergen, N. (1974). *Curious Naturalists*. Harmondsworth: Penguin.

Vlaeyen, J. W. S., Morley, S., Linton, S., Boersma, K. & de Jong, J. (2012). *Pain-Related Fear: Exposure-based Treatment of Chronic Pain*. Seattle: IASPpress.

Waltz, J., Addis, M. E., Koerner, K. & Jacobson, N. S. (1993). Testing the integrity of a psychotherapy protocol: Assessment of adherence and competence. *Journal of Consulting and Clinical Psychology*, 61(4), 620–30.

Wampold, B. E. & Imel, Z. E. (2015). *The Great Psychotherapy Debate: The Evidence for what Make Psychotherapy Work*. Hove: Routledge.

Westen, D., Novotny, C. M. & Thompson-Brenner, H. (2004). The empirical status of empirically supported psychotherapies: Assumptions, findings, and reporting in controlled clinical trials. *Psychological Bulletin*, 130(4), 631–63.

Wolpe, J. (1958). *Psychotherapy by Reciprocal Inhibition*. California: Stanford University Press.

Wright, B., Barry, M., Hughes, E., Trepel, D., Ali, S., Allgar, V. L. et al, . . . Gilbody, S. M. (2015). Clinical effectiveness and cost-effectiveness of parenting interventions for children with severe attachment problems: a systematic review and meta-analysis. *Health Technology Assessment*, 19(52).

Chapter 2
Standardised measures and what you can do with them

In the last 100 years or so, psychologists have developed considerable sophistication in measuring psychological constructs and have amassed a substantial library of measures. This chapter covers basic material on standard measures. Standard measures are those that have been developed and standardised on defined populations and for which we have basic data concerning their psychometric properties, reliability and norms, and information about their validity. In clinical practice these measures are most often multi-item questionnaires and cognitive tests. The chapter covers basic classical test theory of psychometrics to provide the essential background for understanding the rationale for data analysis.

The simplest and probably most frequent sequence of observations in clinical settings is the pre–post design where measurements are made before and after a period of treatment. It is a very weak non-experimental design for determining any causal mechanism of change, because the absence of control conditions means that it is impossible to rule out many of the threats to validity discussed in Chapter 1. Nevertheless, with a little knowledge about measurement we can begin to address two important questions that we pose about a client after therapy: (1) is any change that we observe in the measures genuine, i.e. not an artefact of poor measurement; and (2) what significance can we ascribe to the change? In this chapter we will explore the properties of standardised, normed measures and how such measures may be used in evaluating change in a single individual. This is the material you need to know to begin to answer the two above questions. The main analysis for standard measures used in single cases is the computation of the Reliable Change Index and the application of Clinically Significant Change criteria (Jacobson, Roberts, Berns & McGlinchey, 1999).

FUNDAMENTALS OF STANDARDISED MEASUREMENT

Measures or tests are standardised when the conditions under which they should be administered and scored have been identified and prescribed. Subsequent administration of the measure in the prescribed manner is essential. This is most apparent in the administration of cognitive tests such as the Wechsler family of intelligence tests. Each test comes with a manual of instructions about how to administer and score the various test components. Before such tests can be properly conducted, the tester must learn the protocol and their competence in both administering and scoring the test should be assessed. Violation of the standard protocol will reduce the reliability of the scores; in technical terms it will introduce systematic error and reduce the validity of the test scores.

Although we do not often think of the familiar clinical questionnaires in the same way as cognitive tests, the same principles hold. Questionnaires should be accompanied by explicit instructions about the use of the response scale, such as the time frame the respondent should consider, e.g. 'your experience of the last two weeks', and specific instructions on how to score the items, e.g. how to allocate numerical values to verbal descriptors in the response scale, which items to reverse score, how to allocate items to subscales and what to do with missing data. Ensuring that clients understand the instructions and response scale is an essential part of testing, as is proper scoring and aggregation of the items.

The importance of normative data

The second feature of standardised tests is the development and availability of norms, without which the test scores cannot be interpreted and the test is virtually meaningless. Norms are established by administering the test to a large number of people and computing statistics that summarise the distribution of the scores, the mean, standard deviation, range and estimates of the reliability of the test. Test developers may sample a single generic population, but when the purpose of the test is to discriminate between people who are presumed to differ in key characteristics, developers will explicitly examine sub-populations that are presumed to exemplify these characteristics, e.g. diagnostic groups. In the development of some tests, e.g. tests of cognitive ability, the developer may use an explicit sampling frame to ensure that the final sample includes appropriate representation across variables such as age, sex and socio-economic status. For example, in IQ testing this is important as an individual performance can be referenced with respect to their age. Many questionnaire measures used in clinical settings do not have this sampling pedigree and have been developed on samples of convenience. From a practical perspective it is therefore important to know how the test was developed and the characteristics of the samples used to generate the norms. This information should be found in the test manuals available for well-established tests such as the Wechsler cognitive tests, the CORE-OM, the SCL-90R, and the children's SDQ (a list of acronyms is given at the end of the chapter). These are, however, not always available for many questionnaire measures used in clinical settings and we will look at how to deal with this situation later in the chapter.

Norms, which are usually presented in look-up tables placed at the back of manuals, can be used to match a client's characteristics, e.g. age and sex, to the relevant table with the normative population. When there are more than two or three reference characteristics, the number of tables necessary to provide the relevant information grows quickly. An alternative, but less commonly used, method is to use a multiple regression equation, e.g. Van Breukelen and Vlaeyen (2005). The equation contains the key norm criteria (e.g. age, sex, diagnostic status) and the user enters the client's data for these criteria into the equation. The resulting computation indicates the predicted normative value on the test for the individual, and also shows how much the individual departs from the predicted values. Equations for the computations can be found in either test manuals or journal publications.

The availability of norms for distinct clinical groups and comparative non-clinical samples is extremely useful when considering the status of an individual and the changes that may occur over the course of a therapeutic intervention. We can determine whether the observed change is substantial enough to be relied on rather than the result of measurement error. Normative data can also provide additional information to help us determine the meaning of a score: does it have clinical significance? It is the statistical (mean scores, standard deviation, reliability) properties of standardised, normed tests that give them utility in clinical settings. Before we consider the application of these characteristics we need to review some building blocks of measurement and psychometric theory.

The normal distribution: the importance of z scores

The normal distribution, Figure 2.1, is symmetrical about the mean, so the mean, mode and median all have the same value, and this 'tails' off on either side of the mean. Many natural phenomena approximate rather well to this distribution, e.g. the height of adults, and in the field of measurement in psychology we can often adjust measures so that they are distributed normally. In the normal curve, the x-axis is the dimension of the focus of measurement, e.g. intelligence, catastrophising or other construct, and the y-axis is the frequency with which value on the x-axis is observed. Symmetry means that half the observations are below the midpoint and half are above. So if we sampled at random a single observation would have a 50:50 chance of coming from either half, a probability of 0.5.

A simple equation makes it possible to locate the position of an individual relative to the middle of the distribution. This may be easily translated into a percentile indicating the percentage of observations that fall below and above it and hence the probability of where he or she occurs in the distribution of the population. The device for converting any score into its position on the normal curve is the z score. In order to find a particular z score we need three pieces of information: the observation, the mean of all the observations and the standard deviation of all the observations. We define a z score as the

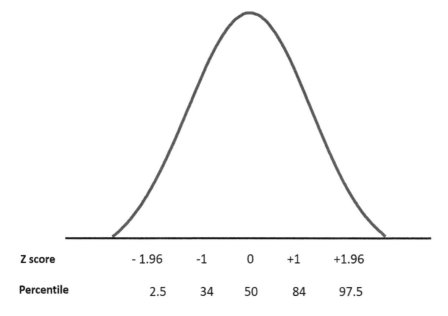

Z score	- 1.96	-1	0	+1	+1.96
Percentile	2.5	34	50	84	97.5

FIGURE 2.1 The normal curve with key z values and corresponding percentile values

deviation of the observed score from the mean (observed score − mean) expressed as a ratio of the standard deviation (SD):

$$z = \frac{\text{Observed score} - \text{Mean score}}{\text{SD}}$$

We can note a number of things when we apply this equation to observations. First, when the observation has the same value as the mean then the z score is 0. So, the mean of our mathematical representation of the normal distribution is 0. The second thing to note is that when the observed score is larger than the mean, the z score will take on a positive value, and when it is smaller it will take on a negative value. So z scores can be either positive or negative and the sign tells us whether the individual score is above or below the mean. The third point to note is that when the observed score is at one standard deviation above or below the mean, the z score will be $+1$ and -1 respectively. In summary the mean of the normal distribution is $= 0$ and it has a standard deviation of ± 1. Once an observed score is expressed as a z score, we can look up its probability value in Normal tables. These can be found at the back of most basic statistics textbooks or you can find them using the NORM.S.DIST function in Excel™ – see Table 2.1.

There is one critical z value that will occur many times in the coming text – 1.96. When we look up that value, $+1.96$ corresponds to the 97.5th percentile, so that only 2.5% of observations will be greater than 1.96. Conversely when we examine the negative tail of the distribution, only 2.5% of observations will be below -1.96. So when we add these two together we know that 95% of our observations will be between a z of ± 1.96.

Z scores have a number of benefits. One, frequently used in psychology, is to translate scores from different scales into a common metric and thus enable us to make comparisons across measures. For example, Table 2.2 shows scores from a single person on three common scales used to measure depression – the BDI-II, PHQ-9 and HAD-D. Each of these scales has a different range. While the HADS depression subscale goes from 0–21, the BDI can take values from 0–63 and the PHQ-9 takes values between 0–27. The scores obtained by a single individual (observed score) range from 38 to 18. How can we compare scores across scales? Translation into a z score will do the trick.

A second function of the z score is that it can be used to turn any measurement into a scale that suits our convenience. The best-known example of this is the scales that measure IQ. If you are familiar with the Wechsler Adult Intelligence Scale you will know that it comprises several subscales, each of which has a variable number of items. When the subscales are scored the tester reads a look-up table and translates each score into a scaled score. For all subscales the scaled scores have a mean of 10 and an SD of 3. The overall sum of the test items is also converted into a total IQ score which has a mean of 100 and an SD of 15. Our culture is now very familiar with the IQ and many people will know that a score of 100 represents an average IQ, and it is unlikely a psychologist will have to explain this. The translation of the raw score into a scaled score is made using the z score. First, the raw scores are converted to z scores and then the new scaled score is computed. The test developer can decide the value of the subtest and test means and SDs, 10 and 3 and 100 and 15, respectively in the case of the Wechsler tests.

New Score $= z \times$ *New SD* $+$ *New Mean*

TABLE 2.1 The normal distribution function

	0.00	0.01	0.02	0.03	0.04	0.05	0.06	0.07	0.08	0.09
0.0	0.0000	0.0040	0.0080	0.0120	0.0160	0.0199	0.0239	0.0279	0.0319	0.0359
0.1	0.0398	0.0438	0.0478	0.0517	0.0557	0.0596	0.0636	0.0675	0.0714	0.0753
0.2	0.0793	0.0832	0.0871	0.0910	0.0948	0.0987	0.1026	0.1064	0.1103	0.1141
0.3	0.1179	0.1217	0.1255	0.1293	0.1331	0.1368	0.1406	0.1443	0.1480	0.1517
0.4	0.1554	0.1591	0.1628	0.1664	0.1700	0.1736	0.1772	0.1808	0.1844	0.1879
0.5	0.1915	0.1950	0.1985	0.2019	0.2054	0.2088	0.2123	0.2157	0.2190	0.2224
0.6	0.2257	0.2291	0.2324	0.2357	0.2389	0.2422	0.2454	0.2486	0.2517	0.2549
0.7	0.2580	0.2611	0.2642	0.2673	0.2704	0.2734	0.2764	0.2794	0.2823	0.2852
0.8	0.2881	0.2910	0.2939	0.2967	0.2995	0.3023	0.3051	0.3078	0.3106	0.3133
0.9	0.3159	0.3186	0.3212	0.3238	0.3264	0.3289	0.3315	0.3340	0.3365	0.3389
1.0	0.3413	0.3438	0.3461	0.3485	0.3508	0.3531	0.3554	0.3577	0.3599	0.3621
1.1	0.3643	0.3665	0.3686	0.3708	0.3729	0.3749	0.3770	0.3790	0.3810	0.3830
1.2	0.3849	0.3869	0.3888	0.3907	0.3925	0.3944	0.3962	0.3980	0.3997	0.4015
1.3	0.4032	0.4049	0.4066	0.4082	0.4099	0.4115	0.4131	0.4147	0.4162	0.4177
1.4	0.4192	0.4207	0.4222	0.4236	0.4251	0.4265	0.4279	0.4292	0.4306	0.4319
1.5	0.4332	0.4345	0.4357	0.4370	0.4382	0.4394	0.4406	0.4418	0.4429	0.4441
1.6	0.4452	0.4463	0.4474	0.4484	0.4495	0.4505	0.4515	0.4525	0.4535	0.4545
1.7	0.4554	0.4564	0.4573	0.4582	0.4591	0.4599	0.4608	0.4616	0.4625	0.4633
1.8	0.4641	0.4649	0.4656	0.4664	0.4671	0.4678	0.4686	0.4693	0.4699	0.4706
1.9	0.4713	0.4719	0.4726	0.4732	0.4738	0.4744	0.4750	0.4756	0.4761	0.4767
2.0	0.4772	0.4778	0.4783	0.4788	0.4793	0.4798	0.4803	0.4808	0.4812	0.4817

This table shows the positive tail of the z score. You must add a value of 0.50 and then multiply by 100 to find the relevant percentile. For example, a z score of 0.00 will be at the 50th percentile. If the z score is 1.25, the percentile is found by looking at the intersection of the row beginning 1.2 and the column with 0.05. This gives the value 0.3944 and the resulting percentile will be (0.5000 + 0.3944) × 100 = 89.44. The value is easily obtained in Excel™ using the NORM.S.DIST function: simply enter =NORM.S.DIST(z,TRUE)*100 into a blank cell and replace z by the numerical value you have computed.

TABLE 2.2 Comparing scores obtained on different scales

Test	Range	Mean	SD	Observed score	z score	Percentile
BDI-II	0-63	23.30	13.00	38	1.13	87
PHQ-9	0-27	11.50	7.29	19	1.03	85
HAD-D	0-21	8.16	7.62	18	1.29	90

The individual's responses to the measures are in the observed scores column. The estimates of the mean and SD come from a community sample (267 general practice patients in Scotland; 70% female with an average age of 49.8 years; Cameron *et al.*, 2011). BDI-II, Beck depression inventory; PHQ, Patient health questionnaire; HAD-D, Hospital anxiety and depression scale.

The literature is replete with various scales that have been adjusted so that the norms have set values of the mean and SD: for example, you may find Stanine scores (range 1–9, mean = 9, SD = 2) or Sten scores (range 1–10, mean = 5.5, SD = 2). A commonly used scale is the T-score with a mean of 50 and SD = 10, and thus a T score of 70 (2 SD above the mean, i.e. a z score of approximately 1.96) is taken as being clinically exceptional and meaningful.

Classical test theory

Classical test theory underlies many of the tests and measures in behavioural clinical science. It is very well established and influences our idea of measurement, perhaps more than we realise. Detailed accounts of classical test theory can be found in texts such as Nunnally and Bernstein (1994). The present account is limited to the essentials necessary to understand the application to single cases.

Classical test theory starts with the assumption that any observed test score is made up of two components: a true score and an error score. The error score can be further partitioned into systematic and random components:

> Observed score = True score + Error score
> Error score = Systematic error + Random error

As the name suggests, *systematic errors* distort our observations in a predictable way. For example, in computing the total questionnaire score we might fail to adjust for reverse scored items; or the patient might not hold in mind the time frame (2 weeks) over which they are asked to judge the presence of their symptoms. In a cognitive test the administrator might consistently give the benefit of the doubt when answers are not quite according to the manual. These are all systematic errors and the purpose of standardisation is to eliminate them as far as practicable.

Use of the term *random error* implies that the error is not systematically related to any feature of testing, but it also has a more precise mathematical definition. Within classical test theory random errors are defined by several properties: (1) on average they sum to 0; (2) they are independent of the true score, i.e. they are independent of the magnitude of the true score; (3) they have a constant variance for all true scores; and (4) they are distributed normally.

With this in mind we can approach the issue of reliability. Whilst we might define the reliability of a measure as the reproducibility of a particular score under identical conditions, this is not sufficiently precise if we want to determine how to estimate reliability. In classical test theory the definition of reliability is based on the proportion of the true score component relative to the total score, i.e. true + error. It expresses this as ratio of the variance of the score to the variance of the observed score:

$$\frac{\text{Variance (True)}}{\text{Variance (Observed)}} = \frac{\text{Variance (True)}}{\text{Variance (True)} + \text{Variance (Error)}}$$

From this it is easy to see that if the error is zero then the reliability is perfect, i.e. = 1, and that as the error increases the proportion of true score will be smaller and the reliability will decrease accordingly. But how do we find out how to estimate the actual reliability when we only have one set of observed scores? To solve this conundrum, classical test theory proposes a thought experiment. Imagine that two sets of scores, 01 and 02, are obtained on the same people at the same time by identical tests; in the jargon of classical test theory these are perfectly parallel tests. As we know that $01 = 02$, we know that they are made up of the same true score and error score components. If we correlate the two parallel tests a bit of algebra reveals that the correlation rxx between the two sets of observed scores (denoted by x) is given by the following equation: $r_{xx} = \sigma_t^2 / \sigma_x^2$. This is the ratio of the true to observed variance that is our definition of reliability. So under these conditions the well-known Pearson correlation coefficient gives the reliability of the measure for perfectly parallel tests. As we do not have access to perfectly parallel tests we have to 'make do and mend' with what is available. As a consequence we have a set of reliability coefficients that are obtained through different sets of empirical operations. Each of these will have limitations and assumptions (as discussed below) and one needs to be aware of them.

Parallel forms reliability

On the face of it, this is the nearest to our thought experiment. In parallel forms reliability the test developers prepare two or more versions of the same test. Scores from two versions are correlated to compute the reliability. In practice, designing parallel forms is difficult and there are relatively few everyday tests in clinical use where parallel forms are available. Even though parallel forms give the appearance of matching our ideal of perfectly parallel tests, a moment's thought will reveal that it is impossible to take different tests at the same time. The reliability estimated may have been influenced by differences occurring due to the time (occasion) or the individual's performance may have been affected by the increased familiarity on the second occasion of measurement or by a change of state, e.g. fatigue. This might be particularly so in cognitive tests. However, provided these differences are not systematic then we can accept the estimate of reliability.

Test–retest reliability

The familiar test–retest reliability coefficient (also known as the test–retest stability coefficient) is obtained by repeating the same test on two separate occasions. The delay between test occasions for different measures may vary widely from days to weeks, and even within a single measure different investigators may choose different time periods between the original and retest occasions. Imagine a test given on two occasions: in this case we may consider the tests to be parallel across time and, using the same assumption about the errors, the correlation between the tests can be shown to be the test–retest reliability. But there are some obvious practical and conceptual limitations to blanket acceptance of test–retest reliability as the estimate of reliability. First, we may only be able to obtain test data on one occasion. Second, a low coefficient may not mean that the test is inherently unreliable. For example, there are some constructs, such as mood, where we might expect change to occur over a relatively short period of time. So repeating the measure over a longer period of time is unlikely to generate a particularly high test–retest correlation. The appropriate use of the test–retest correlation as a measure of reliability requires that we assume that what we are measuring is reasonably stable over the expected time period.

Split-half reliability and its application to determining test length

An early solution to calculating reliability was to use the correlations between the test items to estimate reliability. In computing the reliability the test is split into two halves – a sort of parallel test. This worked well if the test had items that became progressively more difficult because it was easy to pair successive odd and even item numbers with each other. Cronbach (1951) developed a method for estimating internal consistency when the items were not ordered (see below). Nevertheless, split-half reliability has a statistical problem and solving this problem provided a useful equation that we can use in some situations. The problem is that if we compute the reliability for the test, we are estimating the reliability for each half of the test not for the full test itself. In other words the sample size is reduced. So we must correct our estimate to ensure that the estimate is adequate. The common correction for split-halves is known as the Spearman–Brown 'prophecy formula':

$$r_f = \frac{2r_h}{(1+r_h)}$$

where r_f = reliability coefficient for the whole test and r_h = split-half coefficient. This will correct the reliability and increase the estimate. For example, if a split-half reliability is found to be 0.6 (not very good in conventional terms) then the full-scale test reliability is:

$$r_f = \frac{2\times.6}{(1+.6)} = .75$$

which is a little more satisfactory.

More generally it can be shown that for any test we can estimate what the reliability would be if we increase or decrease the test length by a given number of items. This has two useful practical applications. First, in developing a test you can use this equation to work out how many items you need to add to a test to attain a given reliability coefficient. The formula is:

$$r_{newtest} = \frac{k\times r_{oldtest}}{1+(k-1)\times r_{oldtest}}$$

where k is the factor by which the test length is to be increased or decreased and r is the reliability. So if the original short scale has a reliability of 0.40 and the new long scale is 5 times longer, the reliability of the scale will be 0.77.

$$r_{newtest} = \frac{5 \times 0.4}{1 + (5-1) \times 0.4} = 0.77$$

Note that we don't use the actual number of items in the test: we set a ratio for increasing or decreasing the number of items we need. So in the example above if our original scale had 4 items we need to increase this by a factor of 5, i.e. 20 items.

The second use is where you might wish to shorten an existing test. For example, if you have to collect a large amount of data (several tests) from an individual you might consider shortening the length of tests of subsidiary interest. We can rearrange the previous formula so that you can determine a suitable test length directly. If you know the current reliability and can set a lower reliability with which you will be satisfied, then you can estimate the length (k) of the new test using the following formula:

$$k_{test\ length} = \frac{r_{new} \times (1 - r_{old})}{r_{old} \times (1 - r_{new})}$$

So if the old test has $r_{old} = 0.83$ and the level of reliability you will be satisfied with is $r_{new} = 0.75$, then you can shorten your test to about 60% of its original length:

$$k_{test\ length} = \frac{.75 \times (1-.83)}{.83 \times (1-.75)} = .613$$

The new test length is the old test length × 0.613. So if the old test had 20 items the new test length would be 20 × 0.613. This is near enough 12 items. One occasion when you might use this is in constructing a daily diary for self-monitoring based on an existing measure. If you wish to structure the diary around scales that measure constructs that are important for your client, you might consider incorporating some of the items in the diary (copyright permitting).

Internal consistency (Cronbach's alpha and the Kuder–Richardson formulae)

Split-half reliability has a problem in that if one splits the data in a number of ways, more than one coefficient may be derived. Which one is the reliability coefficient? There is a method of obtaining a general measure of internal consistency from one administration of a test: Cronbach's alpha. Cronbach's solution was to imagine that you could compute the reliability from all possible combinations of test items (Cronbach, 1951). Once the number of items in a test gets beyond more than a few there are so many combinations that computing reliability would be tedious. Cronbach showed that an internal consistency estimate of reliability, which he called alpha, could be derived from an inter-correlation matrix of all the test items:

$$\alpha = \frac{(n \times \bar{r})}{\left(1 + \left(\bar{r} \times (n-1)\right)\right)}$$

where $\bar{r}$ = the mean inter-item correlation and n is the number of items in the test. So if there are 20 items in the test with $\bar{r}$ = 0.6 then:

$$\alpha = \frac{(20 \times .6)}{\left(1 + (.6 \times 19)\right)} = .895$$

Cronbach's α is readily computed and appears in general software suites such as SPSS. The Kuder–Richardson formulae, KR20 and KR21, are earlier versions of Cronbach's α for dichotomously (0/1) scored scales. You will see it mentioned in some texts.

THE STANDARD ERROR OF MEASUREMENT (*SEM*) AND ITS APPLICATION

As measurement is not perfectly reliable, it must mean that it is unlikely that any particular score we observe is an exact estimate of the value. Knowing the reliability and standard deviation of a test enables us to determine the range within which the 'true' answer is likely to fall. This involves computing the standard error of measurement (SEM) in order to set confidence intervals (CI) around a particular observation. The SEM is defined as:

$$SEM = SD \times \sqrt{1 - r}$$

where SD = standard deviation of the test and $\sqrt{1-r}$ = square root of 1 minus the reliability of the test. We place a CI by finding the SEM and multiplying it by ± 1.96, representing the 95% limits in the normal distribution. For example, if we observe a score of 25 on a test with a reliability of 0.8 and an SD of 5.0 the SEM is:

$$SEM = 5 * \sqrt{1 - 0.8} = 2.24$$

and the confidence intervals are 1.96± 2.24 = ±4.4. So we can be reasonably confident that the true score lies between 25 ± 4.4, i.e. 20.6 and 29.4.

Jacobson's Reliable Change Index (RCI)

We have shown that all measurement is likely to be unreliable to some extent and therefore difference between two scores from an individual (i.e. a change score) might be a consequence simply of measurement error. Payne and Jones (1957) initially discussed statistical approaches to analysing changes in individuals, but it was not until Jacobson published a series of articles (Jacobson, Follette & Revenstorf, 1984; Jacobson & Revenstorf, 1988; Jacobson et al., 1999; Jacobson & Truax, 1991) that the procedure became widely known and used in evaluating psychological treatments (Lambert & Ogles, 2009; Ogles, Lunnen & Bonesteel, 2001). Jacobson and his colleagues outlined a method to answer two important questions about the difference between an individual's pre-treatment and post-treatment score on a standard measure. First, we might wish to know whether an individual's change is *reliable* and second, whether it is *clinically significant*.

Determining the reliability of change

Jacobson used classical test theory to set up confidence intervals around the pre-treatment score, and he called this the Reliable Change Index (RCI). He set the RCI at ±1.96, i.e.

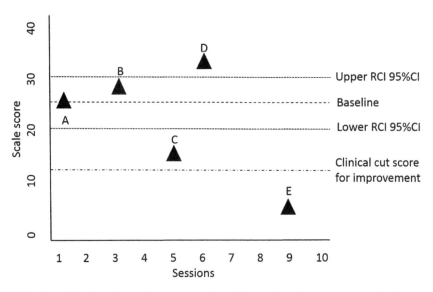

FIGURE 2.2 The Reliable Change Index and clinically significant change: graphical illustration of possible outcomes from a single patient over time

equivalent to the 95% confidence interval around the baseline score. Figure 2.2 illustrates a series of possible outcomes for a single patient over time.

In this figure, the y-axis is the score on the outcome measure and in this case a reduction in the score represents an improvement in status. The x-axis represents various time points over a number of sessions. Each of the data points is labelled A to E. The data point A is at pre-treatment. If the person makes no change then at later time points their score would fall on the dotted line denoting the baseline reference score. The confidence intervals for the RCI are shown as parallel lines either side of the no-change baseline reference. Data point B indicates that the person has not changed significantly because their data fall within the RCI lines. At data point C the person has moved beyond the RCI line marking the lower confidence interval, so they have made a reliable change (improvement). Note that you can also use this method to ask whether a person has deteriorated: are they reliably worse off? In the Figure 2.2 at data point D the person has moved beyond the RCI line marking upper confidence interval, indicating a reliable deterioration.

Computing the RCI

Computing the values of the RCI is relatively easy. Jacobson proposed that the RCI could be established using the simple equation:

$$RCI = \frac{(\text{pre-treatment score} - \text{post-treatment score})}{SE_{diff}}$$

where SE_{diff} is the standard error of the difference, and in turn this is

$$SE_{diff} = \sqrt{2 \times SEM^2}$$

Remember, SEM = standard error of measurement = SD × $\sqrt{(1 - r)}$.

For example, David has a pre-treatment score of 70 on a standardised test of social anxiety, with a mean = 50, SD = 10 and test–retest reliability = 0.8. After eight sessions of therapy his post-treatment score = 55. We want to know whether this change is reliable or whether it might be attributable to measurement error? This can be achieved in three simple steps:

First, compute the $SE_{diff} = 10 \times \sqrt{1 - .8} = 4.47$

Then compute $SE_{diff} = \sqrt{2 \times 4.47^2} = 6.32$

Finally compute the $RCI = \frac{(70 - 55)}{6.32} = 2.37$

As the value of the RCI exceeds 1.96 in the table for z values, we can be reasonably confident that David's improved status is not just due to the inherent unreliability of the test.

Two important questions arise when computing the RCI: (1) which empirical measure of reliability should one use, and (2) from where should one obtain an estimate of the reliability? These points were not always made clear in the original exposition of the method and one can find arguments for the two common forms, test–retest and measures of internal consistency. On balance, the argument for using a measure of internal consistency, usually Cronbach's α, is the more compelling. First, it comes nearer to the conceptual basis for reliability. Recall the imagined two perfectly parallel tests. In contrast, the test–retest measure of reliability compounds the actual reliability of the measure and any actual changes in the measure over time. In practice this means that internal reliability is always (almost) higher than the test–retest reliability and, as a result, the SEM will be smaller and as a consequence it will give a 'tighter' estimate of the RCI and more people will be judged to have changed reliably.

In many publications the estimate of the reliability is made from the available data, but this can only happen when the data comprise a reasonably large data set, at least enough participants to be able to compute Cronbach's α. In clinical settings where one is working on a case-by-case basis it is simply not possible to compute α for a single case. Furthermore, one might argue that the estimate of α from a single sample is likely to be an approximate estimate of the true value. It would be better to obtain α from a much larger set of norms. These data are published for several of the more common measures, but where they are not, you will have to use information available in publications. Some guidance on how to do this is given in the section 'Obtaining norms for the RCI and CSC'.

Variations on Jacobson's theme

Jacobson's original proposal for computing the RCI was simple and elegant, as it only required the pre- and post-treatment scores from a client and two pieces of information about the test – the SD and a reliability coefficient. However, there have been a number of technical criticisms and suggestions for alternative computations. The main focus of the criticisms has been the influence of unreliability on the phenomenon of regression to the mean (briefly discussed in Chapter 1); see Campbell and Kenny (1999) for a clear discussion of this phenomenon. The objection is that Jacobson's method does not take regression to the mean into account. There have been several proposals about how to correct the RCI estimate for regression to the mean (Hageman & Arrindell, 1993, 1999; Hsu, 1989, 1995; Speer, 1992).

All of these methods require additional psychometric information, including estimates of population means and variance, pre- and post-treatment estimates of means, variance and reliabilities, which are often not readily obtainable. Atkins and colleagues (2005) conducted a study where they simulated data sets in which they systematically varied reliability ($r = 0.6 - 0.95$), the magnitude of the pre- to post-treatment change and the correlation between the pre- to post-measure. They computed the RCI using Jacobson's original method and three other methods that incorporated corrections for regression to the mean. They examined how well the methods agreed with each other in classifying 'cases' as reliably changed or not. Combining the six possible comparisons between the measures, the overall level of agreement was high (0.85 using Cohen's Kappa) and this was especially so when the reliability of the measure was high, > 0.85. It is also worth noting that the level of agreement between Jacobson's method and the other three was higher than that between the various combinations of the other three methods for the complete range of reliability coefficients. Lambert and Ogles (2009) reviewed several empirical studies investigating variations in RCI and concluded that 'it has yet to be demonstrated that any of the other approaches is superior, in terms of more accurate estimates of clinically significant change' (p. 494). Given that there appears to be no demonstrable superiority for any of the more complex methods and that Jacobson's method is simple and elegant, the argument for using it in practice is compelling.

Determining the Clinically Significant Change criterion

The second question Jacobson asked was whether the individual had made a sufficiently large change for it to be regarded as clinically meaningful. Jacobson used the term clinical significance, although we will see that his interpretation of clinical significance is defined by the statistical distribution of scores from different clinical groups on the test. The cut points on the measure were called Clinically Significant Change criteria (CSC). Figure 2.2 shows the inclusion of a clinical cut score representing a clinical improvement. Data point E is therefore not only a reliable improvement but also a clinically significant one.

Figure 2.3 shows the essential features of Jacobson's approach to defining a clinical significant change criterion. This figure represents the distribution of scores from a clinical group and a non-clinical contrast (reference) group. In this case, lower scores on the test represent non-clinical status and higher scores represent the clinical state. We assume that the data are derived from a measure where the scores for the clinical and non-clinical groups are normally distributed and that the test has reasonable construct validity and can discriminate between the two groups. This is shown by the degree to which the distributions do not overlap. The upper panel of Figure 2.3 shows the situation when the distributions of the clinical and non-clinical groups show a modest overlap, which is typical of many measures. Jacobson proposed three statistically defined criteria by which clinical significance may be operationalised. He labelled these as criteria **a**, **b** and **c**. Each criterion places a cut point (score) on the measurement scale that effectively splits the observations into 'dysfunctional'/'clinical' and 'functional'/'non-clinical' categories.

Criterion *a*

For criterion **a** the cut score is set so that functional scores after therapy should fall outside the range of the dysfunctional population defined as the extreme end of the dysfunctional distribution, more than 2 standard deviations in the direction of the normal reference group. The criterion **a** is therefore:

$$a = \text{Mean}_{\text{dysfunctional group}} - 2 \times \text{SD}_{\text{dysfunctional group}}$$

Jacobson's choice of 2 standard deviations is a close approximation (and slightly more conservative) to the familiar value of 1.96.

Criterion *b*

The level of functioning should fall within the range of the non-dysfunctional group. For criterion **b** the cut score is set so that score after therapy should fall within the range of the functional population, i.e. with the extreme end of the functional group in the direction of the dysfunctional group. This time we use the mean and SD of the functional group to define the cut point:

$$b = \text{Mean}_{\text{functional group}} + 2 \times \text{SD}_{\text{functional group}}$$

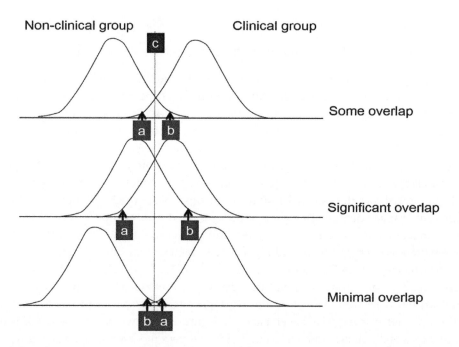

FIGURE 2.3 Schematic representation of Jacobson's statistical approach to defining clinically significant change

Criterion c

The final criterion, **c**, was defined so that it should place the client closer to the mean of the functional group than to the mean of the dysfunctional group. The formula for this is a little more complex because it takes account of, and adjusts for, the likelihood that the variances of the functional and dysfunctional groups are often different:

$$c = \frac{\text{Mean}_{\text{function group}} \times \text{SD}_{\text{dysfunctional group}} + \text{Mean}_{\text{dysfunctional group}} \times \text{SD}_{\text{functional group}}}{\text{SD}_{\text{dysfunctional group}} + \text{SD}_{\text{functional group}}}$$

Obviously the question arises as to which of these three criteria one should chose in evaluating a case. Jacobson and others have discussed this question in some detail (Jacobson et al., 1999; Kendall, Marrs-Garcia, Nath & Sheldrick, 1999). The answers depend on what information you have about the distributions, the degree to which they overlap and the extent to which you wish to make a conservative judgement. Before exploring this further it is worth commenting on the relatively straightforward case that arises when only information on the clinical population is available. This might arise when investigating a phenomenon that is apparently rarely present in a non-clinical group. For example, consider an intervention to reduce the distress experienced by people who have command hallucinations. Ideally a successful treatment would reduce the distress to zero, but one might be willing to accept a degree of change that resulted in the end of treatment score being at the extreme end of the clinical distribution. Under these circumstances criterion **a** is the only criterion available.

In contrast, where the distributions do not or hardly overlap – bottom panel of Figure 2.3 – criterion **a** will be too lenient as it is very clear that this cut score is either not or only just encompassed by the non-clinical distribution. Under these conditions, criteria **b** and **c** would be more likely to represent a shift into the non-clinical range. On the other hand, in situations where the two distributions overlap considerably, both **b** and **c** will not be conservative enough and **a** might be a better option. Thus, it might be wiser not to use measures where there is a known significant overlap between the scores from the clinical and non-clinical groups, as it is apparent that the tests may not have sufficient discriminant validity, i.e. they cannot separate the clinical groups.

Under many circumstances when the distributions show a modest overlap, criterion **c** will be the most appropriate to use and it takes into account all the known information about the test and the performance of the clinical and non-clinical groups. As Jacobson notes (Jacobson et al., 1999, p. 301) '**c** is not arbitrary. It is based on the relative probability of a particular score ending up in one population as opposed to another'.

In practice the selection of a cut score requires some thought. It will depend partly on the data you have to hand and on your willingness to conduct some further analysis – as discussed below. As in all good scientific and clinical practice, it is better for you to select the criterion *before* you conduct your analysis and to avoid a general 'fishing expedition' that tests all the criteria and selectively reports the most favourable one: *post hocery* is generally to be avoided.

Other criteria for determining cut scores

Jacobson's cut scores are determined solely by statistical parameters of the test (mean and variation) rather than any external criterion. A carefully developed and normed test may use other methods, such as standardised diagnostic interviews, to assigning people to clinical and non-clinical groups. Under these conditions criterion **c** may be an optimal point for separating the membership of the group, especially when there is little overlap between the two distributions. Test developers may also use ROC (receiver operating characteristic) methods to determine the sensitivity and specificity of various cut scores. A cut score that is determined by information beyond the mere distribution of the scores is sometimes referred to as an external criterion.

Obtaining norms for the RCI and CSC

Many standard measures in clinical psychology are initially published in journals in a seemingly *ad hoc* manner. For example, you can find measures of health anxiety that have been developed by clinical researchers that are subsequently used by other researchers. As a consequence there may be several studies of a measure that report basic psychometric data (M, SD, reliability) but, unlike well-developed measures such as the CORE-OM or SCL-90R, there is no publication that gives norms by age, gender, diagnostic category and so on. So what should you do? One solution is to use the data from a single paper where the sample more or less corresponds to the one from which your patient might be drawn, e.g. outpatient mental health group. Another solution would be to average the available means, SDs and reliability coefficients, but doing this would ignore important features such as differences in the sample sizes and characteristics. A better solution would be to obtain data from several samples and pool these to form more robust estimates of the parameters in which you are interested. In essence you need to perform a meta-analysis (Borenstein, Hedges & Rothstein, 2009; Field & Gillett, 2010).

Performing a meta-analysis may sound rather daunting and time consuming, but in practice one can perform a basic meta-analysis to obtain pooled estimates of the mean, SD and reliability coefficient relatively quickly using a standard spreadsheet such as Excel™. There are several programmes, both commercial and open source, and routines for SPSS, SAS and other statistical packages, but for a relatively small-scale analysis then a simple spreadsheet is a more than adequate tool.

The basic sequence of a meta-analysis is:

1 Conduct a comprehensive literature search
2 Decide which studies to include
3 Extract the relevant data
4 Calculate the effect size.

The first and last of these steps require some technical knowledge, and completing a meta-analysis requires a series of judgements and decisions to be made. It is therefore sensible to cross-check these judgements and decisions with others. For example, developing a search strategy to obtain all the possible publications on trials in some topics can result in thousands of 'hits' followed by many hours of reading abstracts and titles to make sure that you are only including appropriate papers. There are rules for doing this and, to be frank, most clinicians will have neither the time, inclination, person power (meta-analyses are done by teams of people) nor the expertise to do this. You may have to compromise, and often a 'quick and dirty search' on Google Scholar will reveal several candidate papers (or many if the scale is widely used, e.g. the BDI). You should, however, set criteria for selecting articles (inclusion and exclusion criteria) *before* you begin selection. The studies should include samples from the clinical population that includes your client and also, if possible, from populations that might serve as a control group. These could be other clinical groups but without the clinical condition that your client has, for example, an anxious group without obsessional symptoms, a non-clinical group or a special population such as students. The articles need to report means (M), standard deviations (SD) and sample size (n) and reliability coefficients: test–retest (r) or preferably Cronbach's alpha (α).

One thing to be aware of is the possibility of duplicate publications of the same data. This can occur when authors report a randomised controlled trial and then, in a secondary publication, report a reanalysis of the same data exploring a second set of hypotheses, e.g. the relationship between process measures and outcome. Extracting data from articles can be a frustrating experience, for several reasons. Sometimes the data are simply not there. Authors may say they report them but they are not present in the text. On other occasions the data may not be in the place where you expect them: tables do not always contain the data and you may have to delve into the details of the text. You should also be alert to the fact that decimal points can be in the wrong place, resulting in values that are too large or too small. When these issues arise it is advisable to contact the corresponding author, if possible, to seek clarification. Needless to say it is necessary to double-check your own transcription and data entry.

Combining data in a meta-analysis

The aim of meta-analysis is to aggregate data to provide an estimate of a given statistic, known generically as the *effect size*. In the most common case in meta-analysis, the effect size represents the difference between treated and control groups, e.g. CBT for social anxiety vs treatment as usual. Meta-analysis can also be used to combine other types of data such as those from psychometric tests. In analysing test data we need to compute effect sizes, i.e. the best estimates of aggregated values for the mean, variance (SD^2) and reliability (Cronbach's α is the preferred reliability estimate). There are three important things to consider: (1) whether to use a fixed or random effect model; (2) how to obtain the weights for each observation; and (3) when we should run separate analyses for different types of sample. The standard protocol for combining data involves weighting the observations by the inverse of sample error variance of each observation. Small studies, which are likely to have a bigger error variance, have a smaller weight and therefore contribute less to the estimation of the overall parameter.

Fixed and random effects

In meta-analysis there are two possible models for combining the data from different studies, and a basic understanding of the difference between fixed and random effects in meta-analysis is essential. A good technical introduction is given by Hedges and Vevea (1998) and a very elegant, clear introduction is provided by Borenstein and his colleagues (2009) in their introductory text on meta-analysis.

The *fixed effect* model assumes that any differences between samples are due to sampling error. Each sample estimates the true effect size and the only reason for differences between samples is attributable to sampling error. The statistical model is written as: $T_i = \theta_i + \varepsilon_i$, where T_i = the effect size estimate for the ith sample, θ_i = effect size parameter and ε_i the error: and there are assumptions about the normal distribution of T.

Without any sampling error, the estimates from each study would be exactly the same. The procedure for testing whether this assumption is met is to generate a Q statistic which is tested with the χ^2 distribution with k degrees of freedom, where:

K = number of observations − 1.

If this is significant this suggests that there may be factors other than sampling variance contributing to the variation between the samples.

The alternative is a *random effect* model. This model assumes that the variation in estimates between samples is made up of sampling error + other random effects that vary between samples that may be explained by differences in other parameters, e.g. proportion males, age, comorbidities and source of recruitment (clinic, community). In this case the equation for T is:

$$T_i = \theta_i + \xi_i + \varepsilon_i.$$

The extra ξ incorporates the random effect component. The random effect component can be estimated from the Q value generated in the fixed effect model and the meta-analysis re-run. In a random effect model the estimate of the effect size will be different from the fixed effect model and it will have a wider confidence interval.

Choosing between fixed and random effect models

One approach is to start with the fixed effect model and test the significance of Q. This is just 'brute empiricism' and we really ought to have an *a priori* hypothesis about our analysis. We should only choose a fixed effect model if we believe that all the studies included in the analysis are equivalent: for example, if we have several replications of a study with samples drawn from the same population. The second reason for choosing a fixed effect model is when we want to estimate a common effect size for a prescribed population, and more importantly we do not wish to generalise to other populations. On the other hand when we select data from a set of studies that have been conducted in different settings by different researchers (typical of many clinical situations), it would stretch credibility to assume that they were equivalent. There are many ways in which these studies could differ and these differences may have influenced the data. It would be imprudent to assume they have a common effect size, and using the random effect model would be more credible. I certainly think that this is the case with the sort of data that we are dealing with in this case, i.e. heterogeneous studies from different clinics and settings. Field (2001) also makes the argument that for the 'real world' data that we work with it is probably better (and safer) to assume a random effect model.

Computing weights for means, variance and Cronbach's α

The three weights are relatively easy to compute. The standard error (se) of a mean from a sample size n with standard deviation (Sd) is: $= Sd/\sqrt{n}$. The weight for the ith sample is: $w_i = 1/se^2$. These are easily computed and allow us to compute the effect size for the means.

Less familiar are the standard error estimates for the variance and reliability (Cronbach's α). These are shown in Table 2.3, along with the formula for estimating the weight for combining the means. Whereas the meta-analysis of the mean and variance of a test can be carried out without further ado, the analysis of Cronbach's α should be conducted after the α values have been transformed to a new value T. The equation for the transformation for the ith sample is:

$$T_i = (1 - \alpha_i)^{1/3}$$

After the data have been analysed, the effect size estimate of T must be converted back to an α value using the following equation: $\alpha = |1 - T \circ^3|$ (Botella, Suero & Gambara, 2010; Rodriguez & Maeda, 2006).

Selecting observations for inclusion in the meta-analysis

The final issue to consider is which observations to include in the meta-analysis. Unlike meta-analyses of a specific treatment, in the meta-analysis of test data it will often make sense to run separate meta-analyses for clinical and control groups. After all, we wish to estimate the summary test parameters for both populations to use in the RCI/CSC analyses. We might therefore simply assign observations to either clinical or control populations, but this is often too simplistic. Authors frequently use samples of convenience to develop the measure such as university/college students, but they don't necessarily provide a reasonably matched control group for clinical samples, who are often older and with a different mix of gender and social economic status. A second source of concern is whether the comparisons between control and clinical groups should always be drawn from the same study, i.e. only from studies where authors provide data from clinical and control samples. It might be argued that this strategy will control for 'third variable' differences that might be present if we were to obtain clinical and control samples from entirely different publications.

TABLE 2.3 Computation of weights for the meta-analysis of measures: Means, variance and Cronbach's α

Effect size to be computed	se or variance (v_i)	w_i
Mean	$se = \dfrac{sd}{\sqrt{n}}$	$w_i = \dfrac{1}{se^2}$
Variance	$v_i = \dfrac{2 \times Sd^4}{(n-1)}$	$w_i = \dfrac{1}{v_i}$
Cronbach's α	$v_i = \dfrac{18 \times J_i \times (n_i - 1) \times (1 - \alpha_i)^{2/3}}{(J_i - 1) \times (9 \times n_i - 11)^2}$	$w_i = \dfrac{1}{v_i}$

se, standard error of the mean: *Sd*, standard deviation; *n*, sample size. In the computations relating to Cronbach's α, n_i = sample size of the ith group, J_i = the number of items in the scale for the ith (normally this is the same for each group, e.g. the HAD depression scale has 7 items).

Technically speaking we need to consider whether the samples are truly independent. It would be possible to conduct our meta-analysis using a more sophisticated multi-level modelling approach, but it is unlikely that a practising clinician or clinical team would have the resources to do this. Adopting a more pragmatic approach is probably the best course.

The mathematical techniques of meta-analysis are just that, 'techniques'. They don't replace careful thought and consideration about what to combine. Some time spent considering your clinical setting and obtaining good descriptive information about typical ages, gender distribution and other factors that might contribute to variability in measurement is important. This will allow you to set up plausible selection criteria for selecting data sets to include in your meta-analyses of clinical and non-clinical groups.

Table 2.4 shows the input and output from an Excel spreadsheet of a small meta-analysis. The data are simulated. Imagine you have a patient who has problems with hoarding and you find a measure, 'The tolerance of clutter scale', which has 20 items. The scale appears to be relatively new and you find four publications with data collected from samples of obsessional hoarders and comparison groups drawn from the general population. At the right-hand side of the table the meta-analysed values for the means, the variance and alpha are shown for the clinical and contrast groups. These data can then be used to compute the RCI and CSC analyses for your patients. Note that you will need to take the square root of the variance to find the standard deviation to use in the RCI and CSC calculations.

CONCLUSIONS

Standardised measures are extremely valuable in assessing change in single cases. They allow you to reference your client to the wider population. Generic measures such as the CORE-OM or SCL-90R are particularly useful in this regard, but they will not capture more specific problems such as obsessional features, specific sorts of anxiety and mood disorders, or aspects

TABLE 2.4 Input and output of data needed to meta-analyse test scores

Authors	Year	Mean	Variance	n	Alpha	Number of items in scale	Mean	Variance	Alpha
Clinical group									
Smith & Jones	2013	40.65	95.45	89	0.90	20	37.65	88.68	0.90
Brown *et al.*	2011	35.00	105.06	122	0.91	20			
Kinder *et al.*	2010	37.00	66.42	52	0.86	20			
Jimson *et al.*	2009	38.00	89.11	100	0.89	20			
Comparison Group									
Smith & Jones	2013	21.90	76.74	76	0.90	20	19.81	79.73	0.90
Brown *et al.*	2011	19.45	76.91	101	0.91	20			
Kinder *et al.*	2010	17.66	89.68	65	0.86	20			
Jimson *et al.*	2009	20.12	78.85	87	0.89	20			

The left-hand side of the table shows the data needed for the computations while the right-hand side shows the meta-analysed values for the mean, variance and Cronbach's alpha.

of a physical health problem. Therefore it is strategically sensible to consider supplementing a generic measure with a measure that is specifically designed to sample your client's main problem, e.g. a measure of a key component in OCD or depression.

Wherever possible look for a well-standardised and normed test based with (1) norms based on clearly defined and described clinical and non-clinical groups; (2) good reliability, preferably internal consistency ($\alpha > 0.80$); and (3) large samples, used for establishing norms. It is also helpful if the norms are stratified by key variables likely to influence the estimates of summary data, e.g. sex and age, setting (inpatient vs outpatient) and comorbidity. The presence of a comprehensive test manual is a bonus. It is a relatively sad reflection that there are few specific measures that meet these criteria, so where these data are not available you might consider running a small meta-analysis to improve the quality of your norms if the measure is only available in a few publications.

At the very least you should take measurements pre and post your intervention. If you can obtain measurements on two pre-treatment occasions, do so. This will allow you to check for fluctuation in the baseline and to consider the role of regression to the mean. Similarly, post-treatment and follow-up data are invaluable. Conduct an analysis of reliable and clinically significant change, and specify your preferred CSC criterion in advance. Be careful about the conclusions you draw from these analyses. At the very most you can determine whether someone has made a genuine change that is not the result of measurement error. You cannot conclude that the change was brought about by therapy; you need additional data and another measurement strategy to do that.

Footnote: software for meta-analysis

There is a wide range of software for running meta-analysis, including dedicated commercial programmes such as Comprehensive Meta-Analysis (Borenstein *et al.*, 2009) and RevMan, which is freely available from the Cochrane Collaboration (Cochrane Collaboration, 2015).

Acronyms used in Chapter 2

CORE-OM: CORE outcome measure (CORE: Clinical Outcomes in Routine Evaluation)
BDI-II: Beck depression inventory, 2nd edition
HADS: Hospital anxiety and depression scale
PHQ: Patient health questionnaire
SCL-90R: Symptom checklist, 90-item revised version
SDQ: Strengths and difficulties questionnaire.

REFERENCES

Atkins, D. C., Bedics, J. D., McGlinchey, J. B. & Beauchaine, T. P. (2005). Assessing clinical significance: Does it matter which method we use? *Journal of Consulting and Clinical Psychology*, 73(5), 982–9.

Borenstein, M., Hedges, L. V. & Rothstein, H. (2009). *Introduction to Meta-Analysis*. Chichester: Wiley.

Botella, J., Suero, M. & Gambara, H. (2010). Psychometric inferences from a meta-analysis of reliability and internal consistency coefficients. *Psychological Methods*, 15(4), 386–97.

Cameron, I. M., Cardy, A., Crawford, J. R., du Toit, S. W., Hay, S., Lawton, K., . . . & Reid, I. C. (2011). Measuring depression severity in general practice: discriminatory performance of the PHQ-9, HADS-D, and BDI-II. Br J Gen Pract, 61(588).

Campbell, D. T. & Kenny, D. (1999). A Primer on Regression Artefacts. New York: Guilford.

Cochrane Collaboration (2015). Review Manager (RevMan) (Version 5.3). Oxford: Cochrane Collaboration. Retrieved from http://tech.cochrane.org/revman

Cronbach, L. J. (1951). Coefficient alpha and the internal structure of tests. Psychometrika, 16(3), 297–334.

Field, A. P. (2001). Meta-analysis of correlation coefficients: a Monte Carlo comparison of fixed- and random-effects methods. Psychological Methods, 6(2), 161–80.

Field, A. P. & Gillett, R. (2010). How to do a meta-analysis. British Journal of Mathematical and Statistical Psychology, 63(Pt 3), 665–94.

Hageman, W. J. J. M. & Arrindell, W. A. (1993). A further refinement of the Reliable Change (RC) Index by improving the pre–post difference score: Introducing RC-sub(ID). Behaviour Research and Therapy, 31(7), 693–700.

Hageman, W. J. J. M. & Arrindell, W. A. (1999). Establishing clinically significant change: Increment of precision and the distinction between individual and group level of analysis. Behaviour Research and Therapy, 37(12), 1169–93.

Hedges, L. V. & Vevea, J. L. (1998). Fixed- and random-effects models in meta-analysis. Psychological Methods, 3(4), 486–504.

Hsu, L. M. (1989). Reliable changes in psychotherapy: Taking into account regression toward the mean. Behavioral Assessment, 11(4), 459–467.

Hsu, L. M. (1995). Regression toward the mean associated with measurement error and the identification of improvement and deterioration in psychotherapy. Journal of Consulting and Clinical Psychology, 63(1), 141–4.

Jacobson, N. S., Follette, W. C. & Revenstorf, D. (1984). Psychotherapy outcome research – methods for reporting variability and evaluating clinical significance. Behavior Therapy, 15(4), 336–52.

Jacobson, N. S. & Revenstorf, D. (1988). Statistics for assessing the clinical significance of psychotherapy techniques – issues, problems, and new developments. Behavioral Assessment, 10(2), 133–45.

Jacobson, N. S., Roberts, L. J., Berns, S. B. & McGlinchey, J. B. (1999). Methods for defining and determining the clinical significance of treatment effects: description, application, and alternatives. Journal of Consulting and Clinical Psychology, 67(3), 300–7.

Jacobson, N. S. & Truax, P. (1991). Clinical significance: a statistical approach to defining meaningful change in psychotherapy. Journal of Consulting and Clinical Psychology, 59, 12–19.

Kendall, P. C., Marrs-Garcia, A., Nath, S. R. & Sheldrick, R. C. (1999). Normative comparisons for the evaluation of clinical significance. Journal of Consulting and Clinical Psychology, 67(3), 285–99.

Lambert, M. J. & Ogles, B. M. (2009). Using clinical significance in psychotherapy outcome research: the need for a common procedure and validity data. Psychotherapy Research, 19(4–5), 493–501.

Nunnally, J. & Bernstein, I. H. (1994). Psychometric Theory (3rd edn). New York: McGraw-Hill.

Ogles, B. M., Lunnen, K. M. & Bonesteel, K. (2001). Clinical significance: History, application, and current practice. Clinical Psychology Review, 21, 421–46.

Payne, R. W. & Jones, H. G. (1957). Statistics for the investigation of individual cases. Journal of Clinical Psychology, 13(2), 115–21.

Rodriguez, M. C. & Maeda, Y. (2006). Meta-analysis of coefficient alpha. Psychological Methods, 11(3), 306–22.

Speer, D. C. (1992). Clinically significant change: Jacobson & Truax revisited. Journal of Consulting and Clinical Psychology, 60, 402–8.

Van Breukelen, G. J. & Vlaeyen, J. W. S. (2005). Norming clinical questionnaires with multiple regression: the Pain Cognition List. Psychological Assessment, 17(3), 336–44.

Chapter 3

Target measures: unique measures for the individual

Good measurement is a crucial component in conducting single-case research (Morley, 2015), and Horner and Odom (2014) advise that designing the measurement strategy should be the first step in designing the study. Measurement in single-case research generally focuses on target problems, i.e. problems relevant to the individual, rather than the constructs assessed by standardised measures that are typically used in randomised controlled trials and cohort studies. To some extent the target problems measured in single-case research are idiographic. What is measured is a behaviour or a complaint that is relevant to the individual. The measure therefore aims to capture the content of the problem rather than a psychological construct, which is typically measured using a standardised measure. In this chapter we consider the individual-focused measures that are typically used in single-case research designs. This chapter begins by considering idiographic measurement in general; it then explores the concepts of validity and reliability as applied to idiographic measurement. Direct observational methods are discussed before turning to the measurement of subjective states, where particular attention is paid to personal questionnaire methods because of their strong psychometric properties.

The pragmatic reason for considering individual-focused measures is that these are most likely to accurately capture the key or salient problems brought by the individual or significant others, e.g. parents and carers, to any consultation. These measures often represent the 'target' for treatment. In practice patients do not present their problems as a score on a standardised scale: 'My problem is that I score 32 on the BDI'. They are more likely to report particular symptoms: 'I struggle to get going in the morning'; 'I can't be bothered to do anything'. In many other presentations the complaint will be of specific behavioural problems: 'My daughter gets very distressed when we apply her eczema cream and refuses it half of the time'; 'When I leave the house I have to go through a routine several times, I get really anxious'. Some complaints may be captured by standardised measures but many are not, or are not captured adequately. To illustrate, consider a typical item drawn from a widely used measure in adult mental health services, the CORE-OM, in which the respondent is asked to rate how they have been over the last week using a 5-point scale denoting frequency (*not at all, only occasionally, sometimes, often, most of the time*) for each of the 34 items on the scale. The item 'I have been disturbed by unwanted thoughts and feelings' is very general and might be considered to lack specificity. What does the person do if they have only unwanted thoughts? What sort of thoughts is the person reporting? The thought that their newly married child is unhappy, or a recurrent intrusive thought that they have left the gas cooker on when they leave the house? How should they respond if they have no thought but they do have intrusive images? So in this example the question is not capturing the content that has relevance for the individual. The response scale is also predetermined. It is a general frequency scale and there is no way of knowing what frequency is bothersome or significant for the individual and the response is constrained to frequency. Furthermore we do not know whether the frequency of changes over the week, e.g. whether it is more problematic on work days. In addition, other parameters (intensity or duration of experience) might be equally important for this individual. The challenge is therefore to develop a measure that captures the content of the person's complaint and a scale that satisfactorily characterises the range of likely and desired experience.

When using single-case methods, measures of target problems need to be taken repeatedly and sometimes at close intervals, i.e. more often than the two or three times that is typical of the pre–post and follow-up measurement design discussed in Chapter 2. Chapter 4 outlines several single-case research designs and explains why repeated measurement of target measures is an inherent component of these designs. So an additional requirement of any measure is that it must be readily repeatable. In many clinical settings this means that measurement cannot be overly burdensome for the client. Researchers in the applied behaviour analysis tradition restrict their measurements to observable behaviour and use a range of direct observation methods to obtain the data (Hartmann, 1984; Horner & Odom, 2014). Measurement by direct observation often captures the frequency of a specific behaviour or the proportion of time the behaviour occurs in a given time. Researchers with other theoretical orientations, e.g. cognitive-behavioural and other psychotherapeutic schools, are more likely to measure a variety of thoughts, beliefs, emotional states and behaviour using self-report methods with specially designed questionnaires. These can be incorporated into a diary format to be completed daily or more frequently, or they may be completed at other set times, e.g. during a therapy session.

The frequency of measurement in single-case research varies considerably, from multiple occasions within a single session of observations through to daily diary records and weekly or monthly observations. The exact frequency will depend on the particular problem and the context in which it is being investigated. Similarly there may be considerable variation in what is measured and in the method of data collection. For example, a researcher interested in obsessional behaviour may measure the frequency with which the participant checks or the degree of distress associated with particular intrusive thoughts rather than the overall degree of obsessionality as measured by a standard questionnaire.

The simplest definition of idiographic measurement is one that is uniquely tailored to a specific individual. The uniqueness can be captured in two domains. First, the *content* of the measure may be unique in that it represents a particular behaviour or a statement, or set of statements, representing particular subjective states (thoughts, beliefs or feelings). Second, the *scale* used to measure the extent of the behaviour or subjective state may also be unique and designed for the individual. The personal questionnaire (PQ), discussed later in this chapter, is a fully idiographic measure of subjective states in that both the content and scale are uniquely derived from the client's report of their complaints. There are, however, many examples of measures in the single-case literature where target measures are not fully idiographic. At one extreme a researcher may select particular constructs of particular interest and devise a suitable measure using a subset of items from a standardised questionnaire. For example, Vlaeyen *et al.* (2001) wished to make daily measurements of fear of pain, fear of movement and catastrophising in chronic pain patients with specific fears that making certain movements would result in increased bodily harm. To do this they selected a subset of items from established questionnaire measures and combined these in an easy-to-complete diary format. More commonly the researcher will write items representing target variables of interest, e.g. 'Today my anxiety has been . . .', and these will be paired with response scales to capture the relevant dimension such as frequency or intensity. Commonly used response scales are 10 cm visual analogue scales with defined endpoints such as 'not at all' and 'all the time' (frequency), numerical rating scales, e.g. 0–10, or Likert scales with defined scale points, e.g. not at all, some of the time, much of the time, most of the time, all of the time. Variations in the intensity of a complaint can be captured with phrases such as 'extremely intense', 'very intense', 'moderately intense' and so forth.

One set of objections sometimes voiced about the measures used in single-case research concerns issues of validity and reliability. These are important issues and the main emphasis of this chapter is consideration of validity and reliability for the types of measures used in single-case research. We will consider both measures of subjective states and direct observation of behaviour. The issue of validity is similar in both cases, but the problem of estimating reliability has been tackled differently. We begin by examining validity as it has been addressed in classical test theory.

VALIDITY

The validity of measurement is fundamental to any science or applied measurement in real-world settings. The concept of validity is still debated and developing (Borsboom, Mellenbergh & van Heerden, 2004; Strauss & Smith, 2009), and this section of the chapter provides a précis of its development. Reporting a measure's reliability and validity in a clinical scientific paper is considered essential, but it is often reduced to a simple statement: 'Measure X has adequate reliability and validity (string of citations) and the internal consistency, Cronbach's α, in this sample was 0.86'. According to validity theorists (Messick, 1995; Strauss & Smith, 2009), however, this type of statement somewhat misrepresents the concept of validity. The central plank of measurement validity is *construct validity*, defined as 'the extent to which a measure assesses the construct it is deemed to measure' (Strauss & Smith, 2009, p. 2). Strauss and Smith also define a construct as 'a psychological process or characteristic believed to account for individual or group differences in behavior' (p. 2). A contemporary view of constructs and construct validity has emerged over the past 60–70 years. Its main feature is the recognition that many of the phenomena that interest psychologists, e.g. intelligence, aspects of personality, anxiety and catastrophising, were not directly observable but were hypothetical constructs inferred from various observations. In 1955 Cronbach and Meehl outlined how one might develop evidence for constructs (Cronbach & Meehl, 1955). Central to their argument was the necessity to articulate specific theories and predictions about the relationships between constructs that describe psychological processes. They termed this the 'nomological network', which described and defined the intricate interplay between theoretical explications of the construct and the observations deemed to reflect the implied relationships. At the most basic level one should be able to indicate the extent to which different constructs are correlated and the direction of the correlations. It is even better if one can make more exact predictions about the magnitude of the relationship, but this degree of specificity seems rare in psychology. Once the relationships are described it is then possible to evaluate the performance of measures that are said to represent the constructs against the template of expected relationships.

One important aspect of this viewpoint was the recognition that construct validity subsumed other types of validity that were already recognised. The first of these was content validity: the degree that a measure captures relevant aspects of the construct. To ensure adequate content validity one needs to demonstrate that 'test items are a sample of the universe in which the investigator is interested' (Cronbach & Meehl, 1955, p. 282). Many constructs are multifaceted and require a range of items to capture them. So if a measure does not represent the relevant facets, then inferences about the construct made on the basis of the test scores will be erroneous. For example, a depression scale may lack content validity if it only assesses the affective component of depression but fails to take into account the behavioural component. Conversely a scale may contain items that for the patient or population of interest are irrelevant or better explained by other features. For example, the assessment of depression in people with physical illness is problematic because of the overlap of somatic symptoms in depression and many illnesses. In the applied clinical setting, therefore, one must scrutinise the content of the measure to ensure that it fully captures the facets of the construct of interest and importance for the particular client. Thus a significant element of judgement exists in relation to determining content validity.

The second was criterion validity: the extent to which the measure relates to a specific criterion. Strauss and Smith (2009) give an example of an early psychometric problem that has current resonance. One hundred years ago the US army wished to screen out individuals who were vulnerable to war-neurosis (Post Traumatic Stress Disorder in today's parlance). The criterion was therefore the clinical outcome of neurosis. The aim of this particular screening test was predictive validity of a future event. A measure of concurrent validity may be obtained by correlating the measure of interest to another measure or set of measures taken concurrently. In many settings, defining and measuring the criterion has historically proved to be 'more difficult than obtaining a good predictor' (Nunnally & Bernstein, 1994, p. 97). Often the criterion is a complex construct in its own right, e.g. job performance (a 'good' military officer, competent clinical psychologist), psychiatric diagnosis or 'outcome' in psychotherapy. As before, these problems are solved not merely by the sophistication of psychometric methods but by reasoned judgements about measures and their interpretation. A point, stressed by many validity theorists, is that 'validity is not a property of a test or assessment as such, but rather the meaning of the test scores' (Messick, 1995, p. 741). In his seminal article, Messick argues that not only must one take into account the interpretation of a score but also any implications for action that result from this interpretation.

Arguably Messick's elaborated view of validity represents the high watermark of a hundred years of developing the traditional concept of validity (Strauss & Smith, 2009). The tradition is alive and well, and Strauss and Smith note that the development of more advanced correlational methods such as structured equation modelling can further contribute to the understanding of validity. On the other hand, this elaborated view of validity has not been immune from criticism. For example, Borsboom et al. (2004) argue that the concept of validity based on the nomological network and its associated reliance on correlational methods is overcomplicated and unworkable for the 'practically oriented' (p. 1,061). Instead they argue that reverting to an earlier, more basic, view that a 'test is valid when it measures what it purports to measure' would be beneficial. They propose that a test is valid for measuring an attribute if the attribute exists and if variations in the attribute causally produce variations in the measure. Their critique contrasts their conception of validity based on ontology (the existence of something), reference (that the measure references a real attribute) and causality, with the pervasive current view implied by the nomological network, which, in contrast, emphasises epistemology, meaning and correlation.

In summary, most familiar measures in clinical settings have been developed in the nomothetic tradition using classical test theory. It should be clear from the earlier discussion that no measure is ever completely developed and fixed. We must use the information about a measure that we have at our disposal to make an informed judgement about its validity. Additional information about the performance of the measure in new settings and samples can be incorporated into the available norms and influence the interpretation of measurement validity. Nomothetic measures have great utility in assessing an individual. The norms can be used to identify the person's relative standing with respect to reference groups, clinical and non-clinical at assessment. The test reliability and standard deviation allow us to estimate confidence intervals for a score, and to determine whether an observed difference between two scores over time is genuine (reliable) rather than explained by error in the test. Furthermore the availability of norms allows us to set criteria for determining whether any observed change is 'clinically' meaningful.

The issue of validity in idiographic measurement

The simplest answer to the issue of validity in idiographic measurement is that it is equivalent to criterion validity in nomothetic terms. In most applied clinical contexts, especially those related to outcomes, the focus of measurement is a specific behaviour, complaint or set of complaints, not a construct. It is somewhat ironic that the development of validity theory originated with attempts to predict an outcome ('war neurosis') (Strauss & Smith, 2009). Problems with establishing a strong correlation led to the development of validity theory. One feature of development was the attention given to the measurement of the criterion which itself often required validation in its own right. The problem of validity is greatly simplified when what is measured has direct relevance for the individual concerned. Idiographic measurement can fulfil this condition relatively easily. We do not need to measure a construct – just the relevant clinical targets. Essentially we adopt a behavioural approach and measure only that which is directly relevant, whether it is behaviour or a person's subjective report. We do not need recourse to a construct for the purposes of measurement (Hartmann, 1984; Kazdin, 2010).

What to measure idiographically will often include a person's complaints. Broadly these can be categorised as experiencing too much or too little of behaviour ('I check the gas controls many times before leaving the kitchen'; 'I am unable to go in a lift'), thoughts and images ('I can't get the image of the accident out of my mind') and feelings ('I feel irritable a lot of the time'; 'I find it hard to be kind to myself). These may correspond to symptoms in many cases. Complaints have a *prima facie* quality that is sufficient in most cases to establish their validity. However, clients may also specify treatment goals or targets: 'I want to be able to stand in a supermarket queue without feeling terrified'. The combination of a desired endpoint provides not only the content of the problem but also a guide to the possible response scale that could be developed to measure an outcome.

Idiographic assessment places high priority on the client's definition of what is problematic as representative of criterion validity, but clinicians need to consider their client's proposals with regard to the likely utility of adopting the proposed outcome since there may be occasions when a desired outcome is unlikely to be attainable. For example, in the field of chronic illness the reduction or complete abolition of some symptoms, such as chronic pain, may well be unachievable. All the clinician's skill may be needed to renegotiate and help the client define more appropriate outcomes.

In addition to the individual, the opinion of others may be sought to establish the appropriateness of idiographic measurement. This may be particularly relevant in the case of children, and members of client groups with communication difficulties, such as some people with learning difficulties, older people with dementia, and in group settings (families and care settings). In such cases the consensual agreement of parents, carers and other users should provide a sound basis for establishing the validity of the proposed focus of measurement. Clinical researchers in applied behaviour analysis have developed systematic approaches to establishing 'social validity' (Foster & Mash, 1999; Sarafino, 2001). The questions of the criteria we use to determine what is to be measured do require thought and judgement, just as required in classical validity (Messick, 1995). Validity only becomes a problem when we wish to make claims for the measure that goes beyond what we have measured, e.g. when we make claims that a single measure represents a construct (Kazdin, 2010).

RELIABILITY AND IDIOGRAPHIC MEASUREMENT

Classical test theory provides an explicit model of error and reliability, and it is not obvious how this approach can be generalised to idiographic measures. There are two broad approaches to reliability in idiographic measurement: the first is based on the assessment of inter-observer agreement and the second on the notion of internal consistency.

Direct observation and inter-observer agreement

Direct observation of criterion behaviour is the methodology of choice in some fields of clinical research, e.g. applied behaviour analysis. The application of direct observational methods and reliability coding in real-time in some clinical contexts is unlikely because of the intensive demands on the clinician, and the requirement for a second observer. Nevertheless the extensive methodology for direct observations can be used in the clinical settings to determine how often observations should be taken, and to highlight the need for careful definition of what to observe. Observer agreement can often be obtained in settings where the client is accompanied by one or more carers. For example, it is good clinical practice to negotiate the agreement between a child and their parent about what constitutes the target problem, e.g. bed-wetting, temper tantrum, and conjoint recording of incidents may be the best way of tracking an outcome.

As in classical test theory, measurement can be affected by both systematic and random errors, and behavioural observation methodology has developed to control these errors as much as possible. Developing a direct observation protocol usually begins with an initial consultation with those concerned followed by a period of informal observations to scope the problem and assess the feasibility of making observations. At that stage a careful definition of the target behaviour(s) is drawn up. The definition may focus on the observable features of the behaviour (topographical definition) rather than requiring the observer to make a judgement of intent of the observed person (functional definition). Definitions should be clear, unambiguous and comprehensive and should also define what behaviour is not to be counted. At its simplest an observation schedule may include just a single behaviour – for example, hair-pulling or hitting another – but multiple behaviours can be included in the observation schedule, e.g. when observing interactions in children's playgroup. Observers then need to be trained to use the schedule and decisions made about where and when to observe (Bakeman & Gottman, 1997; Hartmann, 1984; Sarafino, 1996; Suen & Ary, 2014). Table 3.1 provides an outline of the major stages in the development of a direct observation schedule.

An important point is that no measure is inherently reliable or valid, and so our estimation of these qualities should be based on a sceptical analysis that asks 'what other

TABLE 3.1 An outline of the steps in a direct observation

1	Obtain preliminary description of behaviour for client, carers and relevant others: what is the behaviour, how often and when and where it occurs.
	Obtain pilot observation by direct or video recording.
2	Define the target behaviour. The definition should refer to observable behaviour that is clear, unambiguous, exhaustive and boundaries so that the observer can discriminate between different behaviours.
3	Write a code book which includes the definition and examples.
4	Determine your observational strategy, e.g. event recording or some time sampling procedure.
5	Train the observers: they should memorise the code book and practice coding on examples – video records of the behaviour are helpful here.
6	Select a setting where the observations will occur and decide when to observe.
7	Run pilot sessions for further training and to habituate the observers into the setting.
8	Conduct the observations.

factors might explain the observations?' (Elliott, 2002; Lilienfeld, Ritschel, Lynn, Cautin & Latzman, 2014). Even when target behaviours are well defined and observers are trained and have been shown to reach a high level of reliability (inter-rater agreement, see below), there are three significant factors that can affect the data obtained. The first is *reactivity*. Reactivity occurs when the client is aware that they are being observed and alters their behaviour accordingly – for example, they may be less likely to show socially undesirable behaviours and more likely to be socially compliant. As most problem behaviours are socially undesirable, this will result in an underestimation of the problem. Reactivity is also likely to occur when the observers are more conspicuous and when they are novel. Most authorities therefore recommend that observers attempt to minimise their conspicuousness by ensuring that their appearance is not distinctive, locating themselves in a place where they can see but not be seen, not interacting with the client and spending some time in the setting before beginning recording. Wherever possible, adopting less obtrusive observational procedures, such as using video recording or concealing observers, should be considered. Fortunately reactivity to an observer appears to be a temporary state, although the length of time it takes for people to habituate to being observed is not predictable.

The second and third problems that can arise concern the observers. *Observer drift* is an example of the instrumentation threat to validity discussed in Chapter 1. The problem is that over the course of observing over several sessions, an observer's consistency in the application of the agreed coding scheme may shift. This may be because their memory for the definition changes or the observed person's repertoire of behaviour shifts and the observer responds to this. Solutions to this problem include ensuring that observers refresh their memories of the coding scheme, and running recalibration sessions when observers can check their coding against gold standard examples. Where the data have been recorded on video it is recommended that the order in which each session is observed and coded should be randomised. This ensures that any observer drift is not conflated with the time of recording. The third problem is one of *observer fatigue* and motivation. This can be countered by ensuring that observational sessions are not too long and that the choice of observational method (see below) is appropriate for the task at hand.

Observation schedules

Real-time recording

In real-time recording the observer notes the start and ending of every event of interest in a given period of time. The aim is to capture the uninterrupted flow of behaviour. The data obtained can be very rich and, with appropriate analysis, it is possible to capture the relationship between various behaviours in terms of conditional probabilities or one behaviour following another (Bakeman & Gottman, 1997). Real-time recording may be used to build descriptive accounts of behavioural sequences and to begin to unpick possible causal relationships between sequences of behaviour. However, real-time recording is costly, requiring equipment and specialised software and it is exhausting for observers. It is rarely used in studies of treatment outcome other than in the initial stage when the problem is being scoped and defined. Once the specific target behaviour is identified and described, several other observational schedules are available that will capture the behaviour and generate estimates of its frequency of occurrence or the proportion of occasions when it occurs.

Event recording

Event recording can be used when we are interested in the frequency of a behaviour over a given period of time. In event recording, observers simply count the number of times the target behaviour occurs within a particular observational period. Event recording is essentially very simple, and at the end of each observation period each observer reports a single number that summarises the number of times the target behaviour has occurred. Over a number of observation sessions data will accrue from the observers, and the reliability and agreement between the observers can be determined by computing the intra-class correlation coefficient (see below).

One disadvantage of event recording is that unless the observers' records are anchored to a real-time record, i.e. we know the exact times when the behaviour occurs, it is difficult to determine the sources of agreement and disagreement between them. So if two observers report totals of ten and eight events each, we do not know how well their observations overlap. At one extreme it is possible for each observer's observations to be completely independent while at the other extreme they may have observed eight events in common with one observer reporting an additional two events. A second disadvantage is that event recording requires observers to pay continuous attention to the individual. This can be fatiguing. Finally, event recording requires observations from several sessions in order to be able to compute a reliability coefficient. So although event recording has the advantage of being relatively simple, requiring minimal equipment to implement, other direct observation methods have been developed that make it easier for the observers and also enable reliability to be computed from fewer sessions.

When the data are locked to a real-time record, then a more precise estimate of agreement can be made by cross-tabulating agreements and disagreements. The concordance between observers can then be quantified using a variety of agreement coefficients (see below). Two forms of observation – momentary time sampling and partial interval time sampling – meet these requirements.

Momentary time (or scan) sampling

In momentary time sampling the observers are prompted, usually by an electronic timer, to make a single observation and note whether or not the target behaviour is occurring at that moment. They simply record a yes or no response. Momentary time sampling is a flexible method and it can also be applied to situations where there are either several behaviours of interest or where there are several individuals who need to be observed, e.g. a playgroup or school classroom. In momentary time sampling the observer needs to determine how often to sample the environment. In general one needs to sample about twice the frequency with which the behaviour occurs. Even then it is possible to miss low frequency and very briefly occurring behaviours.

Partial interval recording

Partial interval recording is slightly different from momentary time sampling. The observation schedule is split into periods of observation and recording. Observers are prompted to observe for a set period of time, say 10 seconds. This is followed by a time block in which the observed records their observations. The target behaviour is recorded if it occurs at any point in the observation period. Both momentary time sampling and partial interval recording result in an estimate of the proportion (percentage) of recording intervals during which the target behaviour is present. They do not record the frequency or duration of the behaviour. If data about the frequency or duration of a behaviour are required, then either the real-time or event sampling method should be chosen.

Calculating agreement

Where there are two observers and the observations are locked by time, the data can be cross-tabulated to express the extent to which the observers agree or disagree with one another. These methods are applicable to the direct observation methods such as event recording and momentary and partial interval time sampling. Table 3.2 shows the simplest possible 2 × 2 table where there are two observers and each is recording whether the target behaviour was present or absent. The upper left cell (a) shows the *proportion* of occasions when the two observers agree that the behaviour occurred, and the lower right cell (d) the proportion of time when they agreed that the behaviour was absent (non-occurrence). The off-diagonal cells (b and c) show the proportions of disagreement, i.e. when one observer recorded occurrence and one non-occurrence. Table 3.2 also shows the proportions that each observer records regarding the occurrence (p) or non-occurrence (q) of the behaviour. Note that this notation for completing the table makes computations very easy, but it is important that that raw frequency of observations is turned into proportions. This

TABLE 3.2 Computation of agreement coefficients and Cohen's Kappa

		(a) Proportions			(b) Raw data			(c) Observed proportion		
		Observer 2			Observer 2			Observer 2		
		Present	Absent		Present	Absent		Present	Absent	
Observer 1	Present	a	b	p1 = (a+b)	17	3	20	.49	.09	.58
	Absent	c	d	q1 = (c+d)	5	10	15	.14	.29	.43
		p2 = (a+c)	q2 = (b+d)		22	13	35	.63	.38	

The two observers note whether or not the behaviour has occurred (present/absent) in a given interval. Panel (a) represents the proportions algebraically. Panel (b) gives an example data set where the observers made 35 observations. The data are the raw counts. Panel (c) expresses the data in panel (b) as proportions, i.e. each cell in panel (b) is divided by 35.

is simply done by dividing the frequency of observations by the total number of observations. Table 3.2 illustrates this process. Among the various possible agreement coefficients that can be computed from the data in Table 3.2 (Suen & Ary, 2014; Suen, Ary & Covalt, 1990), there are four common ones.

Agreement coefficients

The overall agreement coefficient is the ratio of the number of times the raters agreed $(a + d)$ to the total number of observations $(a + b + c + d)$. This ratio is often multiplied by 100 to give a percentage agreement score:

$$\text{Overall agreement} = \frac{(a+d)}{(a+b+c+d)}$$

When the data are expressed in proportions, the overall agreement is simply $(a + d)$ because the denominator sums to 1. This measure includes both the occasions when they agreed that the event occurred and when they agreed that it was absent. More detailed analysis can be obtained about the relative status of observing occurrence and non-occurrence by treating these two types of event separately. To compute each of these we exclude the occasions on which they agreed that the event was absent in the case of occurrence agreement or present in the case of non-occurrence agreement. The equations for these two are:

$$\text{Occurrence or positive agreement} = \frac{a}{(a+b+c)}$$

$$\text{Non-occurrence or negative agreement} = \frac{d}{(d+b+c)}$$

Agreement coefficients have considerable advantages. They are easy and quick to compute and their meaning is readily apparent. The methods can be easily extended to settings where we have several things we want to observe, e.g. possible activities of a child in a nursery (solitary play, parallel play, cooperative play, aggression). It is also possible to determine whether the agreement is significant (in the statistical sense), but methods for doing this are not often reported. Details of how to do this are given in Uebersax's web pages (Uebersax, 2009), and there are a number of other web-based calculators available.

Cohen's Kappa

While these agreement coefficients are easy to compute and understand, they can be misleading because the formulae do not take into account the probability that the observers may agree merely by chance. Where there is a binary decision, i.e. yes or no, then there is a 25% likelihood that the raters will agree for each of the cells a–d in Table 3.2. This would result in an overall agreement ratio of 0.5 (or 50% agreement) quite by chance. The general preferred index for ascertaining agreement is Cohen's Kappa. Kappa computes agreement by taking the chance probability of agreement into account. It is expressed as the difference between observed and chance agreement expressed as a ratio of perfect agreement (1) minus chance agreement. The following equation summarises this statement:

$$K = \frac{P_o - P_c}{1 - P_c}$$

In this equation Po is the proportion of occasions on which the raters agree with each other, i.e. the overall agreement coefficient, and Pc is the proportion of agreements that are attributable to chance:

$$P_o = \frac{(a+d)}{(a+d+c+d)} \quad P_c = (p1 \times p2) + (q1 \times q2)$$

Like a correlation, Kappa can vary ± 1. Kappa will be 1 if the observed agreement is perfect, as the numerator and denominator will be the same. It is not usual to compute either the confidence intervals or significance of Kappa, but both statistics are possible and can be obtained in SPSS or other proprietary programmes or from online calculators. Kappa is more usually interpreted by referring to the qualitative guidelines suggested by Landis and Koch (1977). They suggest that values of Kappa between 0.00 and 0.20 represent 'slight agreement', 0.21–0.40 'fair agreement', 0.41–0.60 'moderate agreement', 0.61–0.80 'substantial agreement' and values above 0.80 represent 'almost perfect agreement'.

Although Kappa is widely used, there are occasions where it can seriously misrepresent agreement such as when the marginal totals (the values of p and q) are widely discrepant, for example, when both raters show very high levels of agreement and little disagreement, i.e. the values for p are around 0.95 while the values for q are around 0.05. In this case the value of Kappa will be around 0.5, representing moderate agreement, which is clearly counterintuitive. The pragmatic approach to this is to report the Kappa value and to note the very high level of the raw agreement coefficient. Hallgren (2012) provides a brief discussion of this problem and also notes that alternatives to Cohen's Kappa have been developed.

Cohen's Kappa was developed for the case where two observers make binary decisions. It is simple to compute and ideal for those situations where there is a single behaviour to be observed. Kappa has also been extended to situations when there are more than two observers, when there is more than one behaviour to be monitored and when the investigator wishes to weight disagreements differently, i.e. where some disagreements are considered to be of more or less importance. Hallgren (2012) also provides an introduction to the alternative computations.

Intra-class correlation coefficient (ICC)

When the data from two or more observers are expressed as the total number of observations within each session of observation, it will be possible to construct a table such as that in panel (a) of Table 3.3. Panel (a) shows that two observers have been used and they have rated every session. It is possible to extend this by including more observers. If each observer rates each session, it is known as a fully crossed design. This sort of data collection protocol is recommended because it is relatively easy to compute a reliability

TABLE 3.3 The intra-class correlation coefficient

(a) Observations			(b) ANOVA			
Session	Obs 1	Obs 2		SS	df	MS
1	10	11	Between sessions	30.42	5	6.08
2	14	13	Within sessions			
3	11	12	Between observers	.75	1	.75
4	13	12	Residual	3.75	5	.75
5	8	9	Total	4.50	6	.75
6	11	13	Total	34.92	11	3.17

(c) Intra-class correlation coefficients with 95% confidence intervals				
		ICC	Low	High
	Absolute			
	Single	.780	.063	.966
	Average	.877	.119	.983
	Consistency			
	Single	.780	.149	.965
	Average	.877	.260	.985

coefficient that is easily interpretable. The index of reliability that can be applied to this type of data is known as the intra-class correlation coefficient (ICC). Whereas Pearson's and Spearman's correlation coefficients allow us to examine the relationship between two different variables (inter-class correlation), the intra-class correlation is suitable for comparing two sets of data on the same scale. This may be ratings of behaviour on a common scale or, as is often the case in single-case experiments, behaviour observations expressed as counts, frequencies or percentage of time spent doing something. Computing the ICC relies on the analysis of variance and the ability to select the correct model to represent the data. Shrout and Fleiss (1979) outlined three basic models that can apply to reliability data, and McGraw and Wong (1996) elaborated on this. Model 1 can be applied when the raters for each session are different people. It is called the one-way random effects model. So for the data in Table 3.3, model 1 would be applicable if every single rating were to be made by a different observer: we would need 12 observers in this case. Model 1 is not often applicable in single-case research. Model 2, the two-way random effects model, assumes that the same set of observers rate all the sessions and that the observers are selected from a larger population. Model 3, the two-way mixed effect model, assumes that the observers rate all the sessions but that they are fixed, i.e. that they are the only observers we are interested in.

There are two other important considerations in conducting ICC analysis that can help us determine the reliability. The first is whether we wish to compute reliability between the observers as consistent or absolute. When we only want to know whether the observers rate the sessions in the same rank order, we choose the consistency measure. In single-case research we are usually more interested in whether the raters agree with each other, i.e. do they return the same value for each session? In this case we should include the absolute measure of reliability. The best way of considering the difference between consistency and absolute agreement is to consider pairs of scores. If the pairs of data are (10,11), (13,15) and (16,18), they are completely consistent because rater 1's scores are always lower than rater 2's, but the rank order of the observations is consistent. The pairings (10,10), (13,13) and (14,14) show absolute agreement. Note that the data set in panel (a) of Table 3.3 shows neither complete consistency in the rank ordering nor any incidences of absolute agreement: but we should not select the type of analysis on the basis of the pattern of observations we have obtained. For most purposes we should be interested in the absolute agreement measure of reliability.

The second consideration in ICC analysis is whether we want to draw inferences about the reliability of the data on the basis of a single observer's judgements or on the average of judgements made by two or more observers. The average observer option will always be higher than the single observer. If we only use a few of the available sessions to compute reliability between two observers and then use one observer in the other sessions, we should report the single observer reliability. Panel (b) of Table 3.3 shows the data analysed as a two-way analysis of variance, and the results for computing various values of the ICC and shown in panel (c). Values are given for both consistency and absolute agreement and for a single and average observer. In this case the computed values for single and average observers are the same for both the absolute and consistency measure. The value for the single observer is lower than that for the average of the two observers. This is always the case. The main difference between the four values of the ICC is in the range of the confidence intervals. The widest range is obtained in the case of a single observer and with a requirement of absolute agreement.

Reliability and subjective report

Assessing the reliability of idiographic self-report measures presents us with problems not encountered when direct observation is used. With self-report there is only one observer, so we cannot appeal to inter-observer agreement. Where there is more than one item, the strategy of inter-correlating them, as in standardised measures, is not useful because we are interested in specific items. Co-variation between items representing specific complaints does not constitute a test of reliability for an individual item. In some cases clinical researchers have used either complete standardised measures (Wells, White & Carter, 1997) or subsets of items from scales (Vlaeyen et al., 2001). In the latter case reliability can be computed using the Spearman–Brown formula for correcting attenuation (see Chapter 2). Where this approach to measurement is adopted, the reliability of the measure for the individual is inferred from the standardised measure. For many idiographic measures, e.g. a single item in daily diary measures, there is no formal way of computing reliability and we must rely on our interpretation of the pattern of data and the consideration of alternative explanations for the observations. For example, if a person's report over time remains stable, e.g. a baseline period when no intervention is being made, we might consider this to be a reliable record. There are, however, at least two major alternatives that might explain the stability. First, the measure may simply be insensitive to change and second, there may be influences of expectations and demand characteristics on the stability. Refuting insensitivity is possible if the measure shows change as treatment is introduced, but in this case we are still left with the problem of demand characteristics. This has rarely been experimentally investigated in single-case research. One tactic is to include a counter-demand instruction when treatment is introduced. For example, if you have good reason to suspect that your treatment is likely to have a relatively immediate effect and the dependent variable is measured by a daily diary report, then the measure would be expected to show change within a week or two. The problem is to detect whether or not this change is genuine or due to demand characteristics. Issuing counter-demand information – 'we do not expect to see significant change for the first three weeks of this treatment' – provides a way of checking the influence of demand expectations. If the treatment is effective then change will be observed within two weeks. If, however, the demand characteristics are strong then the 'treatment response' will be delayed (Steinmark & Borkovec, 1974).

If self-report is variable during the baseline period (pre-treatment) then the problem is slightly different in that we do not know whether the problem is stable and the variability is attributable to poor reliability, i.e. a badly constructed measure, or whether the target problem is genuinely variable. This is especially likely when we are collecting data from individuals whose environment is relatively varied. The changes in the target variable may be brought about by the changeable behaviour of other people in the environment or by fluctuations in the behaviour of the client. For example, the number of anxiety episodes in a person with social anxiety may fluctuate because of the variable behaviour of others or because the person varies their degree of exposure to situations where anxiety is likely to be elicited, e.g. they may stay at home on some days. Our estimation of the reliability of the measures therefore requires a more nuanced understanding of what we are trying to measure and of the events and conditions that will cause it to fluctuate. In these circumstances there is no number we can assign to reliability. The estimation of reliability relies on our ability to consider and exclude alternative explanations for the pattern of data. (Chapter 8 considers this issue in more detail.)

PERSONAL QUESTIONNAIRES

One measure of subjective report that attempts to deal with the problem of reliability and provide numerical estimate is Shapiro's personal questionnaire (PQ) method. Shapiro was dissatisfied with contemporary approaches to measuring psychological symptoms in the 1950s because they were based either on projective tests of doubtful validity or on multi-item questionnaires, which he believed were psychometrically unsound and did not tap the criterion complaints of patients (Chalkley, 2015; Shapiro, 1975). Shapiro wanted a measure that was able to incorporate both symptoms and complaints that were personally meaningful with a scale that was relevant to the individual, i.e. a truly idiographic measure. He also wanted a measurement technology that could address known problems of questionnaires such as acquiescence (saying 'yes' to each item) and response bias (tending to respond to the middle category on a scale), and also included an assessment of reliability. He developed the PQ to address these issues (Shapiro, 1961).

Personal questionnaires are ideal for monitoring a client's symptoms and complaints over the course of therapy, and are especially useful because they allow the clinician to assess the client's problems using the client's own words in a systematic and structured way. The PQ is also ideally suited for those situations where the client's problems are unusual and cannot be adequately captured by any of the standard measures. Preparation of the PQ involves an explicit sequence of discussions with a client. Both clients and clinicians frequently report that this is a very useful stage. The process ensures that the clinician listens carefully to the clients and the interactive nature of the discussion ensures that the client feels heard. In his initial writing, Shapiro classified patients' complaints about their dysfunctions as having at least one of four features: (1) they are distressing to the person concerned and/or to people they value; (2) they are disabling and interfere with the person's desired level of functioning; (3) they are socially inappropriate in the context of the person's sub-culture; and (4) they are palpably incongruent with reality.

Shapiro's original version

Although others have developed Shapiro's PQ method, the original version remains very usable in clinical and research settings as it can be implemented quickly and efficiently. The PQ does not use pre-selected items that have been pre-tested in a larger sample of patients. It is an idiographic technique that has several distinguishing features. First, the client determines the content of each question. Second, the scale (range) of experience covered in each question is agreed with and calibrated by the individual. Third, the format of the PQ contains a measure of reliability, in the form of internal consistency, that can be assessed on every occasion of administration. Finally, the form of construction and presentation of the PQ is based on an established and robust methodology from the field of psychophysics (pair comparison) and it controls for two common biases – response set and acquiescence.

TABLE 3.4 Example of two personal questionnaire statements

Client's original statement	PQ question	PQ items	Statement level
I am very afraid of my pain	1	I am very afraid of my pain	Illness
		I am moderately afraid of my pain	Improvement
		I am hardly afraid of my pain	Recovery
I often feel tense	2	I often feel tense	Illness
		I sometimes feel tense	Improvement
		I rarely feel tense	Recovery

The client's original statement, slightly reworded, is also the illness statement. Two other statements are developed to reflect recovery and improvement.

The PQ method has several stages in its preparation. In the first stage the clinician-researcher interviews the client to obtain a set of statements that represent the client's distress and complaints in their own words. Following the initial assessment, the clinician reviews the available data and attempts to capture the essential complaints by preparing a statement of each complaint to be used in the PQ. Table 3.4 shows a subset of two statements elicited from a woman with pain related to multiple sclerosis. These statements are known as *illness statements*. These can be slightly rewritten for clarity and checked with the patient at a later stage. The two statements now become two questions (Q1 and Q2) of her personal questionnaire.

In the second stage, the clinician-researcher develops two other statements, shown in Table 3.4, for each of the elicited illness statements. One of these represents an anticipated endpoint of treatment. This is the *recovery statement*. The other is worded so that it is located about midway between the illness and recovery statements. This is the *improvement statement*. The key feature here is the attempt to 'space' the psychological intervals between the items so that they are relatively equal. The English language has a wide range of qualifiers that are capable of subtle reflection of intensity and frequency. Once the illness statements have been tentatively identified and the improvement and recovery statements drafted, they are discussed with the client. This procedure checks whether the statements capture the essence of their concerns, whether the clinician-researcher's judgement about the possible improvement and recovery statements is acceptable to the client, and whether the chosen phrasing of the statements is clear and comprehensible. It is relatively easy to make minor adjustments at this stage.

In stage 3, a deck of cards is prepared. This stage can proceed in conjunction with stage 2. The deck of cards contains all possible pairings of the statements for each question. The three statements for each question are paired with each other, i.e. illness vs improvement, illness vs recovery, and improvement vs recovery, so that one pair is presented on a single card with one statement written above another. In order to control for the positioning of the illness, improvement and recovery statements, they are placed in a counterbalanced way across the separate questions. Within each question a single statement appears on two occasions, once as the top line and once as the bottom. The back of each card contains information that identifies the question number and the positioning of the statements. Shapiro used Roman numerals to represent the three levels of each question: (i) recovery, (ii) improvement and (iii) illness. Thus Q2 iii/ii means that this card contains statements from question 2 and that the illness statement is in the top position and the improvement statement in the bottom position. Across the set of questions the position of the pairs will also be counterbalanced. This simple design is a device for controlling response biases. Figure 3.1 illustrates the layout of the cards for the questions in Table 3.4.

In the fourth stage the cards are shuffled and presented to the client. She is asked to perform a simple sorting task. As each card is read she is instructed to decide which statement of the pair is nearer to their current state. The decision is expressed by placing the card onto one of two piles, labelled TOP and BOTTOM, which correspond to the position of the preferred statement on the card. There are only four ways (out of a possible eight) that the cards can be sorted in a psychologically consistent way. Each of the four consistent sorts corresponds to a single point on a four-point ordinal scale that represents the intensity

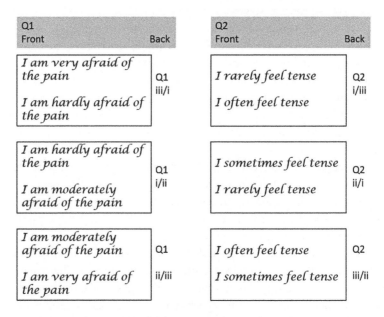

FIGURE 3.1 The layout of two items from a personal questionnaire

Each item has three statements representing a response scale, illness, improvement and recovery (labelled iii, ii and i, respectively) that are paired with each other by locating one statement above the other. These are shown in the left and right hand columns of the Figure. The location of the statements is counterbalanced across a pair of questions so that each level of statement appears equally often in the top and bottom position on the front of the card. The back of the card indicates where each statement is located.

of the symptom/complaint. The four points are shown on the scale in Figure 3.2. The other four sorts contain inconsistencies, such that the choices giving rise to them cannot be made without challenging the prior assumption that the three statements are ranked in severity from the highest (illness statement) through the intermediate (improvement statement) to the lowest severity statement (recovery statement).

Scoring the PQ

The easiest way of understanding the PQ is to imagine that the items are spread along a continuum representing the severity of the symptom. The underlying scale is shown in Figure 3.2. The endpoints correspond to the illness and recovery statements, and the midpoint to the improvement statement, labelled with the Roman numerals i, ii and iii. There are also two points that are the midpoints between the two halves of the scale. This division produces four zones that will correspond to the four points on the scale. Recall that the client is presented with three separate decisions to make about her subjective state:

- illness vs improvement   or iii vs ii
- illness vs recovery   or iii vs i
- improvement vs recovery   or ii vs i.

If the client is at the illness end of the scale she should choose the illness statement in preference to both improvement and recovery statements. She should also choose the

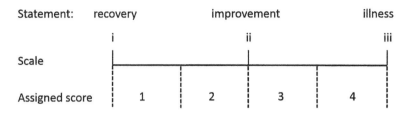

FIGURE 3.2 Personal questionnaire response scale and scoring

improvement statement in preference to the recovery statement. In this case all the choices are consistent with being at the illness end of the scale and we allocate a score of 4. Similarly if the client is at the recovery end she should choose the recovery statement in preference to both the illness and improvement statement. She will also choose the improvement statement in preference to the illness statement. In this case all the choices are consistent with being at the recovery end, and we allocate a score of 1.

If the client is somewhere in the middle, i.e. improving, she should choose the improvement statement in preference to both recovery and illness statements. But she now faces a choice between the two extreme statements – illness vs recovery. This choice essentially forces her to decide which side of the midpoint of the scale she is located. If she chooses illness in preference to recovery she is somewhere between 4 and the middle, and we allocate a score of 3. If she chooses recovery in preference to illness she is somewhere between 1 and the middle, and we allocate a score of 2.

Using the notation i, ii, iii for the statements we can see that these sets of preferences can be written as follows, where pr 'is preferred to': thus i pr ii means that the client prefers i to ii as the better description of their current state: they choose i (recovery) in preference to ii (improvement). The patterns for the valid scores (1–4) are shown in the top half of Table 3.5. There are also four possible inconsistent patterns, shown in the bottom half of Table 3.5. If the PQ is scored immediately, any inconsistent choices can be examined and the cause determined. If one of these occurs it is wise to check the wording of the statements with the client and also to check that you have not misplaced or mislabelled the items. Experience shows that, on the whole, inconsistent sorts are rare and people with high levels of distress, active psychosis or limited cognitive ability can complete the task provided the clinician-researcher has taken the time to develop the items carefully. With a little practice the PQ can be constructed relatively quickly (an hour or so) and administered and scored in a session within a few minutes. Most clients are very accepting of it as it reflects their concerns, and the fact that the clinician demonstrates active listening and monitoring. The scores can be plotted on a session-by-session basis for each question, as a way of actively monitoring specific symptom change. Alternatively one might consider summing across questions as to capture an overall picture of the client's progress on target complaints.

The reliability (internal consistency) of the PQ

With three levels for each question there are four consistent patterns of choices, representing the range from 'ill' to 'recovered', and there are four other patterns of choice that are inconsistent (see Table 3.5). For each question the probability of sorting the cards

TABLE 3.5 Scoring the personal questionnaire

Consistent patterns

	i	ii	iii	i	ii	iii	i	ii	iii	i	ii	iii
i	–			–	x		–	x	x	–	x	x
ii	x	–			–			–			–	x
iii	x	x	–	x	x	–	x		–			–
Score		1			2			3			4	

Inconsistent patterns

	i	ii	iii	i	ii	iii	i	ii	iii	i	ii	iii
i	–			–		x	–	x	x	–		x
ii	x	–	x	x	–			–		x	–	x
iii	x		–		x	–	x		–			–
Score		5 = 1?			6 = 2?			7=3?			8= 4?	

The eight possible ways of sorting the three cards for a single PQ question. The upper half of the table shows the four consistent sorts and the lower half the inconsistent sorts. Each boxed area shows one possible card sort. The x indicates the chosen comparison on which these are entered so that the level indicated in the column is preferred (*pr*) to the level (recovery, improvement and illness) shown in the row. In the first box in the upper part of the table, i *pr* ii, i *pr* iii and ii *pr* iii, this is given a score 1 and indicates that the person has recovered. In the last box the preferences are all reversed so ii *pr* i, iii *pr* i and iii *pr* ii, this is given a score 4 and indicates that the person is 'ill', i.e. at their worst state. The choices in the bottom half of the table are all inconsistent. For example, in the left hand box i *pr* ii, i *pr* iii but iii *pr* ii. These patterns of sorting are given arbitrary scores of 5–8, each of which is near to the pattern shown by the score with a question mark. The dashed lines indicate where there are no data, i.e. where each statement could be paired with itself.

consistently at random is 0.50, which is also the probability of sorting inconsistently. The reliability is $= 1 -$ probability of an inconsistent sort raised to the power of the number of questionnaire items, i.e. $(1 - 0.5^n)$. For a single-item questionnaire the reliability is 0.5, for two items it is 0.75, for three items 0.825 and so on. Thus for a typical 10-item questionnaire the reliability is 0.999.

Other personal questionnaires

There are other approaches to PQs – by Mulhall (1976), Phillips (1963, 1986), Bilsbury and colleagues (Bilsbury & Richman, 2002; Singh & Bilsbury, 1989a, b) and Morley (2004). All of these methods retain the basic ideas of pair comparison, estimation of consistency on each testing and, to a certain degree, the wording of the statements in a unique format, although this is sacrificed to some extent in the Mulhall and Singh and Bilsbury versions. A major aim of these PQs is to overcome the limited 4-point scale for each item that is present in Shapiro's version, thereby making the resulting scale more sensitive to changes in symptoms. Of the various versions Phillips's is the most simple to construct and use.

TABLE 3.6 Phillips's version of the PQ

Item	Consistent choices						Example of an inconsistent choice
I very often feel tense	W	B	B	B	B	B	W
I quite often feel tense	W	W	B	B	B	B	B
I sometimes feel tense	W	W	W	B	B	B	W
I quite rarely feel tense	W	W	W	W	B	B	B
I very rarely feel tense	W	W	W	W	W	B	W
Score	5	4	3	2	1	0	

Phillips observed that it wasn't absolutely necessary to present the pairs of the items. Presenting each item alone and asking the individual to make a judgement about whether they are feeling better or worse than the state described has the same scaling properties. Recall that in Shapiro's version the testee is required to compare two items with their internal state and choose the one that is nearer to that state. Phillips' version simply omits the external pair comparison and asks the person to choose between the state represented by the item and their own state. Table 3.6 shows one of the items taken from the lady with multiple sclerosis ('I often feel tense') and reworked in Phillips' format. In this case it is possible to generate five statements reflecting her level of tension. Each of these can be written on a card. The cards are presented singly in a random order – the client simply has to decide whether they feel worse or better than the statement. They record their response by placing the statement on a pile marked BETTER or WORSE.

Table 3.6 shows the set of all possible consistent scores in columns 2–6. Provided the items are arranged in descending rank of severity, it is very easy to compute the score for each item and to detect whether they are reporting consistently. Assuming that the person is consistent, they will produce a series of Better (B) followed by a Worse (W). Summing the number of Ws gives you the score for that item. If they are inconsistent in their use of the scale then the sequence of Bs and Ws will be broken, as can be seen in the right-hand column of Table 3.6. In the current example the range of possible score is 0 to 5 (5 indicating the worst state). As with Shapiro's method, the number of points on the scale for each item will always be one more than the number of statements. One other advantage of Phillips' method is that you can vary the number of items for each question depending on the client's preference. This gives great flexibility.

CONCLUSIONS

The range of potential target measures that may be used in single-case research is considerable and, unlike the standardised measures considered in Chapter 2, these are generally not available 'off the shelf'. The clinician-researcher must not only select what is to be measured but also decide how to construct and administer a suitable measure. In clinical settings what is to be measured is largely influenced by the problems and complaints brought by the client or those responsible for his or her well-being. In research settings the choice of dependent variables is driven by the research question, and the challenge is to develop a measure that is meaningful vis-à-vis the research question and acceptable to the participant.

Having decided *what* to measure, the next challenge is to decide *how* to measure it. This chapter has discussed, albeit briefly, the two main classes of measurement – direct observation of behaviour and self-report measures of emotional states, beliefs, thoughts and behaviour. We considered how to assess the validity and reliability of these measures. The main contention is that providing the variables are considered at the level of complaint or target problem, then the problem of validity is largely circumvented if we consider the variable of interest as representative of a criterion. It is only when we wish to combine and aggregate several variables and claim that these represent a construct that we need to be more circumspect about our claims. For example, we might aggregate counts of hair-pulling, biting, hitting and kicking behaviours in a preschool child to form an index of aggression. Although we would almost certainly agree that these behaviours are aggressive, we would need to do additional work to ensure that they capture all aspects of aggression – especially if we wish to make claims that generalise beyond our observations (Kazdin, 2010; Primavera, Allison & Alfonso, 1997).

When the target variable is measured by direct observation of behaviour there is a well-tried and tested methodology for developing the measure, designing observational schedules and analysing the reliability of the data. Reliability is considered as the extent to which different observers agree when assessing an individual's performance. One caveat to this is that we assume that everything else is held constant. There may be variables that impact on the observers, e.g. drift and fatigue, that will influence their judgement and recording. Thus it is possible for observers to retain high levels of agreement although their criteria for recording have drifted over time. Our assessment of reliability should therefore be assessed in the context of these other possible confounds. Assessing the reliability of subjective report is, in many instances, dependent on our ability to identify possible alternative explanations and to estimate their likely impact on the obtained data. Most self-report measures do not have in-built reliability checks and assessing reliability remains a significant challenge to clinician-researchers using these measures. Shapiro's PQ methodology offers one way of assessing reliability using an internal consistency criterion. As with direct observation, the clinician-researcher needs to give considerable thought as to how to measure the variable of interest and to reduce the influence of nuisance, confounding influences.

REFERENCES

Bakeman, R. & Gottman, J. M. (1997). *Observing Interaction: An Introduction to Sequential Analysis.* Cambridge: Cambridge University Press.

Bilsbury, C. D. & Richman, A. (2002). A staging approach to measuring patient-centred subjective outcomes. *Acta Psychiatrica Scandinavica, 106,* 5–40.

Borsboom, D., Mellenbergh, G. J. & van Heerden, J. (2004). The concept of validity. *Psychological Review, 111*(4), 1061–71.

Chalkley, A. J. (2015). *The Content of Psychological Distress*. London: Palgrave.

Cronbach, L. J. & Meehl, P. E. (1955). Construct validity in psychological tests. *Psychological Bulletin*, 52(4), 281–302.

Elliott, R. (2002). Hermeneutic single-case efficacy design. *Psychotherapy Research*, 12(1), 1–21.

Foster, S. L. & Mash, E. J. (1999). Assessing social validity in clinical treatment research: Issues and procedures. *Journal of Consulting and Clinical Psychology*, 67(3), 308–19.

Hallgren, K. A. (2012). Computing inter-rater reliability for observational data: An overview and tutorial. *Tutorials in Quantitative Methods in Psychology*, 8(1), 23–34.

Hartmann, D. P. (1984). Assessment Strategies. In D. H. Barlow & M. Hersen (eds), *Single Case Experimental Designs*. Oxford: Pergamon.

Horner, R. H. & Odom, S. L. (2014). Constructing single-case research designs: Logic and options. In J. R. Kratochwill & J. R. Levin (eds), *Single-case Intervention Research: Methodological and Statistical Advances* (pp. 27–51). Washington, DC: American Psychological Association.

Kazdin, A. E. (2010). *Single-Case Research Designs: Methods for Clinical and Applied Settings* (2nd edn). Oxford: Oxford University Press.

Landis, J. R. & Koch, G. G. (1977). The measurement of agreement for categorical data. *Biometrics*, 33(1), 159–74.

Lilienfeld, S. O., Ritschel, L. A., Lynn, S. J., Cautin, R. L. & Latzman, R. D. (2014). Why ineffective psychotherapies appear to work: A taxonomy of causes of spurious therapeutic effectiveness. *Perspectives on Psychological Science*, 9(4), 355–87.

McGraw, K. O. & Wong, S. P. (1996). Forming inferences about some intraclass correlation coefficients. *Psychological Methods*, 1(1), 30–46.

Messick, S. (1995). Validity of psychological-assessment – validation of inferences from persons responses and performances as scientific inquiry into score meaning. *American Psychologist*, 50(9), 741–9.

Morley, S. (2004). EasyPQ – Yet another version of Shapiro's personal questionnaire. Retrieved 9 September 2016 from www.researchgate.net/publication/235463593_EasyPQ_-Yet_another_version_of_Shapiro%27s_Personal_Questionnaire?ev=prf_pub

Morley, S. (2015). Single cases are complex. *Scandinavian Journal of Pain*, 7(1), 55–7.

Mulhall, D. J. (1976). Systematic assessment by PQRST. *Psychological Medicine*, 6, 591–7.

Nunnally, J. & Bernstein, I. H. (1994). *Psychometric Theory* (3rd edn). New York: McGraw-Hill.

Phillips, J. P. N. (1963). Scaling and personal questionnaires. *Nature*, 200, 1347–8.

Phillips, J. P. N. (1986). Shapiro personal questionnaires and generalised personal questionnaire techniques: A repeated measures individualized outcome measurement. In L. S. Greenberg & W. M. Pinsof (eds), *The Psychotherapeutic Process: A Research Handbook* (pp. 557–89). New York: Guilford Press.

Primavera, L. H., Allison, D. B. & Alfonso, V. C. (1997). Measurement of dependent variables. In R. D. Franklin & D. B. Allison (eds), *Design and Analysis of Single-case Research* (pp. 41–91). Mahwah, NJ: Lawrence Erlbaum.

Sarafino, E. P. (1996). *Principles of Behavior Change: Understanding Behavior Modification Techniques*. New York: Wiley.

Sarafino, E. P. (2001). *Behavior Modification: Principles of Behavior Change* (2nd edn). Long Grove, IL: Waveland.

Shapiro, M. B. (1961). A method of measuring psychological changes specific to the individual psychiatric patient. *British Journal of Medical Psychology*, 34, 151–5.

Shapiro, M. B. (1975). The single variable approach to assessing the intensity of feelings of depression. *European Journal of Behaviour Analysis and Modification*, 2, 62–70.

Shrout, P. E. & Fleiss, J. L. (1979). Intraclass correlation: Uses in assessing rater reliability. *Psychological Bulletin*, 86, 420–8.

Singh, A. C. & Bilsbury, C. D. (1989a). Measurement of subjective variables: the Discan method. *Acta Psychiatrica Scandinavica, Supplementum*, 347(1–38).

Singh, A. C. & Bilsbury, C. D. (1989b). Measuring levels of experiential states in clinical applications by DISCAN: a discretised analog method. *Behavioural Psychotherapy*, 17, 27–41.

Steinmark, S. W. & Borkovec, T. D. (1974). Active and placebo treatment effects on moderate insomnia under counterdemand and positive demand instructions. *Journal of Abnormal Psychology*, 83(2), 157–63.

Strauss, M. E. & Smith, G. T. (2009). Construct validity: Advances in theory and methodology. *Annual Review of Clinical Psychology*, 5, 1–25.

Suen, H. K. & Ary, D. (2014). *Analyzing Quantitative Behavioral Observation Data*. New York: Psychology Press.

Suen, H. K., Ary, D. & Covalt, W. C. (1990). A decision tree approach to selecting an appropriate observation reliability index. *Journal of Psychopathology and Behavioral Assessment*, 12(4), 359–63.

Uebersax, J. (2009). Raw agreement coefficients. Retrieved 29 August 2013 from www.john-uebersax.com/stat/raw.htm

Vlaeyen, J. W. S., de Jong, J., Geilen, M., Heuts, P. H. T. G. & van Breukelen, G. (2001). Graded exposure in vivo in the treatment of pain-related fear: A replicated single-case experimental design in four patients with chronic low back pain. *Behaviour Research and Therapy*, 39(2), 151–66.

Wells, A., White, J. & Carter, K. (1997). Attention training: effects on anxiety and beliefs in panic and social phobia. *Clinical Psychology and Psychotherapy*, 4, 226–32.

Chapter 4
Designing single-case experiments

As we saw in Chapter 2, measuring the outcome pre- and post-treatment can, under certain conditions, allow us to interpret any change. However, although we might be tempted to assert that the change is attributable to treatment, we really need more evidence before we can make such a statement with any confidence. Measurement before and after an intervention does not enable us to make causal inferences. Changes in the measures might reflect changes in the conditions of measurement, the sensitivity of the measure, or changes due to extra-therapy events. Figure 4.1 illustrates these issues and the gaps in panels B–E represent the transition point between baseline and treatment periods..

Panel A shows the simplest two observations of pre–post treatment. The main problems with relying solely on pre–post observations are first that we have no information on variation in the outcome over time, and second that we cannot determine whether the change seen in the later observation is uniquely associated with the introduction of treatment. Panels B to E show examples of possible data points over time and offer alternative rival hypotheses for the difference between the single pre- and post-treatment data points. In panel B the presence of all the other data points suggests that there has been no change over time and the single post-treatment data point is anomalous. This data point might simply represent a measurement error, i.e. the participant might have made an error in reporting their state or we might have made a transcription/recording error in our database. Alternatively, the single point of improvement might represent a transient change in the person's state because of the influence of another non-treatment event, e.g. a small win on the lottery. In panel C we can see that there is considerable variability in the measure across the pre- and post-treatment phases and the single pre- and post-treatment data points just happen to coincide with maxima and minima in the baseline and treatment phases. In Panel D a very different pattern is shown. We now have evidence that the person's condition has improved and that we have not been presented with a one-off observation. It is, however, rather more difficult to conclude that this gain is convincingly attributable to treatment because the change occurred well after the introduction of treatment. Again we need to consider possible reasons for this change. It is of course possible that the impact of treatment may not be immediate. Indeed there are precedents for this – for example, pharmacological treatments for mood often require 2 or 3 weeks before their effects are seen, and significant changes in avoidance behaviour may require several

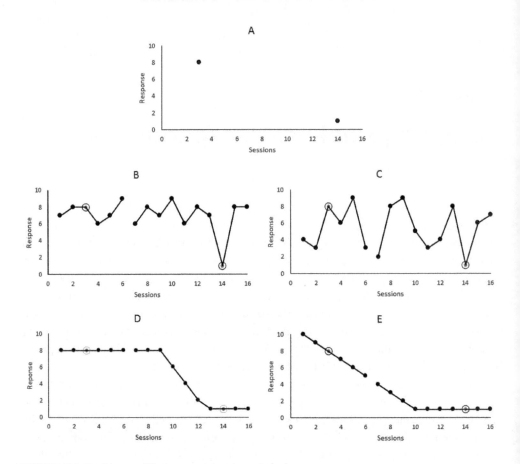

FIGURE 4.1 Problems with pre- post-treatment design

treatment sessions. In Panel E, repeated measurement in the baseline and treatment phases suggests that a reduction in symptoms was occurring before treatment was initiated.

RATIONALE OF SINGLE-CASE DESIGNS

Figure 4.1 shows how increasing the number of measurements taken during baseline and treatment phases can potentially help us consider and eliminate various explanations about change. The cardinal features of single-case design are the use of repeated measures of the criterion variable and the obtaining of data under different conditions, so that the individual is essentially used as their own control. All the designs have the same underlying logic: if the introduction of the intervention is uniquely associated with changes in the target variable, i.e. there are no changes in the target variable at other times, then there is less likelihood that other explanations for the change are true. Group designs rely on inter-group differences to rule out the effects of history, maturation, statistical regression and other threats to internal validity, but single-case designs rely on systematic changes in the pattern of data within an individual to achieve the same ends.

This chapter will illustrate and discuss the basic core of single-case designs. We will use somewhat idealised artificial data sets, rather than include too many references to particular studies, and we will rely in this chapter entirely on visual displays.

Single-case designs have their terminology, the most notable of which is the use of capital (upper case) letters to mark the separation of different conditions, e.g. no treatment and treatment conditions. In the terminology of single-case designs, separate conditions are known as phases and referred to by a sequence of capital letters: A, B, C. Rather confusingly baseline, or no-treatment, is always badged as A and the subsequent treatment conditions as B, C, D, etc. Variations within a treatment condition are signified by the treatment letter with a number sub- or superscripted, e.g. B_1 or B^2. Table 4.1 summarises the basic single-case designs discussed in this chapter.

At the outset it should be stressed that single-case designs should not be applied in a formulaic manner. Like all research, considerable thought is needed about several aspects of the design such as the length of phases, how often to take measurements, when to change condition, intervention manipulation and monitoring context changes. As noted in Chapter 1, these designs can be used in both routine clinical settings and clinical research,

TABLE 4.1 Summary of the basic single-case designs

Name	Abbreviation	Comment
Interrupted time series	AB	Basic repeated measures design. Often considered as a 'pre-experimental' design because there is no manipulation of the treatment or control condition. Widely used in clinical settings.
Reversal	ABAB	Recognised as a powerful experimental design because of the active manipulation (withdrawal and reintroduction) of the treatment component.

Multiple baseline designs
1. Within subject
  1.1. Across behaviours
  1.2. Across settings
2. Between subjects
	MBD	A series of designs in which control is achieved by monitoring target behaviours that are not being treated. The effect of treatment is documented when behaviours change only when they become the focus of treatment. The 'between subjects' option is widely used.

Changing criterion design	CCD	Experimental control is demonstrated by shifts in the target behaviour corresponding with changes in the treatment condition. Unlike the ABAB design full withdrawal of treatment is not necessary.
Alternating treatment designs 1. Without baseline 2. With baseline	ATD	This design comes in two forms, with and without a pre-treatment baseline. It is capable of comparing the impact of two or more treatments.

although it is perhaps harder to use them in routine settings where there are constraints on time and limitations imposed by the characteristics of the case concerned. Ethical issues feature in all clinical and clinical research work and should be considered in both situations.

The AB design or interrupted time-series design

The AB design is sometimes also called the interrupted time-series design. Here we obtain a set of observations prior to treatment, the baseline phase, and set of observations during treatment, the treatment phase. Data can be plotted as in Figure 4.2. Making inferences about the meaning of data in single-case research is no different from the business of drawing inferences in other, more familiar, research designs. In the idealised example in Figure 4.2 the baseline observations are reasonably stable, with a little variation and no obvious marked trend in the data. At the start of the intervention there is a rapid reduction in the dependent variable, followed by a sustained reduction, and we might even suspect a further slight improvement (downward trend). The validity of the conclusion we draw will depend on an understanding of the design and extent to which it can rule out plausible alternative explanations in the context of the study. The major factors which should always be considered are: (1) the length and stability of the baseline; (2) the timing and rapidity with which treatment takes effect; and (3) the likely influence of external events.

With a pattern of data such as that seen in Figure 4.2, we can probably dismiss several major threats to internal validity. The stability of measure in the baseline suggests that regression to the mean is unlikely, as are effects due to testing and instrumentation. Similarly the lack of an overall continuous downward trend probably excludes maturation (spontaneous remission). The other main factor to exclude is history (extra-therapy events), and we have to satisfy ourselves that the observed change did not coincide with an extra-treatment event such as a change in medication or the occurrence of a life event.

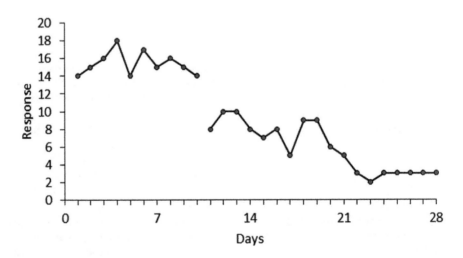

FIGURE 4.2 The AB design

The influence of history on the outcome is easier to dismiss if no changes occurred in the baseline phase despite the presence of other documented changes in the client's life. Factors like these are not under experimental control and interpretation therefore requires that we keep an accurate record of extra-treatment events. Elliott (2002) has suggested a structured method for examining these *post hoc*, and this is discussed in Chapter 8.

The AB design is generally considered as a non-experimental or pre-experimental design, because no attempt is made to manipulate the treatment component in a systematic way by either withdrawing it or adjusting the intensity of treatment. Some experimental control can be achieved however by randomising the point at which treatment starts (Edgington & Onghena, 2007; Onghena & Edgington, 2005). This means that randomisation tests can be used to analyse the data, as discussed below and in Chapter 6.

Extensions and variations of the AB design

There are occasions when one can extend the AB design with the addition of another phase (C) in which a different treatment is tested. In a clinical setting, if no treatment effect is found with the AB design, a second treatment can be offered in an ABC sequence. In this case the B phase becomes a suitable baseline for the evaluation of the C phase, but the interpretation of change in the C phase will need careful thought. It may be difficult to conclude that the treatment in C is entirely responsible for therapeutic gain, as there are two possible alternatives to consider. First, it could be that the impact of the treatment in B is time dependent and that the change observed in the C phase is the delayed effect of B. The second possibility is that the treatment effect of C is dependent on some priming effect of B. Fortunately both of these alternatives can be subject to empirical tests. In the first case one would need to run a series of replications in which the length of phase B is systematically varied. Lengthening B before C is introduced would allow one to test the time dependent nature of the proposed B effect, while reducing the duration of the B phase before C is introduced could demonstrate that treatment coincides with C rather than a time dependency. Testing the priming hypotheses merely requires one to run studies with phases AC, i.e. no B component.

Vlaeyen and his colleagues provide two illustrations of variation of the AB(C) design in a series of studies investigating the effectiveness of a graded exposure treatment for chronic pain. These studies focused on a subgroup of patients with chronic pain who had particular beliefs that engaging in certain activities would have catastrophic effects. For example, a patient might believe that bending over would cause their back to break and they would be subsequently paralysed. In initial studies, Vlaeyen and his colleagues (Vlaeyen, De Jong, Onghena, Kerckhoffs-Hanssen & Kole-Snijders, 2002) used an AB design to demonstrate that patients' fears reduced rapidly and dramatically when they were treated using a graded exposure protocol (Vlaeyen, Morley, Linton, Boersma & de Jong, 2012). In subsequent studies they used an ABC design to rule out two possibilities. The first of these (de Jong *et al.*, 2005) tested the possibility that the change observed might be attributable to a single intensive orientation and education session before actual treatment by graded exposure. This study was designed so that a baseline phase (A) was followed by the education session (B), but the introduction of graded exposure (C) was delayed. The data clearly showed that significant improvement only occurred when graded exposure was introduced. In the second set of studies, Vlaeyen and his colleagues tested the specific effect of graded exposure against an alternative treatment, graded activity, known to be effective for many pain patients (Vlaeyen, de Jong, Geilen, Heuts & van Breukelen, 2001). The treatments are very similar, with the exception that graded activity does not expose individuals to highly feared activities in a structured manner. In these experiments some patients received a baseline period (A) followed by graded exposure (B) and then by graded activity (C), whereas for a second set of patients the sequence of treatment was ACB. The results clearly showed that it was only when graded exposure was introduced that significant changes in fear and behavioural activity occurred.

The ABAB or reversal design

The ABAB design has a stronger claim to be a proper experimental design because the occurrence of the intervention is deliberately manipulated on two occasions, giving the potential of replicating any effect within the individual. The simple elegance of this design is illustrated in Figure 4.3. It can be seen that there is an alternating series of baseline (A) and treatment (B) conditions. The expectation is that therapeutic gain in the problem behaviour will coincide with the introduction of treatment. This is the same expectation as for the AB design, but in the ABAB design the sequence occurs twice. More importantly the ABAB design includes the expectation that when the sequence is reversed, i.e. treatment is withdrawn, the problem behaviour will worsen. This provides evidence that a change in the problem is associated with both the presence and absence of the critical therapeutic event. The replication of the effects in the second AB sequence strengthens the evidence as it becomes increasingly implausible to believe that changes in the problem behaviour just happen to coincide with the presence of extra-treatment events, changes in the natural course of the problem or measurement factors. The causal effect of an intervention is more believable if the effect can be replicated, and the addition of a randomisation element (see Chapter 6) to the ABAB sequence would further strengthen the study.

The ABAB design is simple and it has a strong element of experimental control. This makes it easier to rule out the major threats of history, maturation, statistical regression, testing and instrumentation. This design is commonly used in applied behaviour analysis where it is relatively easy to apply and withdraw reinforcement contingencies, and the effects of the manipulation can be quickly seen. There are, however, occasions when its use is problematic. In some settings it may be considered unethical to withdraw an apparently successful treatment, even for a limited amount of time. For example, one would be reluctant to withdraw treatment from patients being treated for self-harming behaviour. In the clinical setting one might also have to balance the wishes of the patient and their family to continue treatment with the wish to demonstrate the causal impact of treatment, although if appropriate consent has been obtained this problem may be mitigated. Finally, we may face the situation where the treatment is not reversible because the person has learned a new behaviour that is now under self-control. In such cases it may be possible to use another design such as the changing criterion design.

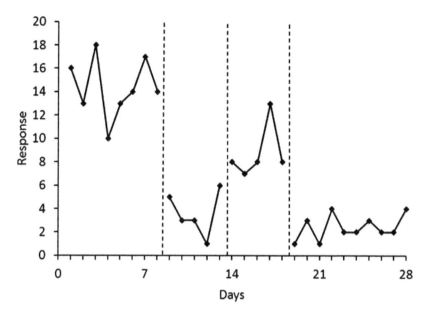

FIGURE 4.3 The ABAB design

Other variants of the ABAB design

As with the AB design, it is possible to add additional phases to the basic ABAB design and thereby to test the effectiveness of two plausible treatment conditions. Barlow, Nock and Hersen (2009) discuss several variations at length and describe testing for possible treatment interactions. The main advantage over the ABC extension to the AB design is the repeated inclusion of return to baseline conditions, as in the sequence ABABACAB.

The changing criterion design

Hartmann and Hall (1976) provided the first accessible account of the changing criterion design (CCD). Hartmann and Hall were advocating this design as applied behaviour analysts, and the typical target behaviours that were the focus of interest were either increases or decreases in the rates of specific behaviours. The changing criterion design can be used when reversal of treatment is considered undesirable or technically implausible. It is particularly suitable when dealing with a single problem behaviour and there is the possibility that changes in the dependent variable can be incrementally graded. Experimental control is demonstrated by manipulating the criterion, specifying when the treatment contingency will be applied. In the standard CCD, after a baseline phase (A), treatment is introduced incrementally across several phases: the treatment phases are often denoted as C_1, C_2, C_3 and so on, where C denotes a change in the criterion. Each treatment phase is defined by a pre-set change in the criterion that the problem behaviour is to meet. In most published examples of the CCD the treatment does not vary across the phases, and only the level of the target problem is adjusted. This is good experimental practice as changing more than one parameter at any time makes interpretation of any subsequent changes in behaviour problematic. Thus in the CCD the treatment element is held constant but the level of expected performance is changed systematically. This will be clearer in the example in the next paragraph. The CCD therefore has replication of the treatment effect built in to its fabric.

Figure 4.4 shows a graphical representation of the changing criterion design. The data in Figure 4.4 are simulated but follow Hartmann and Hall's example (1976, case II, p. 529). For example, imagine you wished to reduce the number of times each day you check your Facebook page. You begin by self-monitoring your daily checking and observe that over a baseline period you checked your page around 18 times per day. This baseline data are then used to set the criterion in the first phase of treatment. The criterion for the first treatment phase is set by referring to the performance level in the baseline sessions. In this case you set the criterion of checking for the first treatment phase as 16. The treatment is a punishment procedure known as a 'response cost' schedule. As the name suggests, response cost procedures result in the loss of a valued activity or item if you make the undesired response. In this case you agree to pay £1.00 every time you check over the criterion, so one additional check will cost you £1.00, two will cost £2.00 and so on. In setting the contract for treatment you might agree that this money can either be donated to a favoured charity, or the incentive might be enhanced, because you will perceive the loss as greater, by agreeing to donate to a non-preferred charity. Once the criterion for the problem behaviour has been met and is stable, a new criterion can be introduced. Experimental control is demonstrated if the changes in the target behaviour closely follow the changes in the set criterion.

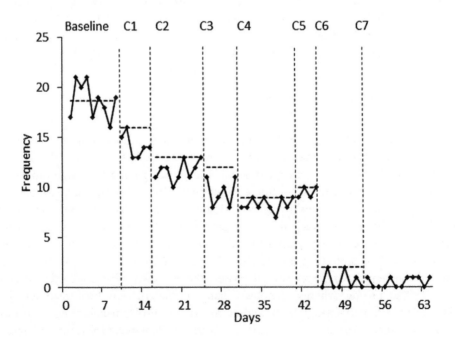

FIGURE 4.4 The changing criterion design

Figure 4.4 shows several important features of the changing criterion design. First, it is generally recommended that there are more than two changes of criterion in the treatment phase. In our example there are nine treatment phases that set criteria for successive reductions in the number of checks of Facebook that can be made without cost. Second, the length of each phase is varied. In this example it ranges from 3 (C_5) to 9 (C_2) days. Varying the length of the phases ensures that any changes do not coincide with regularly occurring extra-treatment events or times such as weekends. Third, the magnitude of the criterion should be varied; in this example it varies from a change of one check between the baseline mean and C_1 and four checks between C_5 and C_6. Large changes in the criterion are unlikely to be successful, at least in the early stages of treatment. Fourth, the phase lengths should be long enough to ensure that successive changes in the therapeutic direction are not naturally occurring, i.e. attributable to the maturation of external events (history) or measurement changes. Hartmann and Hall (1976) explicitly mention this, but the interpretation of data will be dependent on additional documented evidence of extra-treatment events and knowledge of the trajectory of any maturational effects. This might be particularly important if the CCD is used for a problem that has a developmental component, e.g. the acquisition of a cognitive or motor skill. Briefly, one of the conditions for setting the length of the phase is that it should be out of synchrony with any trend in the data, so that the successful implementation of each criterion is shown as a marked discontinuity in the trend. Finally, in this example additional evidence of experimental control, i.e. demonstrating the contingency between the treatment and the criterion, was gained by partly reversing the criterion in phase C_5. Although the CCD is primarily used when reversing the treatment is either implausible or clinically or ethically undesirable, it is always worth considering if criterion changes can be reversed. Complete reversal is usually undesirable, but brief probe withdrawals may be possible and worth implementing in order to enhance evidence for experimental control.

The CCD is an attractive design for many clinical problems in which graded changes in a problem are expected and preferred – for example in many anxiety reduction techniques, but it is among the least reported in the scientific literature. Shadish and Sullivan's survey noted 46 instances out of a total of almost 800 reports of single-case studies, i.e. around 6% (Shadish & Sullivan, 2011).

Other variants of the changing criterion design

There appear to be surprisingly few variants of the CCD. McDougall (2005) proposed a version that fits the clinical context perhaps rather better than the original design. McDougall called it the range-bound changing criterion design. Unlike the standard CCD that sets a single criterion in each phase, McDougall's simple innovation is the setting of upper and lower bound for each criterion. Experimental control is shown if the person's performance stays within the bounds set for each phase. McDougall illustrated this with data showing increased daily exercise time for a runner. He notes several conditions under which the range-bound changing criterion design might be suitably applied. These include examples in which gradual, stepwise changes in behaviour are preferred and conversely when sudden excessive changes might slow or inhibit the development of long-term change.

Many rehabilitation problems such as increasing exercise tolerance (see Main, Keefe, Jensen, Vlaeyen & Vowles, 2015, for examples) or health-promoting behaviours would meet these criteria.

Multiple baseline designs

While the changing criterion design is amongst the least reported in the published literature, the multiple baseline design is the most frequently reported – some 65% of the 800 studies documented by Shadish and Sullivan (2011) fell into this category. The multiple baseline design is really a family of designs that follow the same logic in using the idea of a control variable to demonstrate the effect of an intervention. There are three main variants of the multiple baseline design found in the literature. The logic of the design is most readily understood if we consider a single person with several target variables (the other options are considered later). For example, in a neuro-rehabilitation centre we are asked to help a patient relearn basic self-care skills (shaving, washing, oral hygiene). Figure 4.5 illustrates the use of a multiple baseline design to track the patient's progress and to demonstrate that the specific intervention for each skill is effective. In this case we might assess the patient's competence in shaving skills by observing their performance each day. This serves as the baseline condition which we run for 7 days before introducing training. The training is delivered daily over a week and we continue to monitor perform-ance in the other skills. After a week of consolidation, treatment for washing is introduced, followed by brushing teeth.

Figure 4.5 shows an idealised data plot. The obvious feature of the plot is the step-like pattern of the data, with changes in the target variable occurring only when the treatment is introduced and with no concurrent changes occurring in the untreated variables. The logic of this design is that if treatment effects are specific to the target variable then changes will be observed in only the targeted variable and not in the others that are being measured concurrently. On the other hand, if treatment coincides with an extra-treatment event (history) and it is this that produces the change or spontaneous remission (maturation), then concurrent changes in the control variables will also be observed. Where the ABAB design used replicated withdrawal to establish the specific effect of an intervention, the multiple baseline establishes the effect by replication across behaviours. One might also construe it as a replicated AB design, but the staggering of the intervention offers greater experimental control.

A major requirement of the multiple baseline design is that the target problems should be functionally independent of each other, i.e. a change in one problem does not produce a change in another. Signs of co-variation between the problems in the baseline phase should be attended to as possible indicators of non-independence. A challenge to the independence assumption is also seen in another subtle assumption behind this design: it is assumed that treatment will produce specific changes in behaviour while non-treatment events will produce general changes. The data from the design are interpretable when this assumption holds, but when there are concurrent changes in the variable being treated and the control, variable interpretation is more problematic (Kazdin & Kopel, 1975).

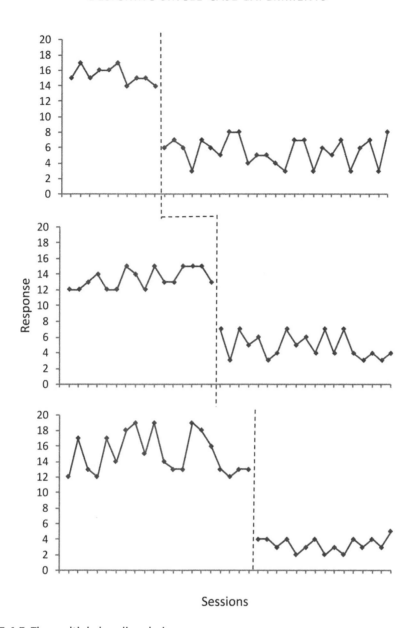

FIGURE 4.5 The multiple baseline design

The example given above is that of a multiple baseline within subject design across different behaviours. The inferences that can be made about the specific causal impact of treatment using this design are relatively strong because the data are collected within the same person at the same time in the same context throughout the study. In other words there is good control of likely extra-treatment effects and confounds. There is another within subject multiple baseline design in which the same target behaviour is observed in different contexts. This is known as the multiple baseline within-subject across-settings design. An example of the application of this design is given in a report by Barmann and Murray (1981), in which they describe the treatment of a young man with severe learning difficulties who made inappropriate sexual displays (self-stimulation) in several settings. The treatment was a simple punishment method called facial screening, in which the therapist lightly pulled a terry cloth bib in front of the patient's face for 5 seconds as soon as he began self-stimulation. This procedure was carried out in the classroom, on the school bus and at home in succession The resulting data plot clearly showed large reductions in the frequency of the sexual behaviour only when the treatment was introduced in the relevant setting.

Perhaps the most frequent applications of multiple baseline designs are those studies that apply the design across several subjects. These are known as multiple baseline designs between subjects. This version of the design has the merit that it is likely to meet the crucial assumption that the target problems are independent of one another. In such studies, participants with the same target problem are included in the study. Only one variable in each subject is measured and evidence of the effectiveness of treatment is obtained when the introduction of treatment produces change only within the treated person and not the others within the study. It is easy to see the parallels between this and a replicated AB design, but the essential difference is the planned staggering of the introduction of the treatment. Ideally, to be consistent with the logic of the design, these subjects should all be treated at the same time and in the same environment so that they are exposed to the same general external events (history). It is not always clear how often this strict assumption is met. Watson and Workman (1981) discussed this issue in greater depth. Although it is highly desirable to conduct the study on all participants concurrently, it may be unfeasible in some circumstances – e.g. when the administrative burden of running each person is considerable or when the problem is relatively rare and one can only obtain cases intermittently. Under these conditions the staggering of baseline length is the essential feature to be retained and the application of randomisation procedures (Chapter 6) will enhance the robustness of the study.

Variants of the MBD design

Both Kazdin (2010) and Barlow et al. (2009) discuss further applications and variants of the multiple baseline design. One particular variant which can be useful in applied settings where resources might constrain extensive data collection is the multiple probe design described by Horner and Baer (1978). They suggest that under certain conditions it might be both possible and advantageous not to collect data on every occasion but to sample, or probe, the target behaviour. This might be advantageous if the measurement procedure is expensive or reactive to repetition. In some clinical cases where there are good case records it might also be possible to obtain historical probes of the target problem. However, this strategy relies on parity between the recording method from case notes and the current observational protocol, and Horner and Baer note that applying probes requires that a strong a priori assumption of stability can be made. The reason for this will become apparent when we discuss the analysis of single cases, but Figure 4.1 at the start of the chapter illustrates that problems of interpretation occur when baselines are unstable.

In summary, multiple baseline designs are extremely flexible and well accepted in the literature. The major attraction is the apparent control built into the design by the staggering of the introduction of treatment without the requirement that treatment should be reversed. For many problems where reversal is neither possible nor desirable for ethical reasons, the multiple baseline design may be the treatment of choice. The second attractive feature of these designs is that replication is built into the fabric of the design. Whereas in the ABAB and changing criterion design replication occurs within a subject for a single problem, replication in the multiple baseline design occurs across behaviours, settings or people, depending on the particular application. The number of replications depends on the number of baselines in the study. Most authorities (Barlow *et al.*, 2009; Kazdin, 2010; Kratochwill *et al.*, 2010) suggest that a minimum number of three baselines, i.e. three baselines within one individual or three individuals, is necessary to establish experimental control, but it is possible to extend this number considerably and developments in data analysis mean that large data sets can be analysed with sophisticated statistical methods (Ferron, Moeyaert, Van den Noortgate & Beretvas, 2014).

Alternating treatment designs (ATD)

In certain circumstances it is possible to design a single-case study that compares the effects of two or more treatments in a single individual. There are several variants of the general design, but the basic principle is that the participant is exposed to two or more treatments on several occasions. Unlike the ABC sequence in the extension of the basic AB design, in the alternating treatment design the interventions are generally quite brief and not presented in distinct phases. The term alternating treatment is a slight misnomer as it suggests that each treatment is alternated in the sequence of presentation. In well-conducted experiments each treatment would be distributed to avoid strict alternation. For example, we might have two treatments B and C and decide that we will conduct an experiment with eight presentations of B and C. The sequence of presentation will be randomised but with the constraint that no more than three sessions of B or C can be presented in one sequence. This might result in the following sequence: B C B B C C C B B C C B B C C B.

The basic features of an ATD are seen in a study by White and Sanders (1986). In this study they demonstrated that an aspect of pain behaviour was functionally related to particular social contingencies. Pain behaviour is a generic term given to behaviour occurring when someone is experiencing pain. The important aspect of this is that unlike the privately experienced, subjective pain (i.e. your experience of the intensity and quality of pain), behaviour that is emitted while in pain is publicly observable, e.g. in a verbal report of pain, in moaning or grimacing, or in a change of gait. In the terms of behaviour theory, publicly observable behaviour is capable of being reinforced, often by changes in the behaviour of other people who may express concern and positively reinforce the behaviour. On the other hand there are other social interactions that effectively punish the expression of pain behaviour. White and Sanders (1986) designed a study to test the hypothesis that a person's ratings of their ongoing pain intensity might be determined by the quality of the immediately preceding social interaction. In this study four chronic pain patients (two with headache and one each with low back pain and chest pain) were interviewed twice a day for 5 minutes for 7 consecutive days. The order of the two conditions was randomly determined within each day. The conversations opened with one of two questions asking about their general state ('How are you feeling/things going'). In one condition the participants were positively reinforced for talking about their pain or how bad they felt (pain talk). Here the therapist expressed their concern for them and admiration for living with pain. In the other condition the therapist responded positively to any talk about feeling better, doing more or reduction in medication use (well talk). At the end of each interview session the therapist asked the participant to complete a single rating of their pain intensity on a 0–5 numerical scale. Across all four patients the data were very clear. After sessions where they had received positive reinforcement for talking about their pain their ratings of pain (a behaviour expression of pain) were notably higher than for the sessions where they had not been reinforced for 'well' talk. Figure 4.6 shows these results.

In the study by White and Sanders no baseline data were needed or obtained. Although it would have been possible to obtain ratings of the patients' pain on random occasions before the onset of the study, this was not strictly necessary. In other circumstances it may

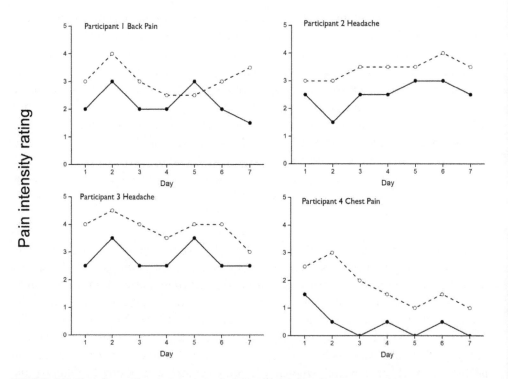

FIGURE 4.6 The alternating treatments design with no baseline

The dotted line represents the "well talk" condition, the solid line represents the "pain talk" condition. Reprinted from *Journal of Behavior Therapy and Experimental Psychiatry*,17(3), White, B., & Sanders, S. H, The influence on patients' pain intensity ratings of antecedent reinforcement of pain talk or well talk, pp.155–159. Copyright (1986), with permission from Elsevier

be more appropriate to include a baseline in the design. Figure 4.7 illustrates this variation in which baseline, phase A, is followed by a treatment phase in which two treatments, T1 and T2, are presented. As before, it is good experimental practice not to alternate the treatments but to present them in a random order. This version of the design is useful if one wishes to test which of two or more alternative treatments produces greater improvement from the baseline. In the example in Figure 4.7, treatment T1 appears to be consistently more effective than treatment T2, and once sufficient evidence of this has been obtained then it should be relatively easy to implement treatment T1 without the need to continue with treatment T2. In an example of this, Ollendick, Shapiro and Barrett (1981) treated a child with severe learning difficulties to reduce his stereotypic hair-pulling. They compared physical restraint and positive practice where the child was guided through a competing activity. Positive practice was shown to be the more effective treatment.

The alternating treatment design is a powerful way of testing the relative efficacy of two or more treatments, but it requires careful planning (as do all experiments). The design is not suitable for all treatments and there are some clear constraints. Interventions should have a relatively immediate effect on the target behaviour. They should also be short acting so that when they are withdrawn there is no carry-over effect (diffusion of treatment effect) that might either hinder the action of the alternative treatment or amplify the impact of same treatment were it to be repeated. The treatments should also be easily discriminable by the participant. Not surprisingly, studies of alternating treatment designs are not often reported in the literature. Shadish and Sullivan's survey (Shadish & Sullivan, 2011) indicated that around 8% of the studies surveyed were ATDs; this figure is close to the 6% observed by Smith (2012).

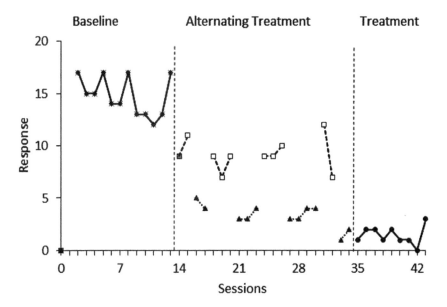

FIGURE 4.7 The alternating treatments design with a baseline. Treatment T1 (filled triangles) is more effective than treatment T2 (open squares)

Other designs

The previous pages have outlined the standard range of designs, but one of the attractions of single-case designs is that it is possible to adapt them to specific problems. An extensive coverage of many of the variants is given in Barlow, Nock and Hersen's (2009) text. For example, they provide detailed coverage of the many possibilities of extending the simple sequence of baseline and treatment conditions in order to test the effects of different treatment components, quantitative variations in a single component, different drug treatments and interaction effects. Single-case designs are very flexible and it is possible to tailor a design by combining various elements of the basic designs. For example, the principle of alternating, or more accurately randomising, different treatments can be incorporated into other experimental designs in order to carry out further checks on threats to the validity of experiments. McKnight, Nelson, Hayes and Jarrett (1984) investigated two treatments for depression on people with different psychological profiles. They identified patients with social skills or cognitive deficits and hypothesised that patients would respond better if the treatment matched their specific problem. They used a hybrid design to test this proposition. First, patients were allocated to a multiple baseline design and secondly the weekly treatments were randomly alternated between a social skills training and a cognitive treatment. The primary outcome was mood as assessed by a standard mood checklist. The data confirmed the investigators' hypothesis: patients with social skills deficits improved more when given social skills training rather than the cognitive treatment, whereas the reverse was true for those with cognitive deficits. It is notable in this study that neither treatment is fast-acting, but the weekly scheduling of treatments ensured enough time for them to be effective.

THE IMPORTANCE OF BASELINES IN SINGLE-CASE DESIGNS

The origins of single-case experiments lie within the behaviour analytic tradition of laboratory-based research on single subjects. Murray Sidman's (1960) classic text clearly articulates the rationale underpinning the principles of experimental design in this setting. A key aspect in the strategy for investigating influences on behaviour is to establish reliable, stable baseline performance under known and highly controlled conditions. It was only when such a stable baseline had been established that experimental manipulations were introduced. Sidman describes in considerable detail various factors that might influence the establishment of stable responding. In the laboratory setting the analysis of external events that might influence responding is relatively easy in comparison to field settings, because one has a good deal of control over the environment and one can limit and constrain events that are likely to influence responding. Sidman called variation in performance due to external events, extrinsic variability. Examples of factors influencing extrinsic variability include problems associated with the reliability of measurement, e.g. defining the target behaviours inconsistently, instrumentation effects, poorly trained observers and variation in reporting practices; and problems in the variation in the environment. Sidman also identified sources of intrinsic variability, i.e. variations within the state of the individual such as fatigue, drug state and diurnal rhythm.

When behaviour analytic principles were applied to humans in clinical settings, applied behaviour analysts transferred the laboratory rationales insofar as it was possible. In reading accounts of applied behaviour analysis studies, it is abundantly clear that considerable attention is given to controlling as many factors likely to influence extrinsic and intrinsic variation as possible. Care is needed in defining and measuring the target problem, and in many studies observations may be carried out in somewhat contrived settings, e.g. observations are limited to fixed periods of time and standardised settings. As a consequence, the chances of obtaining stable responding under baseline conditions can be enhanced. This is not always possible in clinical settings, but nevertheless care should be taken to specify and standardise observations as much as possible. A stable baseline makes it much easier to detect any impact of treatment. In the examples of different designs given earlier in this chapter the data were contrived to show relatively stable baselines and an unambiguous treatment effect. In practice questions arise concerning how to determine the length of baselines, when treatments should be introduced and withdrawn, and how to ensure the integrity of treatments.

The criterion for stability should be explicit

Minimum criteria would appear to be the absence of trend in the baseline and limited variation around the mean value of the data (Gast, 2010). Quantifying the amount of variation around the mean is more contentious. What is an acceptable level? I suggest the following rules of thumb: 5–10% variation around the mean value would probably be considered very acceptable, 10–20% reasonable, 20–30% borderline acceptable and values beyond that questionable. The greater the variability the more difficult it becomes to detect change when treatment is introduced, and greater variability also suggests that there are influences on the target behaviour that may not be understood or controlled.

Determining the length of baselines

How long should a baseline be? Shadish and Sullivan's (2011) survey of single-case experiments published in 2008 reveals considerable variation, with 4% of studies having one data point, 6% with two data points, 20% with three data points, 15% with four data points and 55% with five or more data points. What is not clear from this survey is how decisions about baseline length were taken. Barlow et al. (2009) discuss a range of baselines with variation in trend, variability and the direction of any trend (towards improvement or deterioration). They make several suggestions about how to mitigate problems, including extending the number of observations and attempting to smooth the data by blocking them (averaging), but ultimately they write (p. 73): 'There is no completely satisfactory strategy for dealing with the variable baseline . . .'. The What Works Clearinghouse (Kratochwill et al., 2010) specifies standards for single-case designs and states that three data points per phase are needed to meet the 'standard with reservation', but five data points are needed to meet the standard. Nevertheless, the Clearinghouse documentation also recognises that in some instances, e.g. cases with self-injurious behaviour, shorter baselines may be more appropriate for obvious ethical reasons.

Perhaps we should recognise that there is no definitive answer to the question of how long a baseline should be, other than to state that wherever possible longer baselines are generally preferable to shorter ones and stable baselines preferable to more variable ones. In an applied setting the length of a baseline will be influenced by several factors, and the ideal stable baseline demanded in laboratory settings will not always be attainable. What is important is that the clinician-researcher should be clear and document the criteria used to determine the length of the baseline in any particular study. It is convenient to consider the criteria under two headings, research settings and clinical practice.

Baselines in research settings

When single-case methods are being used as an experimental tool there are three criteria that can be used to decide when to introduce a treatment. The first is the criterion of *stability* (see above). The second is statistical *power analysis*. In group-based experimentation, determining the sample sizes to use in an experiment should be decided by a power analysis. Here the researcher specifies the statistical test they will use, the expected effect size of the intervention and the probability level they will use to assess the effect of the intervention. A similar power analysis can be performed for single-case analysis if the experimenter has made an *a priori* decision to use certain types of statistical analyses, such as time-series analyses, on the data. Recently single-case researchers have paid attention to developing measures of effect size, equivalent to Cohen's d used in group research, that are appropriate for the time series nature of single-case designs. Such measures might form the basis for power analysis in the future (Shadish, Hedges & Pustejovsky, 2014), but with few exceptions the use of power analysis to determine the length of baseline and treatment phases in research appears to be extremely rare and we need statistical models before it can be routinely incorporated into single-case research. A third criterion, also statistical in nature, is based on *randomisation* tests and is more common. To be validly applied these tests require that the length of the baseline should be determined before the experiment begins. Randomisation tests are explained more fully in Chapter 6 and are to be encouraged because they add additional control to the design of an experiment. The ideal would be a stable baseline with the start of the intervention determined by randomly selecting the start point.

Baselines in clinical practice

In clinical practice, where one is using single-case methodology to monitor and evaluate routine clinical practice, there are several possible criteria for deciding when to end baseline observations and begin treatment. In some settings there may be pragmatic reasons for introducing treatment at a given point in time. For example, the clinical service may operate strict protocols and limit client contact to six sessions, of which the first is an assessment and in the remaining five sessions a treatment protocol is adhered to. Under these conditions, when data are collected at each session, obtaining a baseline of more than one data point is impossible and implementing single-case methodology is problematic. If, however, data can be collected more frequently, say by daily diary records, then a longer baseline may be possible but the length will be limited by the number of days between sessions.

Another criterion for introducing treatment might be that the clinician is satisfied that they have completed the case formulation. If this is the case the ethical reason for delaying the introduction of treatment merely to obtain a longer baseline might be regarded as questionable. The initiation of treatment would seem advisable but at the possible cost of an inadequate baseline.

A treatment may also be introduced reactively on the grounds that the target problem is 'out of control'. However, extreme behaviour is rare and it usually returns to a median value without intervention. A reactive intervention is also likely to be confounded with naturally occurring changes in behaviour, which precludes the opportunity for investigating and understanding the problem. Reactive interventions were noted as a threat to validity (Chapter 1) and they require careful consideration. While it is probably true that extremes of behaviour and distress will revert to a more moderate value there are occasions, such as when the patient presents a danger to others or to themselves, when not intervening would be highly questionable. Thus while a sufficiently long and stable baseline in clinical settings is desirable, we must recognise that on occasions there will be practical and ethical reasons why the clinician might choose to terminate the baseline phase and intervene.

TREATMENT FACTORS IN SINGLE-CASE DESIGN

There are two main concerns to be considered with respect to treatment. The first is to ensure that treatment integrity has been maintained, i.e. the treatment has been implemented and delivered as intended. The second is to determine the duration of the treatment during the experimental phase.

The answers to these questions depend in part on the nature of the treatment that is being given and its expected impact: will a large effect be observed almost immediately or is the impact expected to accrue rather more slowly in time? In applied behaviour analysis treatments might be considered to be relatively 'simple' insofar as they comprise a single element, in which there is a clearly specified change in the contingency between the target behaviour and the manipulation of a consequence. Such treatments require a clear protocol specifying the target behaviour and the contingency to be implemented. These should be observable by a third party, and monitoring treatment delivery can be accomplished either in real time or by subsequent analysis of audio or video recordings. Changing the contingency of a target behaviour is also expected to have a relatively immediate and large effect and, as such, it is probably only necessary to replicate the effect over a few sessions to ensure that a change has occurred and that it is robust. In any case one would require more than one treatment session to ensure that any changes are not a transient effect of novelty or a demand characteristic of the experiment.

Other behavioural treatments can be more complex and require several sessions before a significant treatment effect might be observed. For example, Vlaeyen et al. (2012) developed a graded exposure protocol to treat people with pain-related fears. Typically a person with pain-related fear avoids certain movements associated with pain because they fear that executing the movement will result in harm. In the treatment of this problem a hierarchy of feared movements is established using a systematic protocol. Patients then perform each of the feared movements, thus disconfirming their catastrophic beliefs of a harmful outcome. It may take several sessions for them to be exposed to each of the items on the hierarchy and to re-evaluate their belief about the relationship between movement and harm. Establishing treatment fidelity for this protocol seems relatively simple, but it still requires the analysis of video recordings of the sessions for research purposes (Leeuw, Goossens, de Vet & Vlaeyen, 2009).

Many other therapies, including cognitive behavioural treatments where there are established protocols, are truly complex, with multiple treatment components delivered over several sessions. The duration of treatment is determined by the treatment protocol, but under these conditions it is far more difficult to specify the expected course of change. One might anticipate that change would be relatively slow and incremental across sessions, but this might not be so as there is ample evidence of patients making rapid gains early on in the course of treatment (Masterson et al., 2014).

CONCLUSIONS

This chapter surveyed the main designs used in single-case research. Each design attempts to establish experimental control and to account for various plausible rival hypotheses in slightly different ways. The common features of the designs are repeated measurement of the variable of interest under two or more different conditions with the aim of using the individual as their own control. Most often, measurement is at the level of specific behaviours or subjective report – the target variables discussed in Chapter 3. Two recent surveys of published literature on single-case research by Shadish and Sullivan (2011) and Smith (2012) reveal that the most frequent design used is the multiple baseline, where controlled replication is inherent in the design. The alternating treatments and changing criterion designs were relatively rarely reported and, surprisingly, the ABAB (reversal) design, which is probably the strongest design in terms of providing experimental control, was also reported relatively infrequently.

The AB design is regarded by authorities (Barlow et al., 2009; Kazdin, 2010; Kratochwill & Levin, 1992; Kratochwill et al., 2010) as being non- or pre-experimental because it does not include an attempt to manipulate treatment by either reversal (ABAB), repeated change in the criterion (CCD) or multiple comparisons (ATD). Nevertheless it is probable that the AB design is most likely to be employed in everyday clinical settings. Indeed if one regards the multiple baseline design as a series of AB designs, albeit with the added manipulation of varying baseline length (an attempt to control for history, maturation, regression and instrumentation), then this non-experimental sequencing of observations is the most frequently deployed. In clinical settings the AB design is suitable when it is implausible to reverse the treatment, as is the case for many CBT and other psychotherapy interventions. In addition the AB design does not raise the ethical issue of having to reverse or otherwise manipulate the treatment, and this may fit more readily into the standard ethical framework of delivering treatment.

In this chapter we have relied on simple visual inspection of the graphs to illustrate the different designs and the figures have been contrived to be persuasive. Chapters 5 and 6 examine ways in which the data from single-case experiments can be more formally evaluated. Chapter 5 explores several methods for enhancing visual analysis of the data and making inferences about treatment effects. In Chapter 6 we explore two statistical approaches to data analysis and in Chapter 8 we consider an approach to evaluating single-case data that is particularly suitable for non-replicated AB designs and where data may also be gathered at multiple levels of measurement, i.e. using standard (Chapter 2) and target (Chapter 3) measures.

Footnote: where to find examples of single-case research

Detailed commentary on the major experimental designs can be found in two texts on single-case experimental designs, by Barlow, Nock and Hersen (2009) and Kazdin (2010). These texts devote separate chapters to each of the main designs, with the exception of the AB design, covered in this chapter. Examples of single-case experimental designs can be found in journals. Many clinically oriented journals publish manuscripts reporting studies using single-case methods. Some journals focusing on behaviour analysis, such as the *Journal of Applied Behavior Analysis*, emphasise single-case methods as the preferred scientific strategy and contain many examples. Other journals largely focusing on cognitive-behaviour therapy also publish single-case research and cover clinical problems including phobias, psychosis, eating disorders, pain and personality disorders, as well as many others. Among these journals are: *Behavior Therapy*, *Behaviour Research and Therapy*, *Journal of Behavior Therapy and Experimental Psychiatry*, *Cognitive Therapy and Research* and *Cognitive Behavior Therapy*. Other, non-CBT-oriented journals also occasionally publish single-case research, including: *Journal of Consulting and Clinical Psychology*, *Psychotherapy Research* and *Psychotherapy: Theory, Research and Practice*.

REFERENCES

Barlow, D. H., Nock, M. K. & Hersen, M. (2009). *Single Case Experimental Designs* (3rd edn). Boston: Pearson.

Barmann, B. C. & Murray, W. J. (1981). Suppression of inappropriate sexual behavior by facial screening. *Behavior Therapy*, 12(5), 730–5.

de Jong, J. R., Vlaeyen, J. W. S., Onghena, P., Goossens, M. E., Geilen, M. & Mulder, H. (2005). Fear of movement/(re)injury in chronic low back pain: education or exposure in vivo as mediator to fear reduction? *Clinical Journal of Pain*, 21(1), 9–17; discussion 69–72.

Edgington, E. S. & Onghena, P. (2007). *Randomization Tests* (4th edn). London: Chapman & Hall/CRC.

Elliott, R. (2002). Hermeneutic single-case efficacy design. *Psychotherapy Research*, 12(1), 1–21.

Ferron, J. M., Moeyaert, M., Van den Noortgate, W. & Beretvas, N. S. (2014). Estimating causal effects from multiple-baseline studies: implications for design and analysis. *Psychological Methods*, 19(4), 493–510.

Gast, D. L. (2010). *Single Subject Research Methodology in Behavioral Sciences*. New York: Routledge.

Hartmann, D. P. & Hall, R. V. (1976). The changing criterion design. *Journal of Applied Behavior Analysis*, 9, 527.

Horner, R. D. & Baer, D. M. (1978). Multiple probe technique: a variation of the multiple baseline. *Journal of Applied Behavior Analysis*, 11, 189–96.

Kazdin, A. E. (2010). *Single-Case Research Designs: Methods for Clinical and Applied Settings* (2nd edn). Oxford: Oxford University Press.

Kazdin, A. E. & Kopel, S. A. (1975). On resolving ambiguities in the multiple-baseline design: problems and recommendations. *Behavior Therapy*, 6, 601–8.

Kratochwill, T. R., Hitchcock, J., Horner, R., Levin, J., Odom, S. L., Rindskopf, D. & Shadish, W. R. (2010). Single-case technical documentation. Retrieved from What Works Clearinghouse website: http://ies.ed.gov/ncee/wwc/pdf/wwe_scd.pdf

Kratochwill, T. R. & Levin, J. R. (eds) (1992). *Single-Case Research Designs and Analysis*. Hove: Lawrence Erlbaum.

Leeuw, M., Goossens, M. E., de Vet, H. C. & Vlaeyen, J. W. S. (2009). The fidelity of treatment delivery can be assessed in treatment outcome studies: a successful illustration from behavioral medicine. *Journal of Clinical Epidemiology*, 62(1), 81–90.

Main, C. J., Keefe, F. J., Jensen, M. P., Vlaeyen, J. W. S. & Vowles, K. E. (eds) (2015). *Fordyce's Behavioral Methods for Chronic Pain and Illness*. Riverwoods, IL: Wolters Kluwer/IASP.

Masterson, C., Ekers, D., Gilbody, S., Richards, D., Toner-Clewes, B. & McMillan, D. (2014). Sudden gains in behavioural activation for depression. *Behaviour Research and Therapy*, 60, 34–8.

McDougall, D. (2005). The range-bound changing criterion design. *Behavioral Interventions*, 20(2), 129–37.

McKnight, D. L., Nelson, R. O., Hayes, S. C. & Jarrett, R. B. (1984). Importance of treating individually assessed response classes in the amelioration of depression. *Behavior Therapy*, 15(4), 315–35.

Ollendick, T. H., Shapiro, E. S. & Barrett, R. P. (1981). Reducing stereotypic behaviors: an analysis of treatment procedures utilizing an alternating treatments design. *Behavior Therapy*, 12, 570–7.

Onghena, P. & Edgington, E. S. (2005). Customisation of pain treatments: Single-case design and analysis. *Clinical Journal of Pain*, 21(1), 56–68.

Shadish, W. R., Hedges, L. V. & Pustejovsky, J. E. (2014). Analysis and meta-analysis of single-case designs with a standardised mean difference statistic: A primer and applications. *Journal of School Psychology*, 52(2), 123–47.

Shadish, W. R. & Sullivan, K. J. (2011). Characteristics of single-case designs used to assess intervention effects in 2008. *Behavior Research Methods*, 43(4), 971–80.

Sidman, M. (1960). *Tactics of Scientific Research: Evaluating Experimental Data in Psychology*. New York: Basic Books.

Smith, J. D. (2012). Single-case experimental designs: A systematic review of published research and current standards. *Psychological Methods*, 17(4), 510–50.

Vlaeyen, J. W. S., de Jong, J., Geilen, M., Heuts, P. H. & van Breukelen, G. (2001). Graded exposure in vivo in the treatment of pain-related fear: a replicated single-case experimental design in four patients with chronic low back pain. *Behaviour Research and Therapy*, 39(2), 151–66.

Vlaeyen, J. W. S., De Jong, J. R., Onghena, P., Kerckhoffs-Hanssen, M. & Kole-Snijders, A. M. (2002). Can pain-related fear be reduced? The application of cognitive-behavioural exposure in vivo. *Pain Research and Management*, 7(3), 144–53.

Vlaeyen, J. W. S., Morley, S., Linton, S., Boersma, K. & de Jong, J. (2012). *Pain-Related Fear: Exposure-based Treatment of Chronic Pain*. Seattle: IASP.

Watson, P. & Workman, E. A. (1981). The non-concurrent multiple baseline across-individuals design: An extension of the traditional multiple baseline design. *Journal of Behavior Therapy and Experimental Psychiatry*, 12(3), 257–9.

White, B. & Sanders, S. H. (1986). The influence on patients' pain intensity ratings of antecedent reinforcement of pain talk or well talk. *Journal of Behavior Therapy and Experimental Psychiatry*, 17(3), 155–9.

Chapter 5
Visual analysis of single-case data

So far, in discussing single cases we have relied on graphical representation of the data to illustrate the main points. By implication this has relied entirely on your ability to 'read' the figures and be persuaded by the interpretation in the text. This 'visual' analysis has been the mainstay of quantitative single-case methodology and is attributable to the intellectual heritage of single-case designs in the applied behavioural analysis (ABA) tradition. The ABA movement developed from Skinner's behavioural analysis where there were two important characteristics of the research strategy. First, in laboratory and in many early applied settings, a primary requirement was to achieve a steady state of responding prior to any experimental intervention (recall the discussion on how long a baseline should be in Chapter 4). In experiments where animals are studied, this was attained by prolonged periods of training on predetermined schedules of reinforcement. The steady state could be observed in the graphical cumulative record. Second, in order to achieve steady state, responding laboratory studies were conducted in highly restricted, simple environments where external stimuli were controlled and restricted as was the individual's motivational state (hunger, thirst), and the response opportunities limited and contrived. In many applied settings it is impossible, both practically and ethically, to impose this degree of control on an individual. Even if it were possible, the changes imposed would severely threaten the validity and generalisability of any findings.

Notwithstanding this, the astute reader will have noticed that in some of the examples given in Chapter 4 the authors have constrained the setting in some way or other. This might amount to restricting observation sessions to a particular context, restricting the behaviour tasks in which the client/patient is asked to engage or limiting the time period of observation. While it may be very desirable to impose as much experimental control as possible, there are often limitations in practical settings. Data in many clinical settings are very variable, and even if the clinician-researcher has taken steps to understand and control variability we may still be left with considerable variation in the data, and this poses problems for us in drawing conclusions.

This chapter and the next discuss the two major approaches to analysing single-case data: visual and statistical analyses. As single-case designs emerged from applied behaviour analysis and began to be applied by clinicians and researchers with other therapeutic allegiances, it is arguable that data sets became 'messier'. Perhaps this was attributable to reduced environmental control, i.e. clinical settings that were not contrived, greater variability in measurement or interventions that did not have a fast-acting effect (so could not be checked by subsequent withdrawal and reintroduction of interventions). At around the same time researchers became increasingly sophisticated in their understanding of the limitations of simple statistical analysis based on traditional t-tests and F tests, and new methods based on modelling time-series data became more widely known and available (Glass, Willson & Gottman, 1975; Jones, Vaught & Weinrott, 1977). A healthy debate about the alternatives can be seen in the literature with some, predominantly from the ABA school, arguing coherently and persuasively for visual analysis (Baer, 1977, 1988). From the perspective of ABA, Baer's argument is compelling. He emphasises the need for experimental control, understanding variability and establishing stable baselines, and a similar understanding of interventions (based on principles of stimulus control and reinforcement) that produce large and clinically important effects. This approach is consistent with ABA, and the preference for behaviour analysts to work with replicated single-case method-ology is theoretically and methodologically consistent, c.f. Gast (2010) and Sidman (1960). In contrast, others argued for the introduction and development of statistical tests. It has been argued that the statistical approach could perhaps 'trump' visual inspection by removing observer bias from visual judgements (Jones, Weinrott & Vaught, 1978) and be able to reliably detect smaller effects disregarded by visual analysts (Kazdin, 1982). As newer statistical tests were also able to by-pass some of the limitations of traditional methods, objections to the valid application of statistics were also discarded.

THE INTERPRETATION OF VISUAL DISPLAYS

Over the past 20 years there have been a number of empirical enquiries into the merits of visual and statistical tests. Some studies use statistical models to generate data sets with known features and then require observers to make judgements about the presence of change. The observers' performance is compared to the statistically known features of the data. Other studies have compared observers with different levels of experience, e.g. novice vs experienced analysts or statistically skilled vs statistically naive judges. Various summaries of the literature are available and evidence for and against each approach is made (e.g. Barlow, Nock & Hersen, 2009; Brossart, Parker, Olson & Mahadevan, 2006; Busk & Marascuilo, 1992; Manolov, Gast, Perdices & Evans, 2014; Parsonson & Baer, 1992; Spriggs & Gast, 2010; Ximenes, Manolov, Solanas & Quera, 2009). The position adopted here is that visual and statistical analyses are not mutually exclusive. Just as in conventional research, good data analysis should proceed on the basis of careful consideration of the data and exploration of its characteristics, so the same criteria apply in the analysis of single-case data. Researchers often use the graphical tools of exploratory data analysis, such as the box-and-whisker and stem-and-leaf plots found in many software packages. These tools help the data analyst to see the data clearly and to understand its characteristic distribution, the presence of outliers and so on.

This chapter presents a series of graphical tools for exploring single-case data. There are some data sets where an effect is 'obvious'. For example, in an ABAB design when the phases are stable, with little variability or trend, when the intervention produces a large and immediate effect in the response and where withdrawing and reintroducing the intervention produces similar effects. On the other hand there are data sets where trend and variability in the data make it difficult to see what, if anything, is happening but where judicious exploration of the data can reveal interesting findings. It is not necessary to use every technique documented here or other similar methods that can be found in the literature (Spriggs & Gast, 2010). Part of the skill of analysis is learning to select which tool to use. Like all skills this comes through practice and reflection, if possible with a more experienced mentor.

THE IMPORTANCE OF CLEAR AND EFFECTIVE VISUAL DISPLAYS

Despite its apparent simplicity, understanding and making inferences about single-case data can be complex. But unlike group-based research where summary statistics (means and standard deviations) are usually reported and plotted, single-case studies nearly always present the complete data set over time in the form of an x–y plot such as those seen in Chapter 4. In contrast to group research where the test hypothesis is based on a single parameter (are the means of the groups different from each other?), the analysis and interpretation of single-case data considers the pattern of data over the time course of the

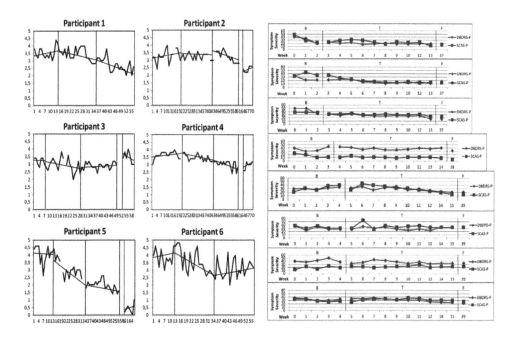

FIGURE 5.1 Examples of poor visual displays

This figure shows two visual displays and their captions from single case series, albeit reduced in size from the original publication. The left panel shows data from six people undergoing a novel treatment for chronic pain. Reprinted from *Behaviour Research and Therapy*, 47(8), Flink, I. K., Nicholas, M. K., Boersma, K., & Linton, S. J. Reducing the threat value of chronic pain: A preliminary replicated single-case study of interoceptive exposure versus distraction in six individuals with chronic back pain. pp.721–728. Copyright (2009), with permission from Elsevier. The right panel shows data from 8 young people treated for comorbid attention-deficit/hyperactivity disorder and anxiety: Copyright © [2012] by the American Psychological Association. Reproduced with permission. The official citation that should be used in referencing this material is Jarrett, M. A., & Ollendick, T. H. (2012). Treatment of comorbid attention-deficit/hyperactivity disorder and anxiety in children: a multiple baseline design analysis. *Journal of Consulting and Clinical Psychology*, 80(2), 239–244. The use of APA information does not imply endorsement by APA.

study. In addition to differences between the means in the different phases, we are also interested in the presence of and changes in trend and variability in the data over time, and particularly in the characteristics of change when an intervention is introduced and withdrawn. Most statistical techniques are only capable of testing one parameter at a time, whereas good visual representation of the data will allow you to see a clear pattern in the data. The remainder of this chapter discusses a number of simple techniques for visualising data plots and facilitating the interpretation of findings.

We begin by considering two data displays that illustrate why spending a little time in producing good visual displays is important. Figure 5.1 shows two data displays from published single-case series by Flink and her colleagues (2009) and Jarrett and Ollendick (2012). They appear to have been produced with two commonly used pieces of software: SPSS (Flink) and Excel™ (Jarrett & Ollendick). They both present data from valuable studies, but the displays themselves are difficult to read.

Flink *et al.*'s study uses a multiple baseline cross-over design to evaluate a technique intended to alter the threat value of persisting pain. They used an ABC/ACB design with the treatments in phases B (interoceptive exposure) and C (relaxation/distraction) counter-balanced across participants. The left panel shows the primary data, daily ratings of pain-related distress made on an 11-point (0–10) numeric scale, and these data are plotted against time (x-axis). The study included a baseline period followed by one of the treatments and then the second treatment and the length of the baseline varied between participants. In addition to plotting the individual data points, Flink *et al.* also plotted a regression line for each phase, although we are not told in the text how this line was fitted. This figure is the main analysis in the study, but it is difficult to read and interpret without a good deal of to-ing and fro-ing between the text and figure. We are being asked to make a judgement about the relative impact of the treatment, across two sets of subjects who received two interventions in different orders. We have to do a lot of additional work to make sense of the data. Reading the figure is made difficult for several reasons:

1   Neither of the axes are labelled
2   The values on the x-axis are particularly difficult to read for some participants
3   Although the length of the x-axis is the same for each participant, the actual duration plotted varies between about 55 and 70 days, i.e. 2 weeks' difference
4   The different phases are not labelled. All we can be sure of is that the first phase is the baseline phase but the sequence of treatment, interoceptive exposure or relaxation/distraction cannot be discerned without recourse to the text
5   The order of the participants in the composite graph is by their identifying number, but this has no relationship to the primary issue, which is the order of treatments they received
6   Finally, the visual aspects of the display are not easily discriminable. The same line thickness is used for the graph frame, and axes, lines separating the phases and the regression lines.

If we rearranged the display it might help us visualise the results more clearly. For example, a new display could also contain six panels but this time the participants could be sequenced to show the multiple baseline aspect of the design for the two orders of treatment. The left column could show the three participants who received interoceptive exposure followed by relaxation/distraction, and the right column the alternative sequence. For each panel the x-axis should be adjusted to the same length, 70 days, so that we can see the alignment across participants. The different graphical elements, axes, data points, their connecting lines, lines separating treatment phases and regression line could be shown using differing widths of line and line types. Finally, we could add an extended legend to the figure that will help the reader understand the data display.

The second example of a graphical display that is difficult to read is given in a study reported by Jarrett and Ollendick (2012). This study evaluated a psychosocial treatment designed for children with attention-deficit/hyperactivity disorder (ADHD) and a comorbid anxiety. They describe a treatment protocol that integrated parent management training for ADHD and family-based cognitive-behavioural therapy for anxiety, and delivered the treatment to eight children who were carefully assessed using standardised measures and diagnostic interviews. They made assessments using two standardised measures, which the children's parents completed weekly. The Disruptive Behavior Disorders Rating Scale (BDRS-P) tracked ADHD symptoms and the Spence Child Anxiety Scale (SCAS-P) tracked anxiety. The children were randomised to receive treatment after baseline periods of 3, 4 or 5 weeks. They had 10 weeks of treatment and were followed up 6 months later. This was a between-subject multiple baseline design.

The original data display is shown in the right-hand panel of Figure 5.1. It was prepared using Excel™. Graphs for each participant have been constructed and then aligned to produce the classic step-like multiple baseline design. While it contains all the data, it is surprisingly difficult to read. The authors seem to have been challenged to put the data into one figure (they may have been constrained by journal requirements). They have followed the traditional way of displaying multiple baseline data by stacking the displays for each participant, but with eight separate charts to stack the vertical scale for the all-important dependent variables is overly compressed, making any differences between phases hard to discern. In contrast the horizontal time axis is somewhat stretched and the follow-up periods for the two conditions overlap with treatment weeks in other plots. The overall impression of the figure is that it is cluttered. For example, there is considerable repetition; the vertical axis is labelled for each case as are the acronyms for the dependent variable (at the right-hand side of each graph); the horizontal reference lines in each graph take up a significant proportion of the data area; and the markers for the data points and the connecting lines are typographically heavy. We could perhaps make some judicious changes to the plot that would eliminate some of the redundancy. For example we could:

1 Remove the frames around each individual graph
2 Plot the data for the two outcome scales separately
3 Remove the key from the right side of each chart. This information can be placed in the legend to the figure
4 Remove the horizontal reference lines in each plot – or reduce the weight of the line used
5 Standardise all the time axes to 39 weeks

6   Remove the x-axis scale value markers (Weeks 0–39) from all but the last (bottom) plot. That will give more vertical height, allowing us to stretch the y-axes and should help us see any changes more clearly

7   We might also experiment with showing a little less information on the y-axes. Perhaps labelling in steps of 20 units rather than 10 units will clean it visually without impacting our ability to read the values

8   The y-axis label 'Symptom Severity' only needs to occur once

9   The legend to the figure is clear and we would not need to adjust that.

Thus although both papers, Flink *et al.* and Jarrett and Ollendick, are interesting and provide valuable clinical research, and they contain valuable data, clear presentation of the data would help the reader appreciate and evaluate the findings.

PREPARING VISUAL DISPLAYS

Good visual displays serve an important function in communicating the findings of research where the essence of the results can be distilled into a condensed space that can form the centrepiece for the narrative reporting the results. For single-case studies, good visual displays are essential because they are also a primary source for the analysis and interpretation of the study. Excellent general introductions to graphical presentation are available and cover the essential factors to bear in mind in preparing good visual displays (Chambers, Cleveland, Kleiner & Tukey, 1983; Cleveland, 1985, 1993). Preparing data displays requires some consideration and planning. This section outlines some of the pitfalls and issues that you might need to take into consideration. There are a number of commonly available software programmes that can be used to prepare displays, e.g. Excel™, the charting facility in Word™ – itself a version of Excel™; in addition, SPSS and many other statistical packages include graphics modules. The advantage of these is their general accessibility; the disadvantage is that their default settings often produce displays that do not do justice to the data and are difficult to read. Preparing visual displays of data is rarely covered in formal courses on methodology.

Graphs are an excellent way of condensing data, and a degree of thoughtfulness in preparing them is required to guide the reader's interpretation. A notable feature of single-case studies is that it is one of the few areas where the reader has access to all the relevant data rather than just summaries of means and variance as is typical of group-based studies. Careful preparation resulting in good graphs should facilitate the reader's reanalysis of the data wherever possible. Figure 5.2 illustrates the main features of a figure constructed to show the results of an AB experiment. The construction of the figure follows Cleveland's advice on plotting data.

1   *Make the data stand out.* Make sure that the data stand out and do not let non-data items clutter the presentation of the data. Tufte (1983) calls the unnecessary non-data items 'chart junk', and common examples of this are the gratuitous and generally unnecessary horizontal reference lines on the y-axis and the grey shading of the data area, produced by default in many Excel charts, c.f. Jarrett and Ollendick's data display in Figure 5.1. Cleveland suggests that for many displays it is advantageous for the graph

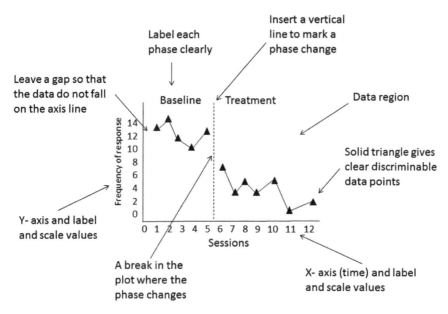

FIGURE 5.2 Main features of a single-case data plot

to be framed on all four sides. This facilitates reading the data values in the upper right hand quadrant of the display. Traditionally this feature has not been the case for single-case plots, and most figures in this text follow this convention.

2   *Only data in the data region.* The four sides of the figure, even if the upper and right side are not drawn, define the data region. A more significant piece of advice is that only data should appear in the data region. In practice this may be difficult to achieve, but minimising intrusion of non-data items (another type of chart junk) such as labels is good practice.

3   *Separate the phases clearly.* In single-case plots one essential non-data feature is the lines used to separate the sequential phases of the study. These need to be presented for us to separate the phases, but they should not intrude and dominate the data points. Many figures produced in the literature use solid vertical lines that have the same weight as the axes and the lines connecting the data points. Although this is established practice in applied behaviour analysis journals, the principle of not letting non-data items compete visually with data points suggests that it would be better to indicate phase change lines by dashed lines with a lesser weight.

4   *Choose symbols with care.* We also need to choose symbols used to plot the data with care. Most software programmes provide a range of squares, diamonds, circles and triangles that can be filled or left in outline and adjusted for size. Judicious experimentation should be used to select clearly discriminable symbols. For example, a triangle and a circle are more easily discriminated than a circle and an octagon, especially when the symbols are small.

5   *Avoid 'spicing up'.* Computer programmes offer a range of additional options to 'spice up' your presentation; these include a range of colours, pseudo-3D effects, shadows

and so on. It is important to appreciate that images that may look good on a large computer screen may not be suitable when reduced in size and printed. Black and white is sufficient for most purposes and is still preferred for many publications. If you must use colours use 'strong' colours like dark blue and red, which provide high contrast with the white background. Do not use yellow and pastel shades that tend to 'blow out' and are difficult to see. This is especially important if you are preparing slides for projection (Duarte, 2008).

6   *Choose appropriate scales.* Choosing appropriate scales for the data is important. These should encompass the range of data and allow the data to fill as much of the data region as possible, preferably without breaks in the scale. Most single-case data plots have a representation of time on the x-axis and the response on the y-axis. Occasionally data plots include two series of data, as in Jarrett and Ollendick's data display in Figure 5.1. If they are on different scales it is necessary to insert a secondary y-axis with an appropriate scale. Needless to say, each scale should be labelled, albeit briefly, and described in the figure legend.

7   *Prepare comprehensive legends.* Figures should enhance the reader's understanding of the data and they should have explicit and comprehensive legends. The legends should identify the variables being plotted, the meaning of the symbols and labels used.

TECHNIQUES FOR SYSTEMATICALLY EXPLORING SINGLE-CASE DATA

The panels in Figure 5.3 show the main features included in the visual analysis of a single-case data plot. The raw data plot of a simple AB study is shown in the upper left panel and the remaining panels each have imposed on them additional data that highlight a key aspect of the data. Analysis and interpretation of the data requires that each of the parameters should be considered before a summary judgement about the data set is made. The main parameters are:

1   The central location, i.e. the mean or median, of each phase and changes in the central location between phases (panel b)

2   The trend, i.e. the systematic shift in location of the central location within each phase, (panel c). Figure 5.3 shows a linear trend imposed on the data, but trends may be nonlinear

3   The variability of the data within phases (panel d). It is important to note that the variability may not be constant within a phase and that it can increase or decrease in time

4   The rate of change between adjacent phases (panel e). How quickly does a feature of the data change between phases, i.e. when a treatment is introduced or withdrawn?

5   Overlap, or how many areas of the data in adjacent phases overlap with each other (panel f)? The extent of overlap will be considered in the next chapter, as several statistical tests have been proposed on the basis of overlap data.

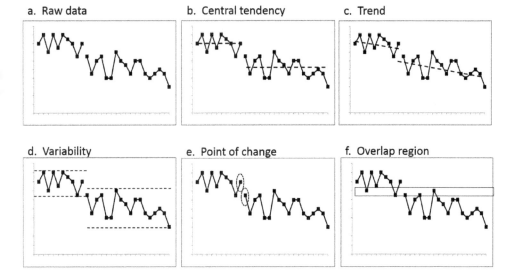

FIGURE 5.3 The main parameters to consider when evaluating single-case data

Panel (a) shows the raw data plot for an AB design. Panel (b) shows an estimate of central tendency (the middle point of the data) for each phase. In panel (c) a linear trend line has been superimposed for each phase. Panel (d) shows one way (range lines) of representing the variability in each phase. Panel (e) marks the point of change between the two phases by circling the last point in the baseline and first in the treatment phase. Finally panel (f) gives an indication of how much the data overlap between the adjacent phases, shown as a shaded area.

Preparing the data prior to plotting

Although the exploratory methods discussed here are graphical, many of them require some basic statistical manipulation of the data to transform the raw data series plot into a plot of one of the summary features of the data. The statistical manipulations are generally simple and can be done by hand or with the aid of a simple calculator. They are also easily performed in a Microsoft Excel datasheet using a few of Excel's functions. The graphics in this chapter were developed in Excel.

One important feature in exploring single-case data using graphical techniques is the ability to present both the original data set and the graphical analysis of a particular feature on a single plot. This is evident in Figure 5.3, where the analysed feature has been superimposed on the original data set. Keeping the original and transformed data set on one display is strongly encouraged, but imposing more than one analysis onto a single figure can result in an overcomplicated display that is difficult to read.

Before we consider a range of exploratory techniques we need to highlight features of single-case data that do not usually apply to group data. Consider a set of observations with one observation per week – for example, the sum of personal questionnaire items measuring a person's symptomatic complaints – shown in Table 5.1. The first four numbers were taken as a baseline and the remaining seven were taken during treatment, with the last at 3 months' follow-up. The original data are shown in the row labelled 'observation' and ordered by

TABLE 5.1 Properties of time-series data

	Baseline				Treatment					FU		
Time (week)	1	2	3	4	5	6	7	8	9	10	11	24
Observation	15	18	14	18	14	12	10	7	6	4	5	2
Rank order	10	11.5	8.5	11.5	8.5	7	6	5	4	2	3	1
Rank within phase	2	3.3	1	3.5	7	6	5	4	3	1	2	1

Note that when rank ordering the observations there may be ties in the data, i.e. two or more observations of the same value. In this case we have two data values of 14 and 18. Their ranks will be an average of the rank values, e.g. the two 14s were at positions 8 and 9 and their rank will be 8.5. FU, follow-up at 3 months.

the time (week) they were collected. In addition to the value of the observation, the observations can be rank ordered across the whole data set by arranging them in order of magnitude. The data can also be rank ordered within each phase. Thus each observation has two other properties: its rank order within the data set or subset and its temporal location. Several of the exploratory graphical methods make use of these properties.

Investigating central tendency (mean)

The most common summary statistic for a set of data is probably the mean, and it is not unusual to see this value plotted as a horizontal line for each phase of a single-case study. With a small sample it may not represent the data very well. Consider the series:
4, 18, 5, 8, 7, 6, 10. The mean value is 8.29, but there are only two numbers greater than this in the set. In small data sets the estimate of the mean is affected more by extreme scores because all scores are given equal weight. A more robust estimator is the median, the number in the middle of the data when they are rank ordered (4, 5, 6, 7, 8, 10, 18), which in this case is 7. When a series has equal numbers of observations the median is estimated by taking the average of the middle two numbers. However, the median is based on only one or two numbers and we can improve on the estimate of the central tendency by computing a median based on more than one or two numbers. The broadened median (BMed) is one solution. Rosenberger & Gasko (1983) suggest the following rules for combining data to produce a broadened median. This involves assigning weights to each observation. Weighting each observation is not a controversial procedure. When we compute a mean of a series of numbers we give each number an initial weight of 1, sum the numbers and divide by the sample size, n. This is the same as giving each number of an initial weight of $1/n$, i.e. multiplying each number by $1/n$ and then adding them together. Giving each number a weight of 1 simply means that we are allowing each number to make the same contribution to estimating the average. In computing the BMed we want to give the middle numbers more importance than those on the outside, and weighting allows us to do this. You will note that in any set of weights that they will add up to 1.

1   For odd-numbered series, when the number of data points is 5 or more but less than 12 then BMed is the average of the three middle values (weight = 0.333). Note that

the middle is the middle of the data when they are ranked in order of magnitude, not its temporal order. When n ≥ 13 then BMed is the average of the middle 5 values (weight = 0.2).

2   For even-numbered series, when n > 5 and ≤ 12 BMed is the average of the four middle values; but in this case we weight the central two numbers by 1/3 (weight = 0.333) and the outer 2 by 1/6 (weight = 0.167). When n > 13 then BMed is the weighted average of the middle 6 values, with the middle 4 weighted by 1/5 (weight = 0.2) and the outer two weighted by 1/10 (weight = 0.1).

Table 5.2 shows the computation of the broadened median for the two phases of an AB design. The baseline phase (upper panel) consists of 9 time points and the treatment phase (lower panel) has 16. The first column indicates the session number (time) and the second is the measurement of the response, the outcome measure of interest. In the third column the numbers have been rank ordered within each phase from lowest to highest. In the fourth column the weights have been assigned to each position in the series. So, in the baseline phase there are 9 observations and, following Rosenberger & Gasko's recommendations, we weight the middle three values by 1/3 and all the other points by 0. This means that the BMed value will be 9*0.33 + 10*0.33 + 12*0.33 = 10.33. If you use Excel it is convenient to insert the BMed value in all the time points of the phase, as this will help in plotting BMed for the phase. The broadened medians for both phases of the data are shown in Figure 5.4. This plot suggests a marked reduction in the central tendency between the phases.

Exploring the linear trend

When several data points are arranged in time, i.e. by the order in which the observations occurred, it is possible that there might be a trend in the data. A trend is a systematic shift in the value of the central location of the data over time. For example, the baseline phase in Table 5.2 shows 9 data points in time. As this set cannot be divided into two equal sets we will simply drop the middle observation and make a quick estimate. In this case, averaging the first four points (9, 12, 7, 8 = 9) and last four points (10, 14, 12, 7 = 10.77) suggests a slight increase in the central location over time. A linear trend is one in which the underlying shift in central location is best represented by a straight line, showing either an increase or decrease. When we estimate only two points from the data, as we have in this example, we can only plot a linear trend but there are other trends that can occur. We also need to distinguish between systematic shifts in the mean, whether they are linear or non-linear, from shifts in variability over time. This aspect of data exploration is also considered later in the chapter.

The simplest way of fitting a straight line is to eyeball the data and draw a line so that it appears to bisect the distribution. Unfortunately, people tend to be rather poor judges of where best to place a linear trend line (Mosteller, Siegel & Trapdo, 1983) because outlying data points seem to exert undue influence on visual perception. Fortunately there are two techniques which, with a little data manipulation, can help us get a better grasp on the presence of trends: the split-middle method and Tukey's three-group method.

TABLE 5.2 Computing the broadened median

	A	B	C	D	E	F
1	Phase	Sessions	Response	Rank Ordered	Weight	Bmed
2		0				
3	Baseline	1	9	7	0	10.33
4		2	12	7	0	10.33
5		3	7	8	0	10.33
6		4	8	9	0.33	10.33
7		5	12	10	0.33	10.33
8		6	10	12	0.33	10.33
9		7	14	12	0	10.33
10		8	12	12	0	10.33
11		9	7	14	0	10.33
12	Treatment	10	2	1	0	3.00
13		11	7	1	0	3.00
14		12	3	1	0	3.00
15		13	2	2	0	3.00
16		14	4	2	0	3.00
17		15	3	2	0.1	3.00
18		16	5	3	0.2	3.00
19		17	5	3	0.2	3.00
20		18	1	3	0.2	3.00
21		19	5	3	0.2	3.00
22		20	3	4	0.1	3.00
23		21	3	5	0	3.00
24		22	1	5	0	3.00
25		23	2	5	0	3.00
26		24	5	5	0	3.00
27		25	1	7	0	3.00

The table illustrates how you might set out an Excel sheet to compute the broadened median (BMed) for both phases of an AB data set with 9 points in the baseline phase and 16 in the treatment phase. The first column and row show the Excel cell references. Row 1 shows the titles for each column of data. Note that 0 is entered in cell B2. This is done to facilitate data plotting as the data values B2–B27 are used to provide the values on the x-axis of the graph. This ensures that the data from the first session are not plotted on the y-axis. In each phase the session number is in the second column (B) and the response is given in the third column (C). The response data have been rank ordered within each phase and rearranged in ascending order across time – column D. This makes it easier to compute BMed using an Excel function. The weights for computing the BMed are entered in the fifth column (E). Note that 0 is entered for the 'outer' responses that do not contribute to computing the BMed. The BMed values for the two phases are shown in the last column (F). The Excel 'SUMPRODUCT' function was used to generate the BMed values, e.g. SUMPRODUCT(C3:C11,E3:E11). This function is entered in cells F3:F11 to return the baseline value of BMed. The reason for this is that in order to plot the value of BMed across the phase as a whole, we need to enter its value at each time point.

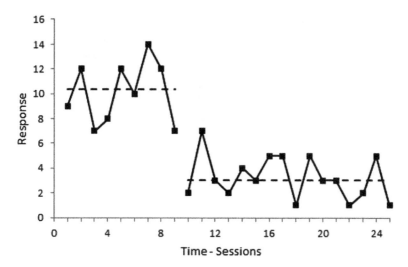

FIGURE 5.4 Plot of broadened median for an AB design. Shown as dashed line; data from Table 5.2

The split-middle method

The split-middle method is a simple way of constructing a linear plot without having to compute a regression line. It also has the merit of being resistant to the influence of outliers, i.e. points that are markedly deviant from the main trend, and this is valuable in small data sets. It was developed by White (see Kazdin (1982)). The idea is to find two data points that best represent the 'average' in each half of a phase. As before, when estimating the central location of a data set we will use medians rather than an average score. The split-middle line is easily fitted by finding the median data value and the median time point in each half. This will give two coordinates that can be plotted and connected with a straight line. The split middle is easy to calculate approximately from any printed graph, and a rough linear fit can be made with a pencil and straight edge.

Table 5.3 contains all the data and computations needed to plot the split-middle trend for each phase of the AB data set that we have used to compute the broadened median. This example illustrates some of the rules of thumb that we can adopt in the data analysis.

Step 1: Split each phase of the data into two halves based on the time axis (x-axis). We can do this by finding the midpoint of the time series in each phase. If the series contains an odd number of data points, the midpoint will coincide with a real-time value. In our example the baseline phase has 9 time points and the midpoint will be at session 5. There will be 4 data points either side of this, and we need to decide where to allocate the midpoint itself. There are two solutions to this conundrum: we can simply drop this data point from the analysis or we can do the analysis twice with the data point allocated to each 'half' in turn. In this case we have dropped the data point. If the series has an even number of points, the midpoint will be a point halfway between the middle numbers. In Table 5.3 the treatment phase has 16 time points and the midpoint will be between the 8th and 9th (session 8.5). We have now split each phase into two halves based on the time point, which for convenience we can refer to as the left and right halves.

TABLE 5.3 Computing the split-middle line

Phase	Sessions	Response	Response ranked within each split	Split-middle time point	Split-middle response
	0				
Baseline	1	9	7		
	2	12	8		
				2.5	8.5
	3	7	9		
	4	8	12		
	5	12			
	6	10	7		
	7	14	10		
				7.5	11
	8	12	12		
	9	7	14		
Treatment	10	2	2		
	11	7	2		
	12	3	3		
	13	2	3		
				13.5	3.5
	14	4	4		
	15	3	5		
	16	5	5		
	17	5	7		
	18	1	1		
	19	5	1		
	20	3	1		
	21	3	2		
				21.5	2.5
	22	1	3		
	23	2	3		
	24	5	5		
	25	1	5		

This table shows the computations for the split-middle method for producing a straight line fit to the data. To compute this, the rank order of the data within each half of the phase is needed – shown in the 4th column. In each phase of the data the temporal midpoint (x-values) is shown in the second column by a grey bar. For the baseline phase this is at session 5 (shown by the shaded area) and for the treatment phase this is between sessions 17 and 18 – these are separated by a horizontal line. See the text for details of computing the split-middle values.

Step 2: We now need to find the time midpoint of each half of the data within each phase by repeating the above process. So in the baseline phase the time midpoints will be $x_L = 2.5$ and $x_R = 7.5$: the lower case L and R denote the left- and right-hand portions of the data, respectively. For the treatment phase the time points for the two halves will be $x_L = 13.5$ and $x_R = 21.5$. These values are shown in the penultimate column of Table 5.3.

Step 3: Now find the middle value of the response data (y-axis) in each half phase. First, arrange the data by rank within each split of the data. If you have arranged the data by rank order within each half phase, as in Table 5.3, the middle values will be the average of the two rank-ordered data points. The values are $y_L = 8.5$ and $y_R = 11$ for the baseline and $y_L = 3.5$ and $y_R = 2.5$ for the treatment phases. These values are shown in the right-hand column of Table 5.3.

Step 4: Finally we plot these coordinates on the graph and join them with a line (Figure 5.5). This plot suggests an upward trend in the baseline despite the presence of a low final value, which, if we had drawn the trend by eye might have led us to draw a line with no trend in it. Nevertheless we need to be cautious in our interpretation of this as there are few data points. There is virtually no trend in the treatment phase. The split-middle method is quick and easy to use and can be implemented on published graphs fitting the line with a pencil and ruler. It is a useful way of checking whether there is any apparent trend in the data. It is easy to implement with small samples, say when N is between 5 and 12.

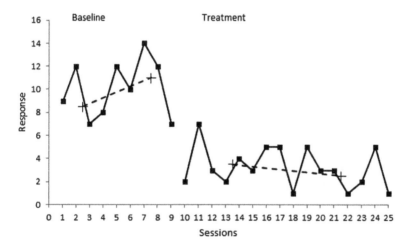

FIGURE 5.5 Split-middle plot for an AB design

Data set from Table 5.3. The plot has been made in Excel. The lines are drawn between the x_L and x_R values for each phase. They can be extended across the whole phase by extending the line if necessary. The present plot indicates a slight upward trend in the baseline and a very slight downward trend in the treatment phase.

Tukey's robust line from three groups

For larger samples, Tukey (1977) developed a similar method which splits the data into three parts. This method uses the standard equation of linear regression, $y = a + bx$, to compute a line and we need to estimate a, the intercept, and b, the slope. We split the data

TABLE 5.4 Computing a robust line from three groups using Tukey's method

Phase and subdivisions	Time	Number of seizures (y)	Data ranked within each subdivision	Split middle time	Split middle	Robust trend	Residual
	0						
Baseline	1	12	5			8.31	3.69
Left	2	15	6			8.35	6.65
	3	5	7			8.40	−3.40
	4	7	8	3.5	7.5	8.44	−1.44
	5	8	12			8.48	−0.48
	6	6	15			8.52	−2.52
Middle	7	11	3			8.56	2.44
	8	11	4			8.60	2.40
	9	10	10			8.65	1.35
	10	4	11	9.5	10.5	8.69	−4.69
	11	13	11			8.73	4.27
	12	3	13			8.77	−5.77
Right	13	21	2			8.81	12.19
	14	13	5			8.85	4.15
	15	9	7			8.90	0.10
	16	2	9	15.5	8	8.94	−6.94
	17	7	13			8.98	−1.98
	18	5	21			9.02	−4.02
Treatment	19	8	5			14.40	6.40
Left	20	9	8			13.67	4.67
	21	15	9			12.93	−2.07
	22	19	12			12.20	−6.80
	23	18	14	4.5	13	11.47	−6.53
	24	14	15			10.73	−3.27
	25	12	18			10.00	−2.00
	26	5	19			9.27	4.27
	27	8	0			8.53	0.53
Middle	28	6	3			7.80	1.80
	29	0	4			7.07	7.07
	30	6	4	12	4	6.33	0.33
	31	4	6			5.60	1.60
	32	4	6			4.87	0.87
	33	3	8			4.13	1.13
	34	2	0			3.40	1.40

TABLE 5.4 *continued*

Phase and subdivisions	Time	Number of seizures (y)	Data ranked within each subdivision	Split middle time	Split middle	Robust trend	Residual
Right	35	0	1			2.67	2.67
	36	1	1			1.93	0.93
	37	3	2			1.20	−1.80
	38	6	2	19.5	2	0.47	−5.53
	39	8	3			−0.27	−8.27
	40	2	6			−1.00	−3.00
	41	1	8			−1.73	−2.73

Columns 1–6 are the same layout as in Table 5.3 and the procedure for finding the midpoints in each third of the data within a phase mirror is that used in the split-middle method. The penultimate column shows the predicted value of response (robust trend). The final column contains the residuals – the difference between the observed and predicted values of y.

Data extracted from Lavender (1981)

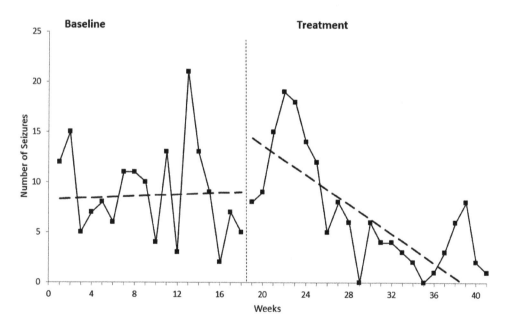

FIGURE 5.6 A plot of the linear trend

into three equal parts to represent the left-, middle and right-hand sides of the plot. When a sample is equally divisible by 3 then the groups will have an equal number in them. When the remainder is 2, Tukey suggests that the additional points should be allocated to the left and right groups. When the remainder is 1 then we allocate the middle group an extra data point. Table 5.4 shows part of a data set from a single-case series in which Lavender (1981) tested a behavioural intervention for serious chronic epilepsy using a simple AB design. The study lasted for almost a year and the total number of seizures per week was recorded. The data in Table 5.4 comprise 18 successive weeks in the baseline followed by 23 weeks of treatment. The data are plotted in Figure 5.6.

The method uses the same procedure as the split-middle technique to find the midpoints for the y-values (number of seizures) at each midpoint of the three parts and the x-values of the data (time). The left, middle and right thirds are denoted by the subscripts of their initial letter, e.g. y_M is the median value of the number of seizures for the middle portion of data. For the baseline phase the three pairs of values are: left: $y_L = 7.5$, $x_L = 3.5$; middle: $y_M = 10.5$, $x_M = 9.5$; right: $y_R = 8$, $x_R = 15.5$.

To compute the slope of the data, indicated by b, we use the left- and right-hand portions of the data:

$$b = (y_R - y_L)/(x_R - x_L) \qquad\qquad b = (8 - 7.5)/(15.5 - 3.5) = 0.04$$

This computes the amount of change in the y-value for the period of time on the x-axis. In this case it is very small and indicates that there is no real trend in the data.

The equation for estimating the value of a is a little more complex:

$$a = 1/3*[(y_L + y_M + y_R) - b*(x_L + x_M + x_R)]$$

The * means multiply. In this example we substitute the values as follows:

$$a = 1/3* [(7.5 + 10.5 + 8) - 0.04*(3.5 + 10.5 + 15.5)] = 8.28$$

and our final equation for computing the best fit line is:

$$y = 8.28 + 0.04x$$

where x is the time (week). If we repeat the process for the treatment phase, the robust line is given by the equation:

$$y = 15.13 - 0.73x.$$

Here the slope is both negative and larger than that observed in the baseline. However, when we compute the values for the treatment phase we must remember to start the week values at week 1 rather than at week 19 where the treatment phase starts. This is because we have computed the trend within the phase but not across the whole series. We can therefore find the robust trend values of y for every value of x (time) by just entering it into the equation and plotting it. The plot of both phases is shown in Figure 5.6. The superimposition of the robust trend onto the original data plot suggests that, despite the initial increase in the number of fits at the beginning of treatment, there is a consistent decline over the weeks of treatment[1]. Nevertheless, there is considerable variability in the data and we might wish to be a little circumspect in our conclusions and explore the data further. The next section gives one method for doing this.

Considering residuals: the vertical line or icicle plot

Residuals are the difference between the observed value and a fitted line that summarises the data. The two fitted lines we have looked at are a representation of the central tendency, e.g. mean, median or BMed, or a representation of the linear trend of the data. The analysis of residuals can be important in helping us to detect how well the fitted line represents the data and whether there are any additional features in the data that might be worth exploring. Standard statistical methods of regression analysis have sophisticated ways of analysing residuals but in small data a simple visual plot, known as a vertical line or icicle plot, of residuals over time can be informative.

Table 5.5 shows a simple data set for a phase containing 8 observations. The broadened median has been calculated and the difference between the observation and the BMed values, the residual, is shown in the final column. It is fairly obvious that the scores seem to increase in time and plotting the residuals, shown in Figure 5.7, makes it clear that most of the negative residuals, i.e. those hanging below the median line, are in the left-hand part of the data whereas the positive ones are in the right-hand part, indicating a positive trend to the data. If there were no trend we would expect the deviations to be randomly dispersed across the time period.

The vertical line plot is very simple and versatile because it can also be used to investigate non-linear trend once a linear trend has been fitted. This can be seen in a plot of Lavender's data in Figure 5.8. This plot shows the residuals computed from the two robust lines computed for the baseline and treatment phases. It is obvious that there is considerable unexplained variability in the data in both phases. As such, the robust (linear fit) line doesn't appear to be a particularly good fit. In fact there appears to be cycling and this is especially true in the treatment phase where the sequence of negative, positive and negative deviations is quite marked. The same phenomenon may also be present in the baseline phase and we might wish to investigate this rhythmic change using a statistical test (Morley & Adams, 1989).

TABLE 5.5 A simple data set to illustrate a vertical line plot

Time	Response	Ranked	BMed	Residual
0				
1	4	4	8.33	−4.33
2	8	7	8.33	−1.33
3	7	7	8.33	−1.33
4	9	8	8.33	−0.33
5	7	9	8.33	0.67
6	9	9	8.33	0.67
7	12	10	8.33	1.67
8	10	12	8.33	3.67

The response data are ranked to aid computation of the BMed parameter shown in column 4, and the residual (column 5) = response − BMed.

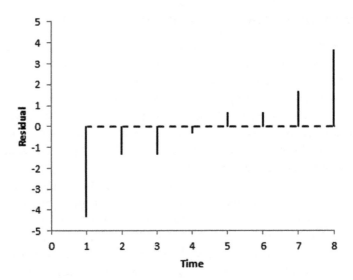

FIGURE 5.7 Simple vertical line plot

Data from Table 5.5. The trend in the data is made very obvious by the non-random pattern of the deviations: negative deviations in the left half and positive ones in the right half. Vertical line plots are also useful to detect non-linear patterns in the data.

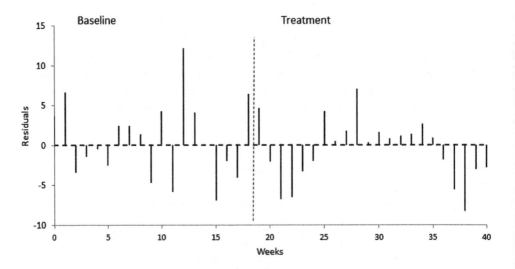

FIGURE 5.8 Vertical line plot for Lavender's (1981) data. The residuals are shown in the right hand column of Table 5.4

INVESTIGATING A TREND WHEN THE DATA ARE NON-LINEAR OR VERY VARIABLE

In situations like this, especially where there is substantial variability in the data, we may obtain a better visual representation of a trend by 'smoothing' the data using running medians. Recall that a trend is defined as a systematic shift in the central tendency of the data in time. Plotting repeated estimates of the central estimate over time will therefore provide an estimate of the trend. As in single-case data, where we often have small n series, it is preferable to take the median of a set of numbers as an estimate because it will be resistant to the influence of outliers and it also makes computations very easy (Velleman & Hoaglin, 1981).

Panel (a) in Figure 5.9 shows a data set where there is marked variability in the data and the immediate visual impression is that there might be a positive trend, i.e. the magnitude of the response is greater as time progresses. The other panels in Figure 5.9 (b, c and d) show the result of a successive series of smoothing operations. Table 5.6 shows the raw data and the smoothed data.

Running medians of 3 successive points (RM3)

In Figure 5.9 panel (b), the data have been smoothed using running medians of 3, denoted as RM3. The computations are seen in Table 5.6. To compute RM3 we take successive batches of 3 numbers and find the middle value. The first number in the series, 15 in this case, has only one number next to it so a value for time point 1 cannot be estimated and we just leave that slot blank. For time point 2 the value is 40 and the values either side are 15 and 55, so the median value is 40 and we enter that value at time point 2. For time point 3 the three values are (40, 55, 40) and the median is 40. This set of data contains two

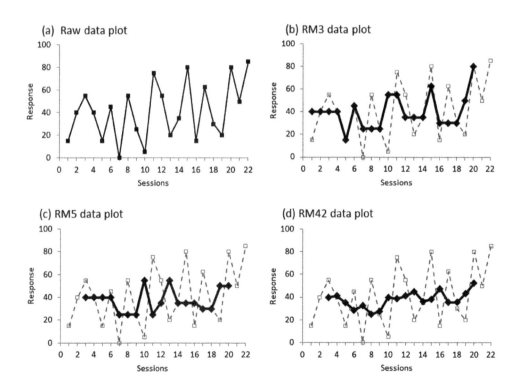

FIGURE 5.9 A series of running median plots showing the effect of ever-increasing smoothing

values that are identical or tied and the convention is that the median is the tied value, i.e. 40. We continue in this manner to the penultimate time point (21) where the series values are (80, 50, 85) and the median value is 80. Panel (b) shows the plot of the RM3 data and the original data set for comparison. The main visual impression is that the smoothed data are a little flatter but retain an impression of an upward trajectory. When the data series is relatively short, say $6 \leq n < 10$, then RM3 can be a useful way of exploring the trend.

TABLE 5.6 Smoothing a series of data points

	A	B	C	D	E
1	Time	Response	RM3	RM5	RM42
2	0				
3	1	15	**15**	**15**	15
4	2	40	40	**40**	**40**
5	3	55	40	40	40.00
6	4	40	40	40	41.25
7	5	15	40	40	35.00
8	6	45	15	40	28.75
9	7	0	45	25	32.50
10	8	55	25	25	25.00
11	9	25	25	25	27.50
12	10	5	25	55	40.00
13	11	75	55	25	38.75
14	12	55	55	35	41.25
15	13	20	35	55	45.00
16	14	35	35	35	36.25
17	15	80	35	35	38.13
18	16	15	63	35	47.50
19	17	63	30	30	35.63
20	18	30	30	30	35.63
22	19	20	30	50	43.13
23	20	80	50	50	52.50
24	21	50	80	**80**	**80**
25	22	85	**85**	**85**	85

The raw data are shown in the column headed Response and the successive smoothing operations using running medians (RM) are in the columns headed RM3, RM5 and RM42. See the text for details of how these are computed. Note: the numbers in bold at time points 1, 2, 24 and 25 are not smoothed, see the text for details. The Excel cell references are shown in the first row and column to illustrate computation. For example the formula in C4 for computing the first RM3 value is = MEDIAN(B3:B5); D5 computes RM5, the value is = MEDIAN(B3:B7); E5 computes RM42, the value is = (MEDIAN(C3:C6)+MEDIAN(C4:C7))/2.

Running medians of 5 successive points (RM5)

When a series has more than 10 data points it can be worthwhile considering plotting running medians of 5 successive points (RM5). In computing RM5, successive batches of 5 data points are considered, so the first data point will be at time t = 3 and final RM5 value will be at point t = n −2. In the example in Figure 5.9 and Table 5.6 the time points will be t = 2 and t = 20, and their values are 40 (median of 15, 40, 55, 40, 15) and 50 (median of 30, 20, 80, 50, 85). Panel (c) in Figure 5.9 shows the RM5 plot; to the eye the sequence of data is a little smoother than the RM3 plot and the suggestion of a linear trend is somewhat lessened.

Running medians of 4 averaged by pairs (RM42)

We can smooth the data even further. Both RM3 and RM5 smoothing tend to produce plots with a rather step-like quality ('plateaus and plains') as is apparent in panels (b) and (c) of Figure 5.9. This is because two or three points with equal values in the same batch will exert an influence over successive estimates of the median. One way of smoothing the curve is to use the average of successive pairs of running medians of 4 data points. Running medians of 4 (RM4) are easily computed but they do contain a small problem. The problem is that the midpoint for the time value is at time 2.5 (halfway between t_2 and t_3). We could interpolate this value on the graph if we so wished. In the present data set the first RM4 value is 40 (15, 40, 50, 40) – the average of the two middle values, which just happen to be the same. The second RM4 is, just by coincidence, also 40 (40, 55, 40, 15) and the corresponding midpoint for time is $t_{3.5}$. When we combine these two estimates the data point will be 40 and the midpoint for time will be t_3, which is much easier to plot. The third value of RM4 will be 42.5 (55, 40, 15, 45) and the next estimate of RM42 will be the average of this and the preceding RM4 value (40), i.e. 41.25. RM42 is really another estimate of RM5 but with the data further smoothed. The plot of RM42 shown in panel (d) of Figure 5.9 is smoother than RM3 and RM5 and although the final point is the maximum in the plot, the overall impression of trend is attenuated and we might wish to be circumspect in making any firm conclusion about this aspect of the data. These computations are easy to do without a computer but they are also easy to express on a spreadsheet.

Some issues with running medians

1   The problem of the missing endpoints. One potential problem with running medians is that there are fewer estimates of the values than there are time points. As we noted for RM3, there is no value for the first or last time points and the length of the series is reduced by 2. For both RM5 and RM42 the two initial and final values cannot be computed and the series is shortened by four time points. The solutions offered by Velleman and Hoaglin (1981) are as follows:
   a) For RM3 simply copy the initial and last data points into the RM3 series
   b) For RM5 and RM42 copy the initial and last data points into the series, but for the second and penultimate value of the series copy the RM3 values.
   Table 5.6 shows these substitutions in bold text. Velleman and Hoaglin (1981) make additional suggestions for further smoothing of these endpoints that requires a little

more computation, but for our relatively rough-and-ready exploratory purposes simply plotting the estimated values and inspecting the raw and smoothed values will usually be sufficient.

2   What to do with very small samples, n < 6? Many data sets found in clinical practice contain small numbers in each phase, especially the baseline phase (Shadish & Sullivan, 2011; Smith, 2012). Statistical analysis of these data can be suspect and the graphical methods for examining trend have for the most part been applied to somewhat larger data sets. Nevertheless it is probably worthwhile attempting some graphical exploration of small data sets because extreme points can obscure trends and mislead the eye. Even computing running medians of 2 (the average of successive data points) will smooth the data a little and reduce the impact of outliers.

Examining variability

If you are familiar with elementary statistics, one basic idea is the variability of the data. This is normally captured by the standard deviation. As we saw in Chapter 2, estimates of variability are central to statistical testing. Research on visual inference, how individuals perceive and form judgements about single-case data, suggests that they are not necessarily very good at taking the variability of the data into account. There are a number of simple ways in which data can be displayed that ensure that you pay attention and describe variability when interpreting the data plot. Figure 5.10 shows a set of visual displays that can be used to explore variability in a data set. The upper left panel (a) shows data from an AB study. The other panels show a variety of visual aids for looking at variability.

The range bar and range line plots

The simplest 'analysis' is to impose the measure of central tendency on each phase and draw bars that capture the range of the data. This is shown in panel (b). If you are familiar with the box-and-whisker plot, this is identical but there is no box, just a median bar. The construction is simple. For each phase the estimate of the median is plotted as a thick bar and the range bars as a pair of 'whiskers' connecting the lowest and highest data values. The plot provides a simple indication of data overlap between the phases of data, but it does not convey any information about the time dimension. This can be easily addressed if we extend the endpoints of the range bars parallel to the x-axis to cover the extent of each phase. This will produce a pair of parallel lines for each phase, as is evident from panel (c) of Figure 5.10. This plot gives the same information as the range bar plot but it can also highlight any shift in the distribution of variability over time. For example, if the series becomes less variable over time this should be perceived as increasing 'white space' around the data points.

Neither the range bar or range line is entirely satisfactory for three reasons. First, a single outlying value will have undue influence on the display. In panel (d) of Figure 5.10 the single value at time point 13 gives an extended upper range value as all the other values lie between 2 and 15. Second, variability may be confounded with trend as in panel (e): the data seem more variable at the beginning than at the end of the phase. Finally, changes in variability within phases are not displayed.

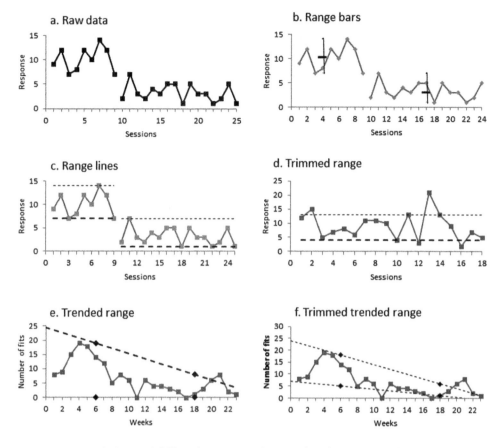

FIGURE 5.10 Exploring variability. Shows several ways of exploring variability within and across phases of a single-case study. Panels (e) and (f) are from data in Table 5.4

The trimmed range

For data sets usually encountered in clinical contexts where phase lengths are often less than $n \leq 15$, the outer values of the range can be trimmed, i.e. removed from any calculation, but kept in the display. A rule of thumb is to trim a sample by around 10–20% to produce a trimmed range display. Morley and Adams (1991) suggested the following guidelines:

1   When $n < 6$ keep all the data in the phase
2   When $n \geq 6$ and ≤ 12, take out one extreme value from each end of the data, i.e. the lowest and highest values
3   When $n > 12$ then take out the two extreme values from each end of the data set.

If we do this for the data in panel (d) of Figure 5.10, the range lines are repositioned.

Trended range

Panels (e) and (f) of Figure 5.10 show data where there appears to be greater variability in the first part than in the second part. This pattern is quite common in clinical and it may reflect the client's increasing mastery and control of their problem as a consequence of treatment. There are two methods that can help us see the data pattern a little more clearly.

The trimmed range will remove the influence of outliers, but it cannot show changes in variation within phases or remove the influence of a trend in central tendency within a phase. A trended range display is able to do this. The idea behind this display is to draw upper and lower lines around the data that capture the change in value over time. To do this we split each phase into halves, based on the sequence of points (time) rather than the magnitude of the data (as in the split-middle method). In each half we locate the two extreme high and low range points and then connect them across the whole of the phase. The bottom right panel shows the method applied to the treatment phase of Lavender's study. The following steps are carried out.

Step 1. Divide the data into two equal time intervals. If the number of time points is even, as is the case here, then there will be equal numbers in each half of the data set. If the number of data points is odd, e.g. 15, then there will be two equal sets of 7 either side of the midpoint (time point 8). In this case there are three options to consider: (1) simply drop the middle data point – this seems plausible if the point is not at the extreme of the data set; (2) randomly allocate the midpoint to one of the halves with a toss of a coin; or (3) repeat the analysis with the midpoint included in each half.

Step 2. Find the midpoints of each half on the time axis. In the current example there are 23 data (time) points and thus 11 in each half, and the midpoint of each half will be time points 6 and 18, respectively. If the number of time points in each half is equal, e.g. 6 and 6, then the midpoints for each half will be 3.5 and 9.5, i.e. (t_{n+1}) $/2$. This is the standard way of finding the median.

Step 3. Within each half of the data find the maximum and minimum values of the data. In the current data set these values are: left half values are $L_{Min} = 0$, $L_{Max} = 19$; right half values are $R_{Min} = 0$, $R_{Max} = 8$.

Step 4. Plot the data points. Left half $x = 6$ $y = 0$ and $y = 19$; right half $x = 18$, $y = 0$ and $y = 8$.

Step 5. Draw a line connecting the two maximum values and the two minimum values.

Panel (e) shows this but you will note that the minimum range point is obscured by the x-axis as there are observations of 0 in each half of the data. This display suggests that over time the variability of the data changes so that in the second part there are fewer epileptic attacks.

We might wish to check that this is not merely the result of extreme outliers, so the figure can be redrawn as a trimmed trended range. We repeat the same process as above but eliminate the extreme points in each half of the data set. The values we plot are: left half $x = 6$ $y = 5$ and $y = 18$; right half $x = 18$, $y = 1$ and $y = 6$. The resulting plot is shown in panel (f) of Figure 5.10. Inspection of the data plot suggests that although variation appears to reduce over time it is not quite as marked as the effect suggested in the trended range plot.

SEEING DATA MORE CLEARLY – AN EXAMPLE

Figure 5.11 has been reconstructed from an article by Derrickson and her colleagues (1993). The clinical problem was the presence of signs of distress in a 9-month-old infant who had been hospitalised since birth in a neonatal care environment. As might be expected, this little boy had received a range of aversive medical interventions, all necessary to preserve his life and well-being. He was showing distress even when no aversive procedure was being carried out. Derrickson and her colleagues reported on the effects of using a combined visual and auditory stimulus that signalled an impending painful medical procedure. They reasoned that being able to predict the occurrence of an aversive procedure should reduce distressed (negative) behaviour. They used a time sampling procedure in which they recorded negative, positive and neutral behaviour every 10 seconds for 5 minutes, i.e. 30 observations per session, and they recorded three sessions per day. Derrickson *et al.* used an ABAB design where no signal was present in the A phase but it was present in the B phase. The signal was a plywood box fitted to the end of the baby's crib. When a staff member performed an aversive procedure, e.g. injection, they pressed a button which resulted in a red light and low buzz. They turned it off as soon as the procedure was completed. In the no-signal phase the box was removed. It is important to note that none of the observations were taken while an aversive procedure was being conducted.

Figure 5.11 shows the percentage of intervals in which positive and negative behaviours were shown in the two conditions. The obvious feature of this display is the co-occurrence of both positive and negative measures represented as superimposed data points using line

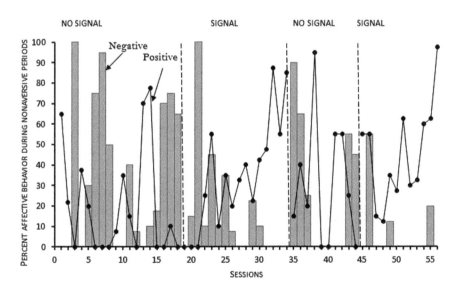

FIGURE 5.11 Positive and negative affective behaviours across four phases of an ABAB design

Lines are positive behaviours and the bar chart is negative behaviour. Figure redrawn with permission from (Wiley) Derrickson, J. G., Neef, N. A., & Cataldo, M. F. (1993). Effects of signaling invasive procedures on a hospitalized infant's affective behaviors. *Journal of Applied Behavior Analysis*, 26(1), 133–134.

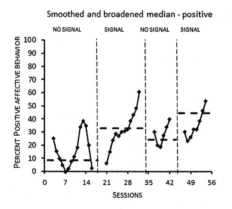
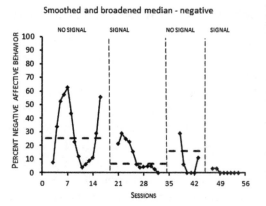

FIGURE 5.12 Reanalysis of the data from Figure 5.11

The left hand panel shows changes in positive behaviour and the right hand panel shows changes in negative behaviour. The data shown are the broadened median (dashed lines) to illustrate the central tendency in each phase and the running median (solid line) to depict trends. For clarity the raw data have not been plotted.

and bar chart. It is not terribly easy to read and we cannot easily discern the mean and trends in each phase, and thus comparing these parameters is tricky. Derrickson *et al.*'s article provides summaries of each of the phases in terms of average percentages and range, which were reported in their text. However, the purpose of a figure is to show more than just an estimate of the mean – especially in a case like this where there is clearly significant variability.

The two panels in Figure 5.12 show the effect of some judicious transformations to explore the possible underlying patterns of behaviour. First, the display of positive and negative behaviours was separated. The broadened median for each phase of the data was computed and plotted phase by phase. The systematic shifts in the median were computed using the RM42 smoothing technique. The broadened median plot suggests that the introduction of the signal condition is associated with an increase in behaviour denoting positive affect. Although there was a slight reduction in this with reversing to the non-signal condition, it did not revert to baseline. There was a further increase when the signal condition was reinstituted. The reverse pattern is observed when we look at the negative affective behaviour plot. One point to note is that the broadened median plot in the final phase is not visible as it coincided with the x-axis, i.e. it has a value of 0. Overall these broadened median plots tend to suggest that the introduction of the signal manipulation was successful in reducing negative affect and there was an associated increase in positive behaviour.

Imposing a trend on the data using the RM42 method reveals a couple of features not immediately apparent from the original raw data plot. First, in the initial no-signal phase the co-variation between positive and negative behaviour is quite marked. This is not entirely surprising as one is partly a reciprocal of the other, but it does suggest that the behaviour is controlled by factors that are unaccounted for. The second feature is that in both phases where the signal was used, the effect was not instantaneous. The data plots suggest an increase in positive and a decrease in negative behaviour within the phase. This is particularly marked in the first signal phase and for positive behaviour overall. The data also suggest that in the second signal phase the effect on reducing negative affective behaviour was very fast.

COMPARING DATA ACROSS PHASES

The final two methods for examining the data, inspecting the point of change and the overlap in data between phases, bring us to the aim of visual analysis. Whereas the other methods featured have focused on describing the data within phases, these two techniques force us to consider differences between the phases and to begin to answer questions about the change and the possible impact of treatment.

Point of change

One of the parameters to consider when evaluating single-case data is the change in the response when treatment is introduced and withdrawn in the case of ABAB designs. Panel (e) of Figure 5.3 shows a very simple way of capturing this by simply encircling the two adjacent points. In this case the magnitude of change is quite small and certainly no larger than change between any two adjacent points in the baseline. We could extend our analysis a little by inspecting two or three points either side of the introduction of treatment. In this case the three points either side do appear to be different although there is an overlap between a couple of them. The importance of the point of change is probably related to the type of treatment. Within applied behavioural analysis, interventions often act rapidly and generate a significant impact within one or two sessions, but this is not necessarily the case when other types of treatment are applied. Even when a relatively 'simple' treatment (in the sense of having few components), such as exposure for anxiety is applied, there may be a time lag before the treatment has an effect. An example of this can be seen in a form of exposure therapy used to treat people with chronic regional pain syndrome where the intervention typically does not show benefits for 4–5 weeks after the treatment has begun (de Jong et al., 2005). Point of change should be considered but the interpretation of change, or the lack of change, will depend on knowledge about the intervention and its likely temporal effect.

Overlap between phases

Panel (f) of Figure 5.3 includes a boxed and shaded area running across the graph. Finding the minimum value in the baseline phase and the maximum value in the treatment phase sets the lower and upper boundaries of the box. Data points in the box represent the degree of overlap in the phases of the study. With designs such as the ABAB the overlap lines must be drawn for successive pairs of phases: AB; BA; AB. An example of this is shown in Figure 5.13, and additional boxes have been superimposed to highlight each pair of overlap lines. Reading the figure from left to right, there is an overlap in the first AB pair and in the BA pair but not in the final AB pair. The question is: how much overlap would be considered as evidence against the interpretation that the treatment has been effective? We will consider this in the next chapter.

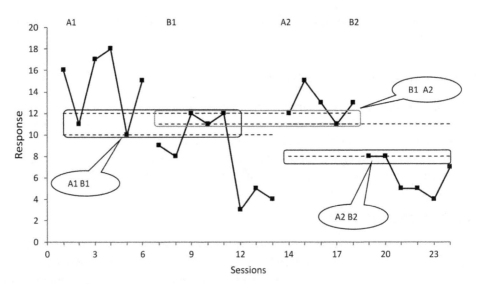

FIGURE 5.13 Examining overlap in an AB design

This illustrates the sequential comparison of phases by examining the degree of overlap between phases. With four phases (A[1], B[1], A[1], B[1]) here are three sets of overlap to consider; A[1] to B[1], B[1] to A[2] and A[2] to B[2] (where there is no overlap). For each overlap the parallel lines marking the upper and lower points of successive phases are drawn. These have been circled and labelled for each pair of phases.

The Conservative Dual Criterion (CDC) method

Fisher and his colleagues (Fisher, Kelley & Lomas, 2003) developed a method for enhancing the visual analysis of AB single-case designs. A practical guide for implementing the method for AB, ABAB and multiple baseline designs has also been prepared (Swoboda, Kratochwill & Levin, 2010). The essence of comparing differences between phases is the need to make a judgement about the difference in the pattern of the data in the second phase. We are asked to determine whether the pattern of the data in the second phase represents a discontinuity from the first phase. This requires the ability to project the mean, trend and variability seen in the first phase onto the second phase and, in the mind's eye, to form a judgement about whether the patterns of the two data sets are sufficiently different to warrant the conclusion that a change has occurred. Fisher *et al.* experimented with several methods for projecting the central tendency (they used the mean) and linear trend from the baseline to the treatment phase of an AB design. They used computer simulations to produce data sets with known characteristics: differences in phase lengths, the magnitude of change and the presence of autocorrelation (autocorrelation is discussed in the next chapter). They were then able to compare judgements about whether or not change had occurred to known characteristics of change. Their results suggested that plotting a mean and trend from the baseline phase onto the treatment phase as visual aids could improve the reliability and validity of judgements about change. A typical plot is shown in Figure 5.14.

Fisher and colleagues found that by plotting a slightly adjusted mean and trend, the reliability and validity was improved. They found that adjusting the mean by shifting it

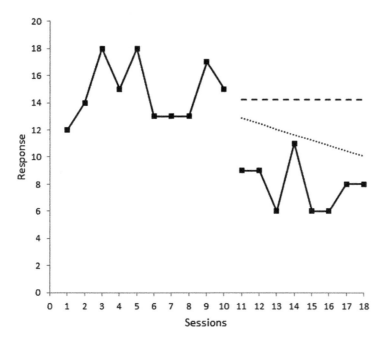

FIGURE 5.14 Analysing an AB design using the Conservative Dual Criterion method

The baseline data are plotted as usual and the mean and linear trend for the baseline data are computed and adjusted by 0.25*SD units (see text for details). The lines representing the mean of the baseline (dashed horizontal line) and trend (dotted sloping line) are plotted in the treatment phase. It is then easy to compare the actual treatment data with the mean and trend data predicted from the baseline.

by a quarter (0.25) of the standard deviation of the baseline, the validity of judgements of change was improved. The method requires that the standard deviation for the baseline phase is computed and added to the baseline mean. This adjusted baseline is plotted in the treatment phase. The trend line is also adjusted by shifting the intercept value a by 0.25 standard deviation. A critical point is the direction of the adjustment. When the treatment is expected to reduce the targeted response, the adjusted mean is the observed mean minus 0.25*SD. When the expected response is an increase, then the baseline value is adjusted upwards by adding 0.25*SD to the observed value. The same direction of adjustment is applied to the intercept (a) used to compute the trend line. Figure 5.14 shows a data set for an AB study with the mean and trend line from the baseline phase imposed on the treatment phase. In this plot it is apparent that all the data points in the treatment phase fall below both the mean and trend line. Fisher *et al.* generated empirical rules for determining how many points should meet the dual criteria – beyond the limits set by the two lines – for different phase lengths. A summary of these is shown in Table 5.7. Once the data have been plotted, it is a matter of seconds to determine whether the pattern meets the conservative dual criteria. Using this method to interpret the data in Figure 5.14, it is clear that we can conclude that change has occurred.

Figure 5.15 shows a data plot for an ABAB study. The first two phases are the same as in Figure 5.14. In the third phase, i.e. the second baseline period, the mean and trend

TABLE 5.7 The criteria for change between two phases

Number of points in the treatment phase	Number of points in the predicted direction needed to conclude that there has been a change
5	5
6,7	6
8	7
9,10	8
11,12	9
13	10
14	11
15,17	12
18,19	13
20,21	14
22,23	15

Data from Fisher, W. W., Kelley, M. E., & Lomas, J. E. (2003). Visual aids and structured criteria for improving visual inspection and interpretation of single-case designs. *Journal of Applied Behavior Analysis*, 36(3), 387–406. doi: 10.1901/jaba.2003.36-387

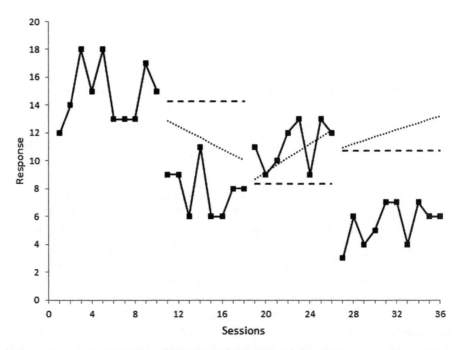

FIGURE 5.15 Using the Conservative Dual Criterion method to evaluate an ABAB design

The data for the first two phases are plotted as in Figure 5.12. In the third phase the lines for the mean and linear tend from the second phase are plotted in phase i.e. the second baseline period. In the final (treatment) phase the mean and linear trend lines from the second baseline period are plotted.

from the first treatment (B) phase have been plotted. Note that because we expect the number of responses in this phase to increase, the mean and trend line are adjusted upwards by 0.25*SD. Five of the 8 data points in this phase exceed the dual criteria, and the data in Table 5.7 suggest that we would need 7 data points to exceed the criteria in order to conclude that a change had occurred. A cautious conclusion would therefore be that reversing the treatment condition did not have the desired effect. On the other hand, data from the final phase in which the mean and trend from the second baseline period have been plotted suggest that the reintroduction of treatment changed responding reliably. So our interpretation of the full data set will need to be slightly nuanced. Lane and Gast (2014; see also Spriggs & Gast, 2010) offer a similar guide to visual analysis, using slightly different principles based on the idea of constructing a 'stability envelope' (confidence intervals) around mean and trend lines.

The CDC method highlights the essence of visual analysis: the comparison of patterns of data over adjacent phases. It illustrates the value of explicitly projecting characteristics of data from one phase to the adjacent one, and it also includes a decision rule based on empirical testing with data of known characteristics. The rules were developed with AB data sets of 10 and 20 points in which the length of each phase was 5 and 10, respectively. These values were later extended to between 8 and 40 data points. At present we do not know how robust the decision rules are for data sets with different characteristics, such as the one reported by Derrickson *et al.* (1993) and shown in Figures 5.11 and 5.12. Nevertheless the CDC is a useful tool in visual analysis. Astute readers will have noted that the CDC method is not purely visual, as there are statistical procedures involved in both plotting the criteria and in the decision criterion itself. In the next chapter we will examine some basic statistical methods for analysing single-case data.

EVALUATING VISUAL ANALYSIS

Visual analysis can contribute towards answering several questions about the data. First, is *there evidence of a change between the phases?* We need to make this more precise by specifying which particular parameter we are interested in: central tendency (mean/median), trend (linear/non-linear) or variability. Note that it is possible to have changes in one parameter but not another. Three simple examples of this are shown in Figure 5.16. This question is equivalent to making a judgement about a reliable change (Chapter 2), but we do not have a formal statistical criterion for making the decision.

The methods for exploring the data discussed in this chapter can help us look at the data in several ways. Firstly, they encourage us to describe various aspects of the data as accurately as possible. Many of the experimental studies on the visual analysis of single cases ask judges to make a single summary decision, change vs no change, without allowing the judges to thoroughly explore the data and describe their various components. This is a bit like running a statistical test such as a regression model without first checking the nature of the data. There are many data sets where change looks obvious – it 'hits you between the eyes' (Bulte & Onghena, 2012b). Even then we might want to engage in a more formal analysis using something like the CDC method. When data are 'messy', the methods described in this chapter can help you describe the basic shape of the data, as we

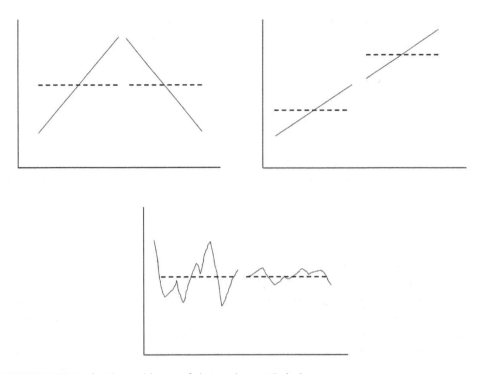

FIGURE 5.16 Evaluating evidence of change in an AB design

The three main parameters (central tendency, trend and variability) can change independently of each other. Panel (a) shows a marked change in trend between the phases but no change in central tendency. In panel (b) there is no change in trend but a marked shift in central tendency. Panel (c) shows a reduction in variability between the phases but no apparent shift in central tendency. In every case we should be cautious about concluding whether the intervention has had any effect as there are plausible alternative explanations to be considered.

saw with Derrickson *et al.*'s data set (Derrickson *et al.*, 1993). In cases like this we might be able to arrive at a tentative conclusion – for example, there is evidence that the number of negative responses did change during the experiment, but the marked variability in the response and the robust underlying trends shown by the RM42 plots suggest that there are other, unidentified factors to take into account.

The second question is, is this change important? We should not confuse this with the question of whether or not change has occurred. Just as in Chapter 2, when we considered the analysis of standardised measures, we need to separate our 'reliable' change from 'clinical' significance. Agreement, on the basis of a visual analysis, that a change has occurred is not enough to determine whether a clinically important change has been made. The criterion for clinical importance must be set externally. In a clinical setting we can set our criterion of importance in consultation with the patient or a significant other. This point was considered in Chapter 3. The criterion depends on a complex social and clinical judgement rather than on any inherent level of the parameter. It is important that it should be specified *a priori* rather than imposed *post hoc*, otherwise our claims will be influenced by what we found rather than what we aimed to do. However, even a part change to a desired outcome might be valuable in guiding a further study.

The third question is, can the change we observe be attributed to the treatment alone? Remember that this is the *raison d'être* of single-case designs, so being able to exclude plausible rival hypotheses about the change is central to visual analysis. The answer to this question therefore depends on the design used and relevant contextual information that can rule out other plausible explanations. For this we need to consider the logic of the design as discussed in the previous chapter.

We might ask a fourth question: do others come to the same conclusion about these data? In other words, how reliable is our analysis of the data and can others replicate it? Research on agreement between judges of single-case data plots could give rise to a degree of scepticism on this issue. Several studies in which both naive and experienced judges have been presented with artificially generated data sets[2] have documented relatively poor inter-rater agreement (Brossart *et al.*, 2006; Deprospero & Cohen, 1979; Ottenbacher, 1990; Ximenes *et al.*, 2009). This should give us cause for concern, but we should note that these studies require judges to make decisions in conditions that are very different from those facing the clinician or researcher. In these studies the judges are presented with a set of graphical plots and are asked to make a single judgement about whether or not change has occurred. The data plots are decontextualised, i.e. they are just data plots; there is no information about the individual, the conditions of treatment or any other relevant information. Furthermore, the judges do not have the opportunity to explore the data in detail using the methods described in this chapter. Their decisions are based on an overall appreciation of the data rather than a detailed analysis and knowledge of the data. These and other more detailed points have been discussed by Baer, a leading advocate of visual analysis (Baer, 1977; Parsonson & Baer, 1992). One argument against the provision of detailed contextual information is that it might bias the visual analyst's decision making. While this may be true, we cannot escape the fact that in most single-case studies the primary analyst(s) will be the investigators and we must therefore consider ways in which biases might be understood and detected. There appears to be little, if any, research on this question.

A practical solution to the problem of visual analysis is to use more than one analyst. Each data analyst should keep a record of how they analysed the data, what factors they considered as threats to the interpretation and why these were either discounted or nullified. The analysts' records can then be examined, either by the analysts exchanging notes or by a third party and a consensus agreement reached. Elliott and his colleagues (2009) have suggested that the analysis of complex case studies could proceed along similar lines, with pairs of analysts arguing for and against the conclusion of change and the interpretations contingent on that (questions 1 to 3, above) in the presence of a judge, i.e. treating the process as a court of law would do and taking into account all the available evidence. One strong feature of single-case data is that all the data are present and available for inspection, and reanalysis and each step of the analysis can be articulated clearly.

CONCLUSIONS

Preparing good graphs is an essential part of the analysis of single-case data, even if you also choose to conduct further statistical analyses of the data. The significant feature of single-case data is the pattern of data over time and between phases. Unlike many group designs where the focus of interest is often a difference in the mean values obtained, it is the pattern of data in single cases that requires interpretation. Sometimes the differences are easy to see but where there is variability and trend, interpretation may be more complex. The ease of access to software graphing facilities is both a benefit and a curse. The temptation to enter the data onto a spreadsheet and hand over the construction of the graph to the software is seductive, but as we have seen this does not always result in high-quality figures.

Data sets in single-case research are usually small, and in the initial stage of analysis they do not need manipulating and transforming by software. At the beginning of analysis it is worth using simple tried-and-tested technology, i.e. pencil, paper and a straight edge; sketch out the graphs that you think will display the data most appropriately. An alternative is to use software to generate a graph of the raw data and to print several copies. It is then easy to pencil in additional graphical items – for example, split-middle, central location, various range bars – onto the graphs as you explore the data. Similarly, rough sketches can be made on a tablet and there are some excellent applications available. When you have a clear idea of the figures you wish to create and likely further analyses, only then commit the data to a spreadsheet and plot the data.

Footnote: producing figures

Spreadsheets are extremely versatile in providing a range of graphical options and built-in functions that enable one to compute statistical parameters such as medians and trends quickly and without error. To compute some of the parameters mentioned here (BMed, trend lines and various running median statistics), a little additional skill is required. This is not difficult and can be achieved relatively quickly by experimentation and playing with the features, the best sort of learning. (Some information on the useful functions has been given in the legends to various plots.) Similar functions are available in Google's 'Sheet' and Apple's 'Numbers' applications and graphs may also be produced in MS PowerPoint and Word and their equivalents.

Producing figures in Excel or other software does take time and, like any other skill, repetition and experimentation will produce competence. Basic guidance is available in the many introductions to Excel (other software is less well supplied with texts) and there have been several 'how to do it' accounts specifically written as guides to constructing the standard set of single case figures (Barton & Reichow, 2012; Carr & Burkholder, 1998; Dixon et al., 2009). These guides give step-by-step accounts for particular versions of common software and there are many 'how to do it' instructions on social media such as YouTube (www.YouTube.com). There is also a suite of programmes written for the R programming language SCDA – Single Case Data Analysis (Bulte & Onghena, 2012a, b) is easy to use in a graphical user interface for R, called RCommander[3]. The Single Case Visual Analysis (SCVA) a programme within SCDA implements several of the data exploration methods discussed in this chapter. It will generate graphs for a variety of estimates of central tendency, variability and trend for several designs (AB, ABA, ABAB, multiple baseline and alternating treatments). The advantage of SCDA is that the computations of the various parameters are automated and you do not have to write any code. The relative disadvantage is that you have to learn to use the R programme. This is not difficult, but it is different from the interface with which most people are familiar. Manolov and his colleagues (2015) have written a comprehensive guide to resources for analysing single-case data, which includes help on downloading, installing and using R. Second, the graphs produced by SCVA are not editable and better-quality figures can be produced in Excel although some additional time and effort is needed. Finally, there is an online facility for training in visual analysis as developed by Horner and colleagues (Horner, 2012).

NOTES

1 By analogy it is possible to compute a regression equation from the split-middle fit. In this case the values are: $b = (y_R - y_L)/(x_R - x_L)$; $a = y_L - b*(x_L)$. This is useful for plotting the data.

2 Artificial, i.e. investigator-generated, data sets are often used because they can be generated to known statistical parameters. Changes in level, trend and variance within and between phases can all be characterised. This allows the researcher to compare the judges' decisions to the predetermined statistical criteria.

3 R and R commander can be downloaded from the R web pages at www.r-project.org/. There are several good guides on how to set them up for Windows, Mac and Linux environments. The article by Manolov et al. (2015) provides one such introduction.

REFERENCES

Baer, D. M. (1977). Perhaps it would be better not to know everything. *Journal of Applied Behavior Analysis*, 10(1), 167–72.

Baer, D. M. (1988). An autocorrelated commentary on the need for a different debate. *Behavioral Assessment*, 10(3), 295–7.

Barlow, D. H., Nock, M. K. & Hersen, M. (2009). *Single Case Experimental Designs* (3rd edn). Boston: Pearson.

Barton, E. E. & Reichow, B. (2012). Guidlines for graphing data with Microsoft Office 2007, Office 2010 and Office for Mac 2008 and 2011. *Journal of Early Intervention*, 34(3), 129–50.

Brossart, D. F., Parker, R. I., Olson, E. A. & Mahadevan, L. (2006). The relationship between visual analysis and five statistical analyses in a simple AB single-case research design. *Behavior Modification*, 30(5), 531–63.

Bulte, I. & Onghena, P. (2012a). The single-case data analysis package: Analysing single-case experiments with R software. *Journal of Modern Applied Statistical Methods*, 12(2). Retrieved from http://digitalcommons.wayne/edu/jmasm/vol12/iss2/28

Bulte, I. & Onghena, P. (2012b). When the truth hits you between the eyes: A software tool for the visual analysis of single-case experimental data. *Methodology*, 8(3), 104–14.

Busk, P. L. & Marascuilo, L. A. (1992). Statistical analysis in single-case research: Issues, procedures, and recommendations, with applications to multiple behaviors. In T. R. Kratochwill & J. R. Levin (eds), *Single-case Research Design and Analysis: New Directions for Psychology and Education* (pp. 159–85). Hillsdale, NJ: Lawrence Erlbaum.

Carr, J. E. & Burkholder, E. O. (1998). Creating single-subject design graphs with Microsoft Excel™. *Journal of Applied Behavior Analysis*, 31(2), 245–51.

Chambers, J. M., Cleveland, W. S., Kleiner, B. & Tukey, P. A. (1983). *Graphical Methods for Data Analysis*. Belmont, CA: Wadsworth.

Cleveland, W. S. (1985). *Elements of Graphing Data*. Monterey, CA: Wadworth.

Cleveland, W. S. (1993). *Visualizing Data*. Summit, NJ: Hobart Press.

de Jong, J. R., Vlaeyen, J. W., Onghena, P., Cuypers, C., den Hollander, M. & Ruijgrok, J. (2005). Reduction of pain-related fear in complex regional pain syndrome type I: the application of graded exposure in vivo. *Pain*, 116(3), 264–75.

Deprospero, A. & Cohen, S. (1979). Inconsistent visual analyses of intrasubject data. *Journal of Applied Behavior Analysis*, 12(4), 573–9.

Derrickson, J. G., Neef, N. A. & Cataldo, M. F. (1993). Effects of signaling invasive procedures on a hospitalized infant's affective behaviors. *Journal of Applied Behavior Analysis*, 26(1), 133–4.

Dixon, M. R., Jackson, J. W., Small, S. L., Horner-King, M. J., Lik, N. M. K., Garcia, Y. & Rosales, R. (2009). Creating single-subject design graphs in Microsoft Excel™ 2007. *Journal of Applied Behavior Analysis*, 42(2), 277–93.

Duarte, N. (2008). *Slide:ology*. North Sacremento: O'Reilly Media.

Elliott, R., Partyka, R., Alperin, R., Dobrenski, R., Wagner, J., Messer, S. B. *et al.* (2009). An adjudicated hermeneutic single-case efficacy design study of experiential therapy for panic/phobia. *Psychotherapy Research*, 19(4–5), 543–57.

Fisher, W. W., Kelley, M. E. & Lomas, J. E. (2003). Visual aids and structured criteria for improving visual inspection and interpretation of single-case designs. *Journal of Applied Behavior Analysis*, 36(3), 387–406.

Flink, I. K., Nicholas, M. K., Boersma, K. & Linton, S. J. (2009). Reducing the threat value of chronic pain: A preliminary replicated single-case study of interoceptive exposure versus distraction in six individuals with chronic back pain. *Behaviour Research and Therapy*, 47(8), 721–8.

Gast, D. L. (2010). *Single Subject Research Methodology in Behavioral Sciences*. New York: Routledge.

Glass, G. V., Willson, V. L. & Gottman, J. M. (1975). *Design and Analysis of Time Series Experiments*. Boulder: Colorado University Press.

Horner, R. H. (2012). Assessing visual analysis of single case research designs. Retrieved 5 June 2015 from www.singlecase.org/#

Jarrett, M. A. & Ollendick, T. H. (2012). Treatment of comorbid attention-deficit/hyperactivity disorder and anxiety in children: a multiple baseline design analysis. *Journal of Consulting and Clinical Psychology*, 80(2), 239–44.

Jones, R. R., Vaught, R. S. & Weinrott, M. R. (1977). Time-series analysis on operant research. *Journal of Applied Behavior Analysis*, 10(1), 151–66.

Jones, R. R., Weinrott, M. R. & Vaught, R. S. (1978). Effects of serial dependency on agreement between visual and statistical inference. *Journal of Applied Behavior Analysis*, 11(2), 277–83.

Kazdin, A. E. (1982). *Single Case Research Designs: Methods for Clinical and Applied Settings*. New York: Oxford University Press.

Lane, J. D. & Gast, D. L. (2014). Visual analysis in single case experimental design studies: brief review and guidelines. *Neuropsychological Rehabilitation*, 24(3–4), 445–63.

Lavender, A. (1981). A behavioural approach to the treatment of epilepsy. *Behavioural Psychotherapy*, 9, 231–43.

Manolov, R., Gast, D. L., Perdices, M. & Evans, J. J. (2014). Single-case experimental designs: reflections on conduct and analysis. *Neuropsychological Rehabilitation*, 24(3–4), 634–60.

Manolov, R., Moeyaert, M. & Evans, J. J. (2015). Single case data analysis: software resources for applied researchers. Retrieved 7 May 2015 from www.researchgate.net/publication/275517964_Single-case_data_analysis_Software_resources_for_applied_researchers

Morley, S. & Adams, M. (1989). Some simple statistical tests for exploring single-case time-series data. *British Journal of Clinical Psychology*, 28(1), 1–18.

Morley, S. & Adams, M. (1991). Graphical analysis of single-case time series data. *British Journal of Clinical Psychology*, 30(2), 97–115.

Mosteller, F., Siegel, A. F. & Trapdo, E. Y. C. (1983). Fitting straight lines by eye. In D. C. Hoaglin, F. Mosteller & J. W. Tukey (eds), *Understanding Robust and Exploratory Data Analysis*. New York: Wiley.

Ottenbacher, K. J. (1990). Clinically relevant designs for rehabilitation research: the idiographic model. *American Journal of Physical Medicine & Rehabilitation*, 69(6), 286–92.

Parsonson, B. S. & Baer, D. M. (1992). The visual analysis of data, and current research into the stimuli controlling it. In T. R. Kratochwill & J. R. Levin (eds), *Single-case Research Design and Analysis: New Directions for Psychology and Education* (pp. 15–40). Hillsdale, NJ: Lawrence Erlbaum.

Rosenberger, J. J. & Gasko, M. (1983). Comparing location estimators: trimmed means, medians and trimean. In D. C. Hoaglin, F. Mosteller & J. W. Tukey (eds), *Understanding Robust and Exploratory Data Analysis*. New York: Wiley.

Shadish, W. R. & Sullivan, K. J. (2011). Characteristics of single-case designs used to assess intervention effects in 2008. *Behavior Research Methods*, 43(4), 971–80.

Sidman, M. (1960). *Tactics of Scientific Research: Evaluating Experimental Data in Psychology*. New York: Basic Books.

Smith, J. D. (2012). Single-case experimental designs: A systematic review of published research and current standards. *Psychological Methods*, 17(4), 510–50.

Spriggs, A. D. & Gast, D. L. (2010). Visual representation of data. In D. L. Gast (ed.), *Single Subject Research Methodology in Behavioral Sciences*. New York: Routledge.

Swoboda, C. M., Kratochwill, T. R. & Levin, J. R. (2010). Conservative dual-criterion method for single case research: A guide for visual analysis of AB, ABA and multiple-baseline designs. (WCER Working Paper No.2010–13). University of Wisconsin-Madison, Wisconsin Center for Educational Research website: www.wcer.wisc.edu/workingPapers/papers.php

Tufte, E. R. (1983). *The Visual Display of Quantitative Information*. Cheshire, CT: Graphics Press.

Tukey, J. W. (1977). *Exploratory Data Analysis*. Cambridge MA: Addison Wesley.

Velleman, P. F. & Hoaglin, D. C. (1981). *Applications, Basics, and Computing of Exploratory Data Analysis*. Boston: Duxbury Press.

Ximenes, V. M., Manolov, R., Solanas, A. & Quera, V. (2009). Factors affecting visual inference in single-case designs. *Spanish Journal of Psychology*, 12(2), 823–32.

Chapter 6
Statistical analysis of single-case data

In this chapter we look at ways of statistically describing and analysing data. For the most part these require no more than the ability to add, subtract, divide and multiply. Many computations can be done by hand, but there is helpful computer software: details are given at the end of the chapter.

The analysis of single-case experimental designs developed in applied behaviour analysis; this eschewed statistical analysis and relied on visual inspection to draw conclusions (Parsonson & Baer, 1992). In implementing applied behaviour analysis experiments, investigators strived to establish a high degree of experimental control by ensuring a stable baseline, accurate measurement and interventions that were likely to have immediate and large effects. The application of statistical analysis, it was argued, was unnecessary. In addition, applying conventional statistical parametric tests such as Student's t and analysis of variance is inappropriate because the data frequently violate the assumption that error terms from successive observations are independent. This is because time-series data are often auto-correlated, i.e. each observation in the series is correlated with previous ones, and the error terms are not independent. There has been considerable debate about the extent of autocorrelation in short time series typically found in single-case methods. It is not always present, but it would seem wise to assume that it is a potential feature and that it would be a threat to the validity of analyses using conventional parametric statistics (Shadish, Rindskopf, Hedges & Sullivan, 2013).

There are, however, specialised time-series analyses that model autocorrelated data and take these into account in the analysis. Time-series analysis was introduced to the analysis of single-case data in the 1970s, but its application is no longer recommended because of the relatively small n used in single-case data. Most authorities suggest that at least 50 measurements per phase are required to identify and test the models. There are some studies where this type of analysis has been legitimately applied (Vlaeyen, de Jong, Geilen, Heuts & van Breukelen, 2001), and it does provide a powerful data analytic tool where there are sufficient data. More recently researchers have investigated a variety of alternative analytic methods such as multi-level modelling, generalised additive modelling and non-linear Bayesian analysis (Kratochwill & Levin, 2014; Shadish, 2014). In general, these and classical time-series methods require a degree of statistical sophistication not yet present in the clinical research community, and the general applicability of some of the methods has yet to be tested.

This chapter focuses on two types of analysis that are suited to the relatively small data sets found in single-case studies: first, the analysis of non-overlap data by a direct comparison of distinct phases (referred to as non-overlap methods) and second, consideration of the whole distribution against all possible distributions using randomisation tests (referred to as randomisation tests). Both methods use non-parametric tests for statistical analysis, so that the problem of correlated error terms is circumvented. The methods are also relatively easy to understand and have the advantage that many of the analyses can be carried out by hand with few computations. There is a variety of computer software available free of charge from the Internet, and details on some of these are appended at the end of the chapter. Before we consider non-overlap and randomisation tests specifically, this chapter outlines some simple methods for exploring time-series data. Prior to considering the use of statistics, it is necessary to carry out an initial exploration of the data.

INITIAL DATA EXPLORATION

Readers may be used to providing summary statistics, e.g. mean, range and standard deviation, and testing for normality of the distribution when investigating differences between groups. In single-case data, means and standard deviations can be misleading when there are small samples and when there is trend in the data. We are interested in the overall pattern of the data rather than just a single parameter such as the mean, but before we consider statistical tests that compare different phases it is worth asking a few questions about each phase. There are several hypotheses that we might wish to consider (Morley & Adams, 1989):

1   That the series is random, i.e. there is no trend in the data
2   That there is a trend in the mean of the series
3   That the series contains cyclical variation
4   That there is a trend in the variability of the series.

Table 6.1 shows four sets of data that illustrate testing these hypotheses, and Figure 6.1 shows the data plotted in four panels. The first two hypotheses are likely to be the most frequently entertained, and two statistical tests that can address them are considered below in some detail, while tests for cyclical variation and change in variance may also be of interest (Morley and Adams, 1989).

TABLE 6.1 Data sets (after Morely and Adams, 1989) to illustrate statistical procedures for exploring the data

Time point Series	1	2	3	4	5	6	7	8	9	10
A	8	3	5	4	2	8	5	6	9	5
B	8	3	1	7	3	0	9	2	0	6
C	2	0	3	4	5	2	6	5	8	7
D	7	6	6	5	6	2	8	1	0	9

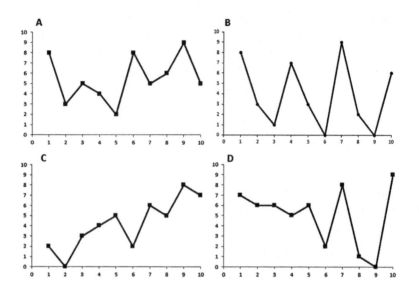

FIGURE 6.1 Plot of data from Table 6.1

Assessing randomness

Non-random traits can be revealed by identifying patterns in the data using the concept of turning points, e.g. up-down-up-down-up suggests something non-random, potentially cyclical, in the same way that up-up-up-up-up suggests a linear trend. With a large number of random samples, each with a large number of observations points, the number of turning points in each of the samples would follow a normal distribution. Morley and Adams (1989) described several tests for randomness in short series, but here we just consider one, the turning points test.

The turning points test

This is a simple test to apply and easily done when the data are presented as a graph. The basic assumption of the test is that if the data are randomly distributed then the number of peaks and troughs in the data will be distributed in a more or less predictable manner. Peaks and troughs are data points that are larger or smaller in value than their immediate neighbours. In the sequence 6, 7, 4, 3, 5, there are two turning points, both underlined: 7 is a peak because it is greater than its neighbours, and 3 is a trough. In a random series the probability of finding a turning point in any three successive observations is 2/3 (0.666), i.e. the probability of a peak plus the probability of a trough. In a series of n data points there are (n − 2) possible starting points for sequences of three numbers, so in our short sequence of 5 numbers there are 3 possible sequences that might contain a turning point (each turning point is underlined): 6, 7, 4; 7, 4, 3 and 4, 3, 5. The expected number of turning points, E(T), in a random series of length n is:

$$E(T) = \frac{2}{3}(n-2)$$

It is possible to test the significance of the observed number of turning points against the expected number. In small samples there are fewer options for T, so we need a more focused test to consider whether the number of observed turning points is random. The left side of Table 6.2 shows the values of T needed to obtain conventional levels of significance ($p < 0.05$) for series of sample sizes 5 to 10. For example, there are 6 turning points in series A and this value is clearly much larger than the criteria in Table 6.2 – either 2, 1 or 0 turning points – so we can tentatively conclude that the series is random (a more detailed table with exact probabilities is produced by Morley and Adams, 1989).

For larger samples (in this example, 12) the distribution of T approximates to the normal distribution: the right side of Table 6.2 shows the test values for series lengths of 11–16. Thus for a series with n = 12 the expected number of turning points is 6.67 (although of course the actual number of turning points can only be a whole number). In practice we would probably conclude that T = 7 is random, but T = <4 and T = > 10 probably are not random. It may contain a trend or other feature that should be explored and taken into account.

So, the turning points test is quick and easy to implement and 'good enough' for an initial exploration of the data, but there are limitations. First, it is insensitive to trend, i.e. it cannot detect trend in the data and may give a false result when a trend is present. This is easily demonstrated with the series 2, 1, 4, 3, 6, 5, 8, 7, 10, 9. Here all but the first and the last numbers are turning points (T = 8). The test of significance would lead us to conclude that the data are random, but there is clearly a strong positive trend in the data. Second, in series B, Figure 6.1, the data give an impression of a regular cycle occurring every 3 points. There is a peak followed by a smooth drop and a sharp rise to the next peak. The lengths between the peaks and the troughs do not appear to be random, although the computed value of T = 6 is not significant and suggests that the series is random.

TABLE 6.2 The turning points test

Series length 5–10			Series length 11–16				
n	T	Criterion	n	T	SD	95% Confidence interval	
5	2.00	0	11	6.00	1.28	3.50	8.50
6	2.67	0	12	6.67	1.35	4.03	9.30
7	3.33	1	13	7.33	1.41	4.57	10.10
8	4.00	1	14	8.00	1.47	5.11	10.89
9	4.67	2	15	8.67	1.53	5.67	11.67
10	5.33	2	16	9.33	1.59	6.22	12.45

The left side of this table shows the number of turning points needed to reject the null hypothesis in series with the value of *n* 5–10. With sample sizes in excess of 10 the distribution approximates to the normal distribution. (In this case the standard deviation (SD) is given by $[(16n - 29)/90]^{1/2}$, where, *n* = sample size). T = expected number of turning points.

Tests for trend in mean

Chapter 5 defined trend in mean as a systematic shift in the value of the central location of the data in time. There are several tests for trend, but the most familiar and useful is Kendall's Tau (τ).

Kendall's Tau (τ)

This is a powerful test, and it is introduced here because it also features in formal tests of non-overlap statistics (discussed later in this chapter) and there are several computer programmes that include Kendall's τ as an option. It is, however, relatively easy to compute by hand with small samples. We will use the data in series C, Table 6.1 to illustrate computation. The simplest method is to construct a table that enables you to compare each number in the data series to every other number. Table 6.3 gives an example. The first column is the series in the order in which the data were observed and the first row is the same data but in reverse order, i.e. the last observed data point is now the first.

We compute τ as follows.

1   Enter 0 in the diagonal cells. These are the cells where each observation is compared with itself. Entering 0 ensures that we do not count them.
2   Starting on the first row, compare each value in the first column with the value in the succeeding columns. In this case the value 2 is compared successively with 7, 8, 5 and so on. For each comparison enter:

   +, if the value in the column is greater than the value in the row, e.g. 7 > 2
   −, if the value in the column is less than the value in the row, e.g. 0 < 2
   T, if the values are tied.

3   Sum the number of +, − and tied observations. In this case there are 37 +, 6 − and 2 ties. As a check on your computations, the sum of all these values should be $n(n-1)/2$, where n is the number of observations in the series. In this case, as n = 10 the resulting value is 45, i.e. $((10 \times 9)/2)$, and the total of 37 + 6 + 2 is indeed 45.

TABLE 6.3 Computing Kendall's Tau for series C in Table 6.1

Session →		10	9	8	7	6	5	4	3	2	1
↓	Data → 7	8	5	6	2	5	4	3	0	2	
1	2	+	+	+	+	T	+	+	+	−	0
2	0	+	+	+	+	+	+	+	+	0	
3	3	+	+	+	+	−	+	+	0		
4	4	+	+	+	+	−	+	0			
5	5	+	+	T	+	−	0				
6	2	+	+	+	+	0					
7	6	+	+	−	0						
8	5	+	+	0							
9	8	−	0								
10	7	0									

4   Compute τ as:

$$\tau = \frac{S}{N(n-1)/2}$$

S = (number of positive values – number of negative values)

In this case the value of $S = 31$ and τ is $(37 - 6)/45 = 0.69$. If there is a negative trend in the data then the value will be negative.

For small sample sizes, when n is between 4 and 10, Kendall (1976) computed the critical values of S, and Table 6.4 shows the values of S needed to obtain the conventional significance values of $p < 0.05$ and $p < 0.01$. In our example the value of $S = 31$, and this exceeds the necessary critical value of 27 for significance at $p < 0.01$.

Like many non-parametric tests, Kendall's test is a form of randomisation test. These tests consider only the data available at hand and computing all possible arrangements of the data. The probability of the observed sequence of data for that particular set can then be calculated exactly. For small samples it is possible to compute all the possibilities by hand, but it soon becomes tedious. For example, when there are only 4 data points there are $4! = 24$ ways in which the 4 points can be arranged. (The ! after a number indicates the factorial, i.e. we multiply $4 \times 3 \times 2 \times 1$.) For 10 observations in the present example, $10! = 3,628,800$ permutations. Fortunately when the sample size is 8 or greater the sampling distribution of τ closely approximates to the normal distribution and the standard deviation of τ is given by the equation:

$$\sigma_\tau = \sqrt{\frac{2(2n+5)}{9n(n-1)}}$$

where n is the sample size. We can test the null hypothesis that $\tau > 0$ using the normal distribution, $z = \tau/\sigma_\tau$.

Other tests for trend

Both the turning points test and Kendall's Tau are easy to compute and can be quickly run to check the basic characteristics of each phase in a study. Panels B and D in Figure 6.1 suggest two other patterns of data that might be found. Panel B shows data where two

TABLE 6.4 Critical values of S

Significance level	Sample size						
	4	5	6	7	8	9	10
0.05	6	8	11	13	16	18	20
0.01	–	10	13	17	20	24	27

S must obtain or be greater than the value shown to meet the criterion for significance at the conventional p values for n between 4 and 10. Note that when the computed value of S is negative, it simply indicates that the trend is negative: its significance may be tested by ignoring the negative sign.

data points separate the peaks and troughs, and it gives the impression that the data might be cyclical. Such a pattern might be expected if a client has a mood disorder or if we are monitoring a known cyclical process such as alertness. It is possible to test for patterns in the phase length. Kendall (1976) reports a test based on the same logic as the turning points test, i.e. comparing the expected number of different phase lengths to the observed number; a worked example is given by Morley and Adams (1989). In panel D the data appear to become more variable as time progresses. Foster and Stuart (1954) developed the Records test as a test for trend and change in variance. This is easy to compute and testing for trend is possible, but unfortunately the test for change in variance is mathematically difficult. Foster and Stuart simply say that the distribution of the statistics is 'troublesome'. On balance therefore I do not recommend it.

The main point of these initial tests is to facilitate exploration of the data and describe them as well as possible before embarking on further tests. If you are reasonably satisfied that there is no trend in the different phases, then the overlap and randomisation tests for differences between the levels of phases can be applied with some confidence. On the other hand, the occurrence of trend will require one to select an analysis that can accommodate this feature of the data, such as the Tau-U test described in this chapter.

Tests for differences between phases 1: non-overlap statistics

Parker and his colleagues (Parker, Vannest & Davis, 2011) reviewed nine non-overlap methods for analysing the difference between phases in single-case designs. All these methods approach the problem of trying to quantify differences between two adjacent phases in a single-case study by computing some statistic that summarises the extent to which data points in the phases do not overlap. Some of the methods are purely descriptive while other more recent ones include statistical tests for differences between phases. This section outlines four of the current methods: percentage of non-overlapping data (PND), percentage of data points exceeding the median (PEM), non-overlap of all pairs (NAP) and Tau-U. The sequence in which the methods are presented is such that we begin with a simple descriptive method to illustrate the basic ideas and this is followed by methods that use more of the available data and include statistical tests. All of the methods are easily implemented by inspecting graphical plots. Indeed one of the advantages of these methods is that they can be applied to graphical plots even when the original data values are not available. The first three methods are illustrated with data from a simple AB time series:

Baseline (n = 7):   17, 12, 14, 18, 14, 16, 13
Intervention (n = 12):   8, 13, 12, 9, 6, 7, 6, 4, 5, 5, 5, 6

and are illustrated graphically in Figures 6.2 to 6.4.

Simple overlap: percentage of non-overlapping data (PND)

The simplest overlap statistic to compute is the percentage of non-overlapping data (PND), proposed by Scruggs, Mastropieri and Casto (1987). PND simply refers to the percentage of data points in the treatment phase that do not overlap with any of the values in the baseline phase. Figure 6.2 shows a plot of the data set and illustrates the computation.

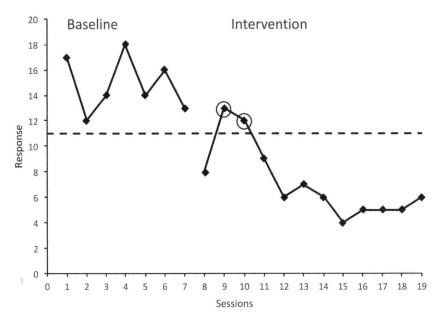

FIGURE 6.2 An AB design illustrating the percentage of non-overlapping data (PND) statistic

The criterion to determine the percentage of non-overlap is set at the extreme data point of the baseline phase. In this example the treatment is expected to reduce the magnitude of the response and the extreme point is therefore the lowest value in the baseline phase. To compute PND we simply count the number of points in the intervention phase that exceed (in this case points that are lower than) the lowest baseline point. There are 12 data points in the intervention phase, of which 2 (circled in Figure 6.2) do not exceed the baseline criterion and 10 do. PND is calculated as 12–2/12 × 100 = 83%. This is a very simple statistic to compute, but there are two problems. First, the method makes use of a single score in the baseline phase. On occasions this score might be highly aberrant and this will result in a very small PND, although most of the data in the intervention phase exceed the other data in the baseline. In the current example a single aberrant baseline observation of 4 would give a PND = 0%, although many of the intervention data points are clearly lower than the majority of the baseline data. The second problem is that the statistical distribution of PND is unknown and there is no associated statistical test associated with it. PND is really just a simple descriptive summary. It is therefore rather limited in its use.

Using the median: percentage of data points exceeding the median (PEM)

An alternative approach that uses more of the data is the percentage of data points exceeding the median (PEM) (Ma, 2006), in which the median value of the baseline data is used as a referent. Figure 6.3 shows the same data as Figure 6.2, but this time a horizontal line representing the median observation from the baseline is superimposed on the data.

The number of data points in the intervention phase that exceed the median are counted and expressed as a percentage. In our example all 12 data points in the intervention phase exceed the median, so PEM = 100%. Ma (2006) did not suggest any formal statistical test for this analysis, but others (Parker, Vannest & Davis, 2011) have suggested that Mood's median test is appropriate (Corder & Foreman, 2014; Seigel & Castellan, 1988).

MOOD'S MEDIAN TEST

Mood's test is essentially the familiar Chi-squared test that can be applied to two or more groups. In our case there are two sets of data (baseline and intervention). Within each group the data are split into those points that fall above or on the median and those that fall below the median, and we count the number of observations falling into each category. We now have a simple 2 × 2 contingency table and a Chi-squared test (χ^2) can be performed on the data. The issue we must consider is which estimate of the median should be used. In Mood's original version of the test the median is derived by pooling all the data across the two phases. The logic is that if the medians of the two samples are equivalent then equal numbers of observations from each group will fall above and below the overall median. In the PEM there is an argument for using the median derived from just the baseline data, because we have set that as a referent for a specific hypothesis that the treatment data will be different from the baseline.

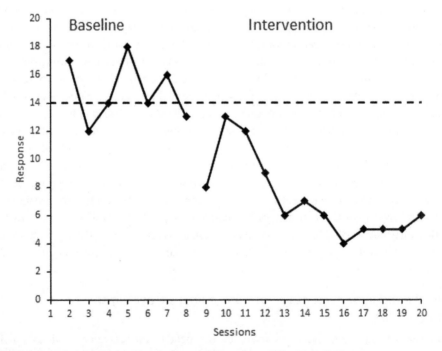

FIGURE 6.3 Percentage of data points exceeding the median (PEM) plot

Note the horizontal line representing the median of the baseline and its projection into the intervention phase. In this example it is very clear that all of the data points in the intervention phase exceed (are lower) than the baseline median.

TABLE 6.5 Mood's median test

Mood's original version Median = 9			Application to PEM Median = 14		
Cut score	Baseline	Intervention	Cut score	Baseline	Intervention
≥ 9	7	3	≥ 14	5	0
< 9	0	9	< 14	2	12
$\chi^2=$		9.975			11.6327
P value =		0.001587			0.000648
Fisher's exact test P =		0.0031			.0018

Table 6.5 shows the distribution of the cells for both the original version of Mood's test and the PEM. In both cases the result reaches the conventional ($p < 0.5$) level of significance. Nevertheless, we should exercise a degree of caution as in this case the cell frequencies are low and the test is not particularly powerful. With small numbers, as is the usual case in single-case research, it is probably better to use Fisher's exact test; the results for this test are shown in the bottom row of Table 6.5.

Using just the median from the baseline has two disadvantages. First, the number of observations in one of the rows will be small, i.e. approximately half of the number of observations in the baseline condition, and this will affect the power of the test. The second issue is that using just the baseline observations means that we are essentially projecting the baseline scores into the treatment phase. This is what we did when we used visual inspection methods (Chapter 5) to draw conclusions about change. The problem with this is that the projected estimates of what might happen in the treatment phase will have a greater degree of error associated with them. You may recall from Chapter 5 that Fisher et al. (2003) recognised this and adjusted the projected trend and level in the conservative dual criterion test. For these reasons it may be better to use Mood's original version of the test, which uses all the available data to estimate an overall median. However, we should recognise that this is not the same as a test on the PEM. Table 6.5 makes it clear that Mood's original version is more conservative, i.e. the χ^2 value will be smaller.

Using all the data: non-overlap of all pairs (NAP)

The PEM method makes use of more data than the original PND method, but it still only uses a single point estimate to characterise the baseline data. Parker and Vannest (2009) suggested a procedure that makes use of all the data: non-overlap of all pairs (NAP). This method compares every point in one phase to every point in the succeeding phase. The number of data points to compare is therefore the product of the number of observations in each phase. In our example this is 7 (Baseline) × 12 (Treatment) = 84 comparisons. Each comparison is scored 0 if the values of the intervention data point represent an improvement, i.e. where the data do not overlap. In the present example, improvement means that the value should be smaller. A score of 1 is given if the value represents a non-improvement and assigned 0.5 if the values are tied. To compute NAP the total

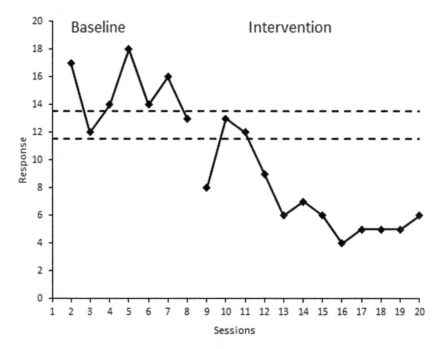

FIGURE 6.4 Computing the non-overlap of all pairs (NAP) statistic

number of improvements is divided by the total number of comparisons ($n_{baseline} \times n_{treatment}$).
Parker and Vannest (2009) suggest that NAP should be rescaled to adjust for chance level
agreement using the following adjustment: $(1 - NAP/0.5)$.

Fortunately in most cases we do not have to construct a matrix of comparisons between
the baseline and treatment phases and we can work out the number of non-overlap pairs
from the graph. Figure 6.4 illustrates how to do this. First draw two parallel lines to capture
the zone on the graph where data points in the two phases overlap. In our case, because
improvement is indicated by a reduction in the response, the lower line will pass just below
the minimum response value in the baseline and the upper line will pass through the
maximum observation in the intervention phase. Then locate the first baseline point in the
overlap zone (session 2) and compare it with all of the treatment points in the overlap
zone. In this case they occur at sessions 9 and 10. As the score at session 9 represents non-
improvement, so we score it as 1. The score at session 10 is tied, so score it 0.5. Then repeat
the process for other baseline data points. The only other score is at session 7, which is tied
with session 9. So we have 2 tied scores and one deterioration score in the overlap zone;
the sum of these scores is 2 $(1 + 0.5 + 0.5)$. As we know there are 84 possible comparisons,
the NAP score = 84–2/84 = 0.976 and the adjusted NAP, $(1 - 0.976/0.5)$, is –0.952, which
in this case is hardly noticeable – i.e. there is very little overlap between the phases.

Parker and colleagues (Parker, Vannest, Davis & Sauber, 2011) also noted the use of the
Mann–Whitney U test for measuring the overlap, or non-overlap, between two series of
data. The Mann–Whitney test is a non-parametric test described in many basic statistics

TABLE 6.6 Computing the Mann–Whitney by hand

	Data arranged in descending order																U
Baseline data	18	17	16	14	14	13	12										
Intervention data						13	12	9	8	7	6	6	6	5	5	5	4	
#Baseline value	0	0	0	0	0	0.5	1.5										**2**
#Intervention value						5.5	6.5	7	7	7	7	7	7	7	7	7	7	**82**

textbooks and is available in many software packages. The test is simple enough to compute by hand, as demonstrated here, although it is necessary to look up the significance values of the U statistic in a reference table, which are widely published in textbooks and on the Internet.

To help visualise the overlap, it is helpful to arrange the data in rows by order of magnitude, and this is presented in Table 6.6 for the current data set. The baseline data and intervention data are each listed in rows, and as it is expected that the intervention will reduce the score, the data are in descending order. In this example, we can see that the data overlap at values 12 and 13. To calculate the U statistic, we assign each data point in the series a value. The value will be the count of data points in the comparison series that precedes the observation data point. Where a comparison data point has the same value as the observation data point (a tie), then a value of 0.5 is added. In the baseline data, there are no overlapping points with values of 14 or higher, so these data points have an assigned value of 0. At 13, there is a tie with an intervention data point, and so a value of 0.5 is assigned. At 12, there is one preceding intervention data point (13) and there is a tie (12), so a value of 1.5 is assigned. The sum of the assigned values is the U statistic.

The U statistic can be calculated as a measure of the overlap from the perspective of either data series, and as a measure of overlap it can be calculated with ascending or descending data. So in this case, for the intervention data, there are five baseline data points that precede the first data point of 13, and there is a tie, creating an assigned value of 5.5. At 12, there are six preceding data points and a tie (assigned value = 6.5), and for data points from 9 to 4 all seven baseline data points preceding the observation data point (assigned value = 7).

In this case the baseline U is the smaller value, or U_S, 2, and the intervention U is the larger value, or U_L, 82. Given the number of overlapping possibilities (the range of U) is $n_1.n_2$ then if we know one value we can calculate the other from the formula: $n_1.n_2 = U_S + U_L$. As a check for this case, $n_1.n_2 = 7*12 = 84$; and $U_S + U_L = 2 + 82 = 84$.

Once we have the U_S value, the significance can be looked up in the reference table. In this case, U = 2 and this is significant with a two-tailed test for the minimally conventional level when p = 0.05, so we might conclude that there is a statistically relevant non-overlap in the data set.

Controlling trend: Tau-U

SIMPLE AB COMPARISONS

All of the preceding simple analyses can be done when there is no trend in the baseline data. Figure 6.5 shows four patterns of data (there are many others) where the preceding overlap statistics might be misleading. Each panel represents a simple AB design with the phases separated by the vertical dashed line.

In panel (a) there is a marked upward trend in the baseline followed by a similarly marked downward trend in the treatment phase. The result is that the mean (and median) value in both phases is equivalent and there is no overlap in the data. As a consequence none of the simple tests we have considered would give a statistically significant result. One interpretation of the data is that the intervention is successful in reversing the increase in the baseline. We might be able to test the difference between trends with an appropriate analysis. An alternative hypothesis is that the baseline and treatment phases just happen to coincide with a natural cycling in the participant and there is no real treatment effect. The way to test this is to reverse the treatment, i.e. conduct an ABA experiment but ensure that the second A phase is at least as long as the combined initial AB phase. If there is natural cycling then this should occur in the extended second A phase.

Panel (b) shows a sequence in which the outcome is increasing in the baseline phase, and this continues in the treatment phase. In this case the data barely overlap and the means/medians are obviously different. Our tests would show 'significance', but if

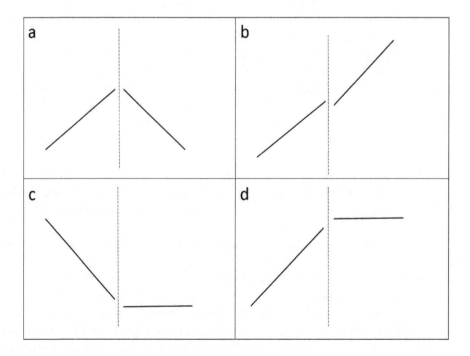

FIGURE 6.5 Problems in interpretation of data patterns

improvement is indexed by an increase it is difficult to discern whether the treatment is effective or whether the person has just continued to improve as time passes. There may be a treatment effect if it could be shown that the slope of the treatment phase is greater than the slope of the baseline phase. Essentially we need to demonstrate that the intervention causes a discontinuity in the trend of the slope.

In panel (c) improvement in the target problem is indicated by low scores, whereas in panel (d) an improvement is indicated by a high score. Panels (c) and (d) show situations where there are marked trends in the baseline followed by a treatment phase characterised by a level slightly below (panel c) or above (panel d) the final data point of the baseline. One of the preceding overlap statistics would record a difference between the two phases, but we would obviously need to exercise caution in our interpretation of the data. The pattern in panel (c) suggests that there is a 'floor effect', i.e. that during the baseline the problem decreased and the treatment just happened to coincide with the natural floor improvement, whereas in panel (d) the baseline ends at the natural ceiling of improvement. In both cases statistical tests would be misleading and we need to consider the alternative that treatment had no effect.

Parker and his colleagues (Parker, Vannest, Davis *et al.*, 2011) developed the Tau-U test in an attempt to control for data with trend in the baseline. The test is called Tau-U because it combines elements of two non-parametric tests: Kendall's rank correlation test (Tau) and the Mann–Whitney U statistic, used to analyse the non-overlap of all pairs statistic (NAP). To illustrate the use of Tau-U we will use the following data set in which improvement is indicated by lower scores. The values of the data are:

> Baseline (n = 7): 15, 12, 16, 15, 11, 14, 10
> Treatment (n = 9): 8, 11, 6, 12, 4, 5, 8, 7, 5

and Figure 6.6 shows a plot of the data. From the plot it appears as if there is a downward trend in the baseline phase. The broadened medians of the two phases are baseline = 13.33 and treatment = 7. The two lines marking the overlap zone suggest a degree of overlap.

Parker and colleagues note that both Tau and U are based on Kendall's S distribution and they are both tests of 'dominance'. Table 6.7 illustrates the basic idea of dominance in the rank order of the data. The basics of the Tau-U analysis can be understood if we construct a table that includes both baseline and treatment data in a particular order. The rows of the table are arranged in descending order, i.e. beginning with the first baseline session and ending with the last treatment session. The columns are arranged in the reverse manner, beginning with the last treatment session and ending with the first baseline session. This means that all pairwise comparisons between data points are made in a 'time forward' direction. We begin by comparing the first baseline point (value = 15) with the last treatment point (value = 5) and record a minus sign if the treatment point is less than the baseline point, a plus sign if it is greater and a T if the data are tied.

As we work across the first row (top line of the shaded portion) we reach a point where we are making comparisons between the baseline data points, in the non-shaded area, and we continue coding the response in the same way. We repeat the process row by row. The 0s represent the comparison of each data point with itself and are not used in the computations. The matrix comprises three distinct areas. The first 7 rows and 9 columns

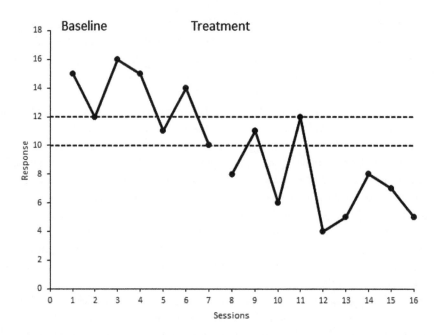

FIGURE 6.6 Simple AB design with apparent trend in the baseline and an overlap between the two phases

Table 6.7 Data layout for the computation of Tau-U

			Treatment (B)									Baseline (A)						
	Session →	16	15	14	13	12	11	10	9	8	7	6	5	4	3	2	1
	↓ Data	5	7	8	5	4	12	6	11	8	10	14	11	15	16	12	15
Baseline	1 15	–	–	–	–	–	–	–	–	–	–	–	–	T	+	–	0
	2 12	–	–	–	–	–	T	–	–	–	–	+	–	+	+	0	
	3 16	–	–	–	–	–	–	–	–	–	–	–	–	–	0		
	4 15	–	–	–	–	–	–	–	–	–	–	–	–	0			
	5 11	–	–	–	–	–	+	–	T	–	–	+	0				
	6 14	–	–	–	–	–	–	–	–	–	–	0					
	7 10	–	–	–	–	–	+	–	+	–	0						
Treatment	8 8	–	–	T	–	–	+	–	+	0							
	9 11	–	–	–	–	–	T	–	0								
	10 6	–	+	+	–	–	+	0									
	11 12	–	–	–	–	–	0										
	12 4	+	+	+	+	0											
	13 5	T	+	+	0												
	14 8	–	–	0													
	15 7	–	0														
	16 5	0															

represent all the comparisons between baseline and treatment points ($n = 63$) as in the computation of the NAP statistic (the Mann–Whitney U), as shown by the grey shading. There are two non-shaded areas in the upper right and lower left representing comparisons within the baseline and treatment phases, and these are used to compute the trend in each phase. For each part of the matrix we find the number of positives, negatives and ties. The number of pairs in each partition is also determined. If n_A is the number of observations in the first phase (baseline) and n_B is the number in the second, treatment, phase then the number of pairs for the comparison between the two phases is the product of the number of data points in each phase ($n_A n_B = 63$) and the number of pairs in the baseline and treatment phases are ($n_A(n_A - 1))/2$ and ($n_B (n_B - 1))/2$, respectively. These data are shown on the left side of Table 6.8.

From the basic data in the table we can compute S and then Tau-U for each part of the matrix and the matrix overall. In the current example the values for Tau-U in the A vs B, and A and B columns are all negative. The interpretation of this is that there is a negative trend in both the phases (−0.48 and −0.28) and the values observed in the B phase are lower than those in the A phase. This really confirms our visual inspection of the graph. The information on the complete data set (full matrix) simply indicates a downward trend overall. The interpretation of whether or not the intervention phase is significantly different from the baseline is therefore compromised by the initial downward trend in the baseline data, and we might reasonably argue that this would have continued in the treatment phase even if we had not implemented treatment. The Tau-U statistic can help us decide between the interpretations of the data. The logic is straightforward: we need to compute a statistic that compares the baseline and treatment phases but removes the influence of the baseline. Tau-U does this by subtracting the data on the trend in phase A from the A vs B comparison. The resulting values are shown in the far right-hand column. Note that the number of pairs remains at 63 because the comparison between phases A and B still remains. It is important to carry out the simple arithmetic in the right order in order to obtain the right signs. For example, the number of positives is $3 - 5 = -2$ and $S = (-2 - 43) = -45$. The value of Tau-U is $-45/63 = -0.71$, which is smaller than the uncorrected comparison of

TABLE 6.8 Computing Tau-U

| | Partitions of the matrix | | | Full matrix | Tau-U |
	A vs B	Trend in A	Trend in B	Total	A vs B − Trend in A
N of pairs	63	21	36	120	63
N of positives	3	5	11	19	−2
N of negatives	58	15	22	98	43
N of ties	2	1	3	5	1
S ($N_{pos} - N_{neg}$)	−55	−10	−10	−79	−45
Tau (S/N of Pairs)	−.87	−.48	−.28	−.66	−.71
z	−2.91	−1.50	−1.09		−2.38
p	0.0036	0.1331	.2971		.017

−0.87. It is possible to test the significance of all the Tau values, and Parker and his colleagues have a freely available online calculator (Vannest, Parker & Gonen, 2011). The values of z and its associated probability are shown in the last two rows of Table 6.8. This analysis shows that despite our visual impression of a downward trend in both A and B phases, neither of these is statistically significant in conventional terms. Nevertheless it might be advisable to remove the influence of the baseline trend so that our analysis is as conservative (cautious) as possible. Inspection of the uncorrected and corrected contrast between the AB phases shows that even when the trend in baseline is removed the contrast remains significant; the value of Tau has dropped from −0.87 to −0.71. As a consequence we might be reasonably confident that the intervention is associated with a statistically significant change.

Beyond simple AB comparisons

So far we have considered the capacity of Tau-U to make comparisons between two phases (A vs B) and to make the same comparison controlling for any trend in phase A. It is also possible to test two other combinations: (1) a comparison of A vs B controlling for the trend in phase B, when we have evidence of trend in phase B; and (2) the comparison between A vs B controlling for trend in phase A and phase B, if both phase A and B contain trends. These four options make the Tau-U procedure very flexible but, as in all data analysis, it is important to have a clear *a priori* plan of analysis and not to 'go fishing' for results using every possible combination.

ABAB DESIGNS

One of the apparent limitations of Tau-U is that it can only make a comparison between adjacent phases of data in an AB design. Parker *et al.* (2011) have suggested a plausible solution to this problem so that it can be applied to ABAB and multiple-baseline designs. For ABAB designs the solution is to break the data into two AB designs, conduct separate analyses on each AB pair and then combine the results in a 'mini' meta-analysis. I would also suggest an intermediate stage, which is to use Tau-U to test for the predicted reversal effect in the middle BA pairing. This is consistent with the logic of experimental control in ABAB designs (Chapter 4), because reversal of the treatment should be associated with a significant change in performance in the direction of the initial baseline observations. Failure to observe a reversal in the BA pair of phases would undermine the validity of the interpretation.

MULTIPLE BASELINES

Multiple baselines can be considered as a series of AB designs with varying baseline and treatment phases, and the solution is to run a separate analysis for each of the AB components and then combine the results. Similarly if an investigator has run a series of AB experiments, separate analysis combining the results will give an omnibus analysis of the series. The online calculator provided by Parker and colleagues (Vannest *et al.*, 2011) includes a facility for combining analyses across phases and subjects.

Tests for differences between phases 2: randomisation tests

The principle of randomisation tests is relatively simple, and it is possible to conduct basic examples by hand. This section will consider randomisation tests available for some of the common single-case designs: AB, ABAB, multiple-baseline and alternating treatments designs. Randomisation tests are well suited to analysing single-case data because they are non-parametric and make no assumptions about the nature of the error structure in the data. The basis for a randomisation test is that it uses only the data gathered in the study and constructs a test that essentially asks: 'given all the possible ways in which the data can be arranged, what is the probability of this particular set of observations occurring?' For example, imagine you have a bag with 10 balls (n) in it, each marked with a number from 1 to 10. You draw two balls with the numbers 3 and 1 from it. What is the chance of the sum of the numbers of the balls you have drawn being 4 or less? It is fairly easy to work out that there are only two possible combinations (r) that meet this criterion – (3 + 1) and (2 + 1) – all other combinations will give totals of 5 or more. In order to work out the probability of drawing balls with a total of 4 or less we need to determine how many ways can we select 2 balls from 10. This can be written symbolically as $\binom{n}{r}$ and it is worked out as

$$\frac{n!}{r!(n-r)!}$$

When we use this equation to work out how many ways we can draw two balls from 10, i.e.

$$\frac{10!}{2!(10-2)!}$$

the answer is 45. To find out the chances of drawing two balls with a total of 4 or less we simply divide $2/45 = 0.044$, so the chance of this happening is less than 1 in 20.

The essential component of randomisation tests is that they are only valid if the decision about when to begin treatment and, in the case of multiple-baseline designs, allocate individuals to a particular 'arm' of the design, is made in advance and decided on the basis of randomisation. Whereas in randomised controlled trials individuals are randomised to treatment groups in an attempt to remove selection bias, the randomisation in single-case designs randomises when treatment is started and is an additional control against several threats to validity (reactive intervention, history, maturation). Because randomisation tests require that the length of baselines and treatment sessions be determined before the start of the study, they may not fit comfortably in pure clinical settings where time may be limited and other criteria for instigating treatment will be more salient. They are, however, ideal for research applications in which pilot studies have already provided information about the likely impact of treatment – an example of this approach is given in Chapter 7. Under these conditions randomisation tests offer a powerful tool (Edgington & Onghena, 2007; Heyvaert & Onghena, 2014; Onghena & Edgington, 2005).

Randomisation test for AB designs

The key features of a randomisation test for a simple AB time-series design are shown in Table 6.9. A number of decisions are required. First, we need to determine the length of the study, including the baseline and intervention. This is made easier if we have already run a number of other single-subject studies beforehand and established baseline and response characteristics. In the example in Table 6.9 the study has been planned to last for 4 weeks with 28 daily observations, shown in row 1. Second, we must decide which research hypothesis we are going to test. In this case we simply expect the average score in the baseline (A) to be greater than the average score in the treatment (B) sessions ($A_{average} > B_{average}$). The differences between the average in phases A and B ($A_{average} - B_{average}$) will form our test statistic and, if our hypothesis is right, we expect this value to be positive. Although we have chosen the average score in the two phases, randomisation tests are very flexible and we could equally well use the median or broadened median, a measure of trend or variability in each phase in order to construct our test statistic.

Third, we must decide the minimum number of data points we are prepared to accept in the baseline and treatment phases. In this case our prior studies suggested that a minimum of five data points was required to obtain a stable baseline and a similar number of points to establish the effect of treatment, i.e. we already know that the treatment effect is likely to occur relatively rapidly after its introduction. The second line of Table 6.9 shows the minimum number of baseline and treatment sessions, i.e. days 1–5 and 24–28, respectively, and the third line indicates the 18 possible days on which treatment can be randomly assigned to begin. We select one of 18 possible points using a random number table or generator: the RANDBETWEEN(6,23) command in Excel will return a value for a possible starting session, or the SCRT (Single-Case Randomisation Test) program within the SCDA (Single-Case Data Analysis) package can be used to design the experiment (Bulté & Onghena, 2013).

In Table 6.9, treatment was randomly assigned to begin on day nine and the sequence of sessions assigned to the AB phase is shown in the row labelled 'Implemented'. Although, in this case, we have chosen five data points as the minimum number for both baseline and treatment phases, the chosen number does not have to be identical. Under other circumstances we might require a longer period to be sure of a treatment effect (e.g. de Jong et al., 2005). We can now begin the experiment and collect data over the 28 days of the study. The data obtained are shown in the 'Data' row in the table, with the baseline points shaded grey and the treatment data devoid of shading.

Having obtained the data, we can construct our randomisation test by computing the test statistic (mean of the baseline − mean of treatment) for all possible 18 combinations that we could have run with shortest to longest baseline. In Table 6.9 these are shown as a series of rows with a step-like characteristic where the baseline phase is shaded light grey and the treatment phase is dark grey. The final column for these rows shows the values for the test statistic and the actual observed value we obtained is shown with a box around it. The observed value is 8.70. If we arrange the final column in order of magnitude it will be obvious that our observed value is the largest of all the possible 18 combinations, so the probability of this ($^1/_{18}$) = 0.055. What we observed was the most extreme possible,

TABLE 6.9 Constructing and analysing a randomisation test for an AB design. The light grey shaded area shows the possible baselines while the dark grey area shows the treatment sessions.

Days	1	2	3	4	5	6	7	8	9	10	11	12	13	14	15	16	17	18	19	20	21	22	23	24	25	26	27	28	
Phase	A	A	A	A	A																			B	B	B	B	B	
Randomise options						R	R	R	R	R	R	R	R	R	R	R	R	R	R	R	R	R	R						
Implemented	A	A	A	A	A	A	A	A	B	B	B	B	B	B	B	B	B	B	B	B	B	B	B	B	B	B	B	B	
Data	10	14	12	14	10	13	13	12	5	1	3	7	3	1	4	2	2	3	2	6	7	1	5	5	3	7	2	2	
Shortest baseline >																													7.26
																													7.80
																													8.33
Observed data >																													8.70
																													7.97
																													6.79
																													6.08
																													6.06
																													5.53
																													2.48
																													4.52
																													4.00
																													3.50
																													3.17
																													2.67
																													2.85
																													3.29
Longest baseline>																													2.59

but it is still higher than the conventional $p < 0.05$. This example neatly illustrates one limitation of the randomisation test if one is concerned with conventional significance levels. This is that the smallest obtainable probability will be the inverse of the number of randomisation options. If one wishes to obtain the conventional level of $p < 0.05$ then there must be at least 20 randomisation options.

In order to be confident that the effect is robust we need to replicate the study; if we do this we may not need to have specific 20 randomisation points because we are able to combine the data across cases to obtain an omnibus p value. For example, in a series of AB experiments in which there are 10 possible randomisation points for each experiment, the smallest obtainable probability is 0.10, not considered significant in conventional terms. If we run a series of 5 replications and obtain individual p values of 0.10, 0.20, 0.20, 0.30 and 0.30 and combine these probabilities in a mini meta-analysis, then the chance of obtaining such an extreme set of p values is 0.0134 (Edgington & Onghena, 2007). The method for doing this is shown in the appendix to this chapter.

Randomisation test for ABAB design

There have been several proposals for randomisation tests for ABAB designs, with that proposed by Onghena (1992) following the logic laid out for the AB design we have just considered. Onghena notes that in the ABAB design there are three points where decisions about changing the phase must be made: (1) the transition between the first baseline period and the first treatment period; (2) the transition between the first treatment and second baseline; and (3) the transition between the second baseline and second treatment. Mathematically these transitions are a set of triplets with each number representing a point of phase change. The randomisation procedure should define all possible sets of triplets within the boundaries that we decide before the experiment is conducted. Onghena gives the example of an ABAB study with 24 measurement points and where there must be a minimum of 4 data points in each phase. In this case there are 165 possible triplets, i.e. points where the transitions between phases can occur. It is possible to work these out by hand, but the SCDA package (Bulté & Onghena, 2013) will compute them more easily. Onghena suggests that a test statistic (T) that compares the combined effects within each phase is the most straightforward. For example, the comparison $T = (A1_{average} + A2_{average})/2 - (B1_{average} + B2_{average})/2$ compares the difference between the sums of the means for the baseline (A) and treatment (B) phases. As before, we can replace the average with other measures, e.g. broadened median or trend, as befits our hypothesis. Table 6.10 shows the data used by Onghena to illustrate the computations.

As in the analysis of the AB design, once the data are collected we need to compute all possible (165) combinations of the data and determine the probability of our observed T or a more extreme value occurring. The means of the four phases are: $A_1 = 4$, $A_2 = 3$, $B_1 = 2$ and $B_2 = 1$, where the subscripts refer to the first and second occurrence of the condition. Our test statistic, $T = (4 + 3)/2 - (2 + 1)/2 = 2$. The complete set of the 165 randomised alternatives is computed and the 10 most extreme values are: 1.886, 1.886, 1.9306, 1.9306, 1.9306, **2.000**, 2.0576, 2.057, 2.057, 2.098.

TABLE 6.10 The randomisation test for an ABAB design

Session	1	2	3	4	5	6	7	8	9	10	11	12
Condition	A1	A1	A1	A1	A1	A1	B1	B1	B1	B1	B1	B1
Data	6	2	5	3	4	4	1	2	3	1	3	2

Session	13	14	15	16	17	18	19	20	21	22	23	24
Condition	A2	A2	A2	A2	A2	A2	B2	B2	B2	B2	B2	B2
Data	2	3	4	2	4	3	0	1	2	0	2	1

Data from Onghena (1992, Table 1) are used to illustrate the application of a randomisation procedure to ABAB design. A1 and A2 are the first and second baseline phases, and B1 and B2 the treatment phases.

The observed value, in bold, is 5th highest in the ranking and thus the probability of it or a larger value occurring by chance is $5/165 = 0.03$.

One feature of randomisation tests, illustrated by the ABAB design, is that as the complexity of the design increases the power of the test is generally better than for an AB design. The example given by Onghena (1992) had 24 observations with a minimum of 4 in each phase, which gave 165 possible randomisations. Even with 21 observations with a minimum of 4 data points per phase, there are 56 possibilities. A second feature, which is not present in the non-overlap methods, is that the randomisation test for the ABAB design uses all of the data to perform an omnibus test whereas non-overlap methods have to break the design down into its constituent parts, run several analyses and then reintegrate the findings. Randomisation tests are superior in this regard.

Randomisation tests for multiple baseline designs

If the number of studies being published is an accurate indicator (Chapter 4), then multiple baseline designs are amongst the most popular in use and there are several proposals for randomisation tests for multiple baseline designs, all with slightly different approaches. In order to compare the methods we need to be sure we have a common terminology. For this purpose it might be helpful to consider multiple baseline designs as a series of replicated AB studies, each of which has a different baseline length. It is convenient to refer to each of these AB sequences as units. Recall too that multiple baseline designs have three general options – between subjects, within subjects across different behaviours and within subjects (same behaviour) across different contexts. For convenience we will simply refer to these as subjects, so in this case a subject can refer to either a between-subject design or one of the within-subject designs.

Wampold and Worsham's (1986) approach to the problem proposed that one specified the number of units, the number of observations within units and the length of baseline for each unit before the start of the experiment. For example, one might design a study lasting for 20 sessions and having four units (subjects or behaviours). The length of baselines for these units could be assigned as 6, 8, 11 and 14 sessions. The units are then randomly allocated. For a design with N units there are N! ways in which subjects can be assigned to the different AB designs. The drawback to this otherwise elegant approach is that the power of the study is limited. For example, with three units, generally regarded as the minimum for a multiple baseline design, there are 6 alternatives, which means that the minimum probability that can be obtained is $1/6 = 0.167$. This number rises to 24 ($p = 0.042$) with four units and 120 ($p = 0.008$) with five units to be randomised.

Marascuilo and Busk (1988) suggested an alternative strategy by proposing that the timing of the intervention should be determined randomly for each unit, as in the AB design (above). If there are k possible points where the intervention might start and N units, then this leads to kN possible start points. This proposal gives greater power than Wampold and Worsham's method. When both k and N are 4 there are 256 possible randomisation points ($p = 0.004$), but the amount of control over when the intervention will occur is less. In addition, staggering of interventions cannot be guaranteed and this undermines the logic of the multiple baseline design (see Chapter 4).

It is not surprising that someone should try and combine the best of both Wampold and Worsham's and Marascuilo and Busk's approaches, keeping the design feature of the former and the power of the latter. Koehler and Levin (1998) suggested a method which they called *regulated randomisation*. In this procedure the investigator can both allocate subject to units and randomise the times at which the intervention is given within each unit. The number of possible randomisations is given by the formula, N! $\Pi_i^N k_i$ (the Π_i^N symbol will be unfamiliar to many but it simply means a product, i.e. multiplication). For example, if we have 4 subjects (N) and for each unit there are 5 (k_i) points where the intervention may randomly start, then the equation N! $\Pi_i^N k_i$, i.e. $4! \times 5 \times 5 \times 5 \times 5 = 24 \times 625$, yields a staggering 15,000 alternatives, a number sufficiently large to take up considerable computer time to generate all the possible test statistics that are needed to compute the exact probability of the obtained result. The solution in this case is to use a Monte Carlo version of the randomisation test. Rather than compute every randomisation alternative, the Monte Carlo method simulates the distribution of the data by randomly sampling them, so rather than computing the test statistics for all 15,000 possibilities the software will compute a specified number, e.g. 1,000 and compare the obtained statistic to this sampled distribution. Even with 3 subjects, probably the minimum number for a multiple baseline design (Kratochwill *et al.*, 2010) and 3 possible start points, there will be 3! $\times$ 3 $\times$ 3 $\times$ 3 = 162 potential randomised assignments. Working out all the possibilities by hand would not only be time consuming but tedious and error prone. Fortunately the SCDA programme (Bulté & Onghena, 2013) will fulfil this task and will also select one of the many alternatives for the researcher to implement.

For example, we plan a between-subjects multiple baseline study with 3 subjects. Our pilot studies have shown that good baseline data can be obtained in 5 sessions and this will be the minimum number of points in the baseline phase. The intervention phase can therefore begin from session 6 onwards. We decide that there are 3 possible start points for the first unit, at sessions 6, 7 and 8. As we want to retain the staggered control of the multiple baseline design, the first possible session that can be a start point for the second unit is 9 and for the third unit the first possible session will be 12. There are 162 possible

TABLE 6.11 Data used to illustrate the randomisation test for a multiple baseline design

Session	1	2	3	4	5	6	7	8	9	10	11	12	13	14	15	16	17	18	19	20
Subject 1	11	9	11	8	12	8	9	8	12	8	8	10	8	6	5	8	6	6	8	5
Subject 2	8	6	7	7	8	6	7	6	3	5	4	7	3	7	5	5	7	6	6	4
Subject 3	13	13	10	11	11	13	9	11	12	6	4	3	6	7	3	6	7	7	6	4

The baseline data are shown in the shaded portion of the rows.

combinations of triplets and subjects and the SCDA software can be used to both generate all the sequences and select one for implementation. In this example the software selected the sequence 13, 7, 10. This means that treatment for the first subject begins at session 13, and for the second and third subjects the treatment will begin at sessions 7 and 10 respectively. The experiment is run and we obtain the data shown in Table 6.11. Our test statistic is the average difference between the baseline and treatment phases aggregated over the three subjects. The observed test statistic is = 3.398, and the last 10 values obtained by randomisation are: 3.311, 3.332, 3.367, 3.385, **3.398,** 3.431, 3.433, 3.451, 3.466, 3.484.

The observed test statistic is shown in bold and is the 6th most extreme value, so the computed p value is $(6/162) = 0.037$. The randomisation test indicated that there is a significant statistical effect of treatment. Of course the data may be plotted to achieve the standard staggered graphical display. Inspection of the data plots shows that although there are differences between the baseline and treatment phases, there is still considerable variability in the treatment phases and we might wish to consider whether, in this case, our clinical criteria have been met.

Randomisation test for alternating treatments designs

In Chapter 4 we noted that alternating treatments designs have two general forms, one with a baseline period before the different treatments are introduced and one without a baseline. In both cases the focus of the analysis is the phase when the treatments are allowed to alternate. It is this latter component where randomisation can help us design and analyse a study. By way of illustration, consider an early experiment investigating a potential therapeutic intervention in cognitive therapy. Teasdale and Fennell (1982) asked the question, 'does the procedure challenging dysfunctional thoughts in people with depression reduce the experience of depression?' More specifically they asked whether the cognitive modification procedure would reduce belief in the thought, the primary outcome, and a reduction in depressive mood (secondary outcome). To do this they compared periods when the therapist engaged the client in the standard thought-challenging protocol with periods when the therapist facilitated the patient in exploring the meaning of the thought. The results of the study were that there was a greater change in belief after the thought-challenging intervention, and it was consistently accompanied by greater reduction in self-rated depressed mood than was obtained in the thought exploration condition.

Let us re-imagine this study from the perspective of a randomised alternating treatments design comparing two conditions, A and B, in which we have decided that each participant (n = 4) will have four sessions of each condition, i.e. total of 8 sessions. If the sequence of these sessions is completely randomised, then there will be $\binom{8}{4}$ = 8!/4!4! = 70 possible assignments. Clearly we may wish to put some constraints on selecting from this list and it might advisable not to select the sequences where either the A or B treatment occurs more than twice. In this case there are 34 possible assignments, also shown in Table 6.11, and we select one of these at random for each of our subjects. These are shown in bold in type in Table 6.12. The smallest probability that can be obtained with 34 permutations is 1/34 = 0.029.

We then conduct the study on 4 patients and the first gives the following data for belief ratings: A = 5, 4, 6, 3 and B = 2, 0, 3, 1.

Condition A is thought challenge and B is the control, thought exploration, intervention. The value given is the within-session change in the strength of the belief, scaled between 0 and 7, so that a positive score represents a decrease in the strength of belief. The test statistic is the difference between the average of the two conditions (A = 4.5 and B = 1.5), which is 3. The probability of this result being observed is $p = 0.059$ if the null hypothesis is true. The other three replications give p values of 0.029, 0.059 and 0.063. When these are combined (see the appendix to this chapter for details), the probability of observing

TABLE 6.12 Randomisation for an alternating treatments design

A A B A B A B B	B A A B A A B B
A A B A B B A B	B A A B A B A B
A A B B A A B B	**B A A B A B B A**
A A B B A B A B	B A A B B A A B
A A B B A B B A	B A A B B A B A
A B A A B A B B	B A B A A B A B
A B A A B B A B	B A B A A B B A
A B A B A A B B	B A B A B A A B
A B A B A B A B	B A B A B A B A
A B A B A B B A	B A B A B B A A
A B A B B A A B	B A B B A A B A
A B A B B A B A	B A B B A B A A
A B B A A B A B	B B A A B A A B
A B B A A B B A	B B A A B A B A
A B B A B A A B	B B A A B B A A
A B B A B A B A	B B A B A A B A
A B B A B B A A	B B A B A B A A

The 34 randomisation options are selected from the possible 70 to ensure that a treatment is not given on more than 2 adjacent occasions. The four randomly selected for the study are shown in bold.

this set of p values in 4 replications is $p < 0.00009$, giving support for the hypothesis that this particular part of the treatment protocol appears to be effective in the predicted manner.

CONCLUSIONS

This chapter has focused on two classes of statistical analysis that are relatively easy to apply and which avoid the problems of having to model correlated error terms that are likely to be present in the data. Both non-overlap and randomisation tests have their place in the analysis of single-case data.

The non-overlap methods are graphically intuitive and can mostly be carried out without specialist software. They are ideal for analysing data where it has not been possible to randomise the timing of onset of different experimental phases. As such, they are the primary tools for analysing data generated by curious clinicians in a clinical setting. At their weakest they add a level of description to the data set and at their strongest it is possible to conduct formal non-parametric statistical tests (Mann–Whitney and Tau-U).

Randomisation tests are a little more complex and require the investigator to plan the study in some detail, and therefore they will be more difficult to apply when spontaneously following one's clinical curiosity. On the other hand, when the investigator has enough information about the likely course of treatment, the additional experimental control and statistical power offered by randomisation tests will enhance the data analysis. Randomisation tests should be seriously considered under these circumstances.

The present chapter describes use of the randomisation test for the AB, ABAB, multiple baseline and alternating treatment designs. As yet there is no test for the changing criterion design, but Onghena (1992) has indicated how such a test might be developed and Edgington and Onghena (2007) give details of other design options as do Dugard, File and Todman (2011). In the illustrative examples in this chapter the test statistic used in all the randomisation tests is the difference in the average response between phases. Randomisation tests are very flexible and it is possible to use test statistics derived from other summary measures, e.g. median, variability or trend, but each of these requires some pre-processing of the data before they can be submitted to the randomisation test. For the most part, randomisation tests require specialist software but most of these programmes are free and relatively easy to use.

Statistical analysis is neither a supplement nor an alternative to visual analysis, and both approaches to analysis are encouraged. Careful construction of visual displays (Chapter 5) is an essential part of the analysis of single-case data. The visual analysis should lead to a description of the data and can give an overall, holistic view. Where necessary, additional exploratory statistical analysis of phases can be conducted using the simple methods discussed at the beginning of this chapter. Thereafter, statistical analyses provide more concise and focused tests of particular aspects of the data testing for between-phase differences and permit the drawing of inferences about the causal impact of treatment. Statistical analysis should contribute to a fuller understanding of the data. It has been argued that there are several advantages of statistical analysis (Kazdin, 2010). Included in these is the fact that statistical analyses can be robustly replicated by other analysts, in contrast to visual analysis where there is evidence of variability between different analysts. It has also been suggested that statistical analysis is capable of detecting small treatment effects that might then become the subject of further development. However, we should remember the distinction between statistical and clinical significance and be aware that they represent different criteria that are not interchangeable. It is possible to have small consistent differences between baseline and treatment phases that are statistically significant but clinically trivial. In the clinical context we will need to pay attention to whether the outcome meets a defined clinical criterion. Chapter 2 discussed how standardised measures could be analysed from this perspective and Chapter 3 considered the sorts of measures, predominantly idiographic ones, used in repeated measurements of single-case experiments. In many cases it is clear what outcomes on these measures will be regarded as clinically important, and these criteria should be used in evaluating the data as a whole. Complete analysis relies on the thoughtful interplay between visual and statistical analysis and a clear statement of what is clinically important.

Methods for statistical analysis of single-case data have developed rapidly over the past few years as researchers have capitalised on developments in general statistical analysis, such as multi-level modelling. Some of the advances have been stimulated by the perceived need to develop an effect size measures for single-case data and to develop robust meta-analytic procedures for combining data across cases. These issues will be discussed in Chapter 7. Most of the new methods require a degree of statistical sophistication and expertise in specialist software, and unless you have a clear need to explore and use these methods they are probably not necessary for a basic analysis of many single-case data sets.

Footnote: software for statistical analysis

Major statistical packages such as SPSS often include non-parametric tests. Alternatives are available as free plug-in modules for Excel, e.g. Real Statistics (www.real-statistics.com for Windows and Mac) and there are several online calculators for several non-parametric statistics, e.g. www.wessa.net/ (Wessa, 2015). Parker and his colleagues recommend StatsDirect (http://statsdirect.com). This is an excellent and easy-to-use programme that works with Excel. It is relatively cheap but only available for Windows.

Computation of the Tau-U statistic and the non-overlap for all pairs analysis can be done with the online calculator at www.singlecaseresearch.org (Vannest *et al.*, 2011). This website also includes a useful YouTube presentation of how to use the software.

The examples of randomisation tests used in the chapter were all conducted using the single-case data analysis package developed by Bulté and Onghena (Bulté & Onghena, 2013). This comprises a suite of three programmes; Single-Case Visual Analysis (SCVA), Single-Case Randomisation Tests (SCRT) and Single-Case Meta-Analysis (SCMA) that run in the R environment. This will run on Windows, Mac and Linux, and the R Commander package provides a more familiar 'point and click' interface. R and all its associated packages are freely available at the Comprehensive R Archive Network (https://cran.r-project.org).

Appendix: combining probabilities

Edgington and Onghena (2007) discuss two procedures (additive and multiplicative) for combining p values. They note that the additive method is a little more conservative if the

p values are dissimilar. The equation for the additive method looks complicated, but in practice it is easy to compute with a calculator and one rarely needs to use more than the first 2 or 3 terms of the numerator.

If the sum of the n independent p values is S, then the probability of getting a sum as small as S is given by:

$$C(n,0)(S-0)^n - C(n,1)(S-1)^n + C(n,2)(S-2)^n - C(n,3)(S-3)^n \ldots n!$$

where $C(n,r) = n!/(-r)!$

Note that as the numerator expands the plus and minus signs between each term alternate. The numerator is expanded until the term (S–n) becomes negative.

Suppose we run six single-case studies in an attempt to replicate the Teasdale and Fennell (1982) experiment. The observed p values for our experiments are: 0.35, 0.25, 0.25, 0.20, 0.25 and 0.20 and the sum of these (S) = 1.5. Although none of the p values for the 6 studies reaches the conventional significance of $p < 0.05$, they are all in the 'right' direction. To evaluate the likelihood of observing these 6 values we use the equation above. As S = 1.5 we only need the first two terms in the numerator before the value of (S–n) becomes negative: $C(6,0)(1.5-0)^6 - C(6,1)(1.5-1)^6 n!$

$$= \frac{1(1.5-0)^6 - (6)(1.5-1)^6}{720!}$$

$$= \frac{11.39 - 0.09375}{720!}$$

$$= 0.01569.$$

The resulting p value is the probability of getting a sum as small as S (1.5 in this case) from six independent p values when each of the six null hypotheses is true, i.e. when the H_0 states that there is no effect. In this case the combined probability is 0.16 (rounded), suggesting that the chance of this occurring is quite small. We might tentatively conclude that the combined studies indicate that we reject the null hypothesis that there is no difference between the two conditions.

REFERENCES

Bulté, I. & Onghena, P. (2013). The single-case data analysis package: Analysing single-case experiments with R software. *Journal of Modern Applied Statistical Methods*, 12(2), 450–78.

Corder, G. W. & Foreman, D. I. (2014). *Non-parametric Statistics: A Step-by-step Approach* (2nd edn). New York: Wiley.

de Jong, J. R., Vlaeyen, J. W. S., Onghena, P., Cuypers, C., den Hollander, M. & Ruijgrok, J. (2005). Reduction of pain-related fear in complex regional pain syndrome type I: the application of graded exposure in vivo. *Pain*, 116(3), 264–75.

Dugard, P., File, P. & Todman, J. (2011). *Small-n Designs: A Practical Guide to Randomisation Tests* (2nd edn). Hove: Routledge – Taylor & Francis Group.

Edgington, E. S. & Onghena, P. (2007). *Randomisation Tests* (4th edn). London: Chapman & Hall/CRC

Fisher, W. W., Kelley, M. E. & Lomas, J. E. (2003). Visual aids and structured criteria for improving visual inspection and interpretation of single-case designs. *Journal of Applied Behavior Analysis*, 36(3), 387–406.

Foster, F. G. & Stuart, A. (1954). Distribution-free tests in time series based on the breaking of records. *Journal of the Royal Statistical Society (Series B)*, 16(1), 1–16.

Heyvaert, M. & Onghena, P. (2014). Randomisation tests for single-case experiments: State of the art, state of the science, and state of the application. *Journal of Contextual Behavioral Science*, 3(1), 51–64.

Kazdin, A. E. (2010). *Single-Case Research Designs: Methods for Clinical and Applied Settings* (2nd edn). Oxford: Oxford University Press.

Kendall, M. (1976). *Time Series*. London: Charles Griffiths.

Koehler, M. J. & Levin, J. R. (1998). Regulated randomisation: A potentially sharper analytical tool for the multiple-baseline design. *Psychological Methods*, 3(2), 206–17.

Kratochwill, T. R., Hitchcock, J., Horner, R., Levin, J., Odom, S. L., Rindskopf, D. & Shadish, W. R. (2010). Single-case technical documentation. Retrieved from *What Works Clearinghouse* website: http://ies.ed.gov/ncee/wwc/pdf/wwe_scd.pdf

Kratochwill, T. R. & Levin, J. R. (eds) (2014). *Single-case Intervention Research: Methodological and Statistical Advances*. Washington, DC: American Psychological Association.

Ma, H. H. (2006). An alternative method for quantitative synthesis of single subject researches: Percentage of data points exceeding the median. *Behavior Modification*, 30(5), 598–617.

Marascuilo, L. A. & Busk, P. L. (1988). Combining statistics for multiple-baseline AB and replicated ABAB designs across subjects. *Behavioral Assessment*, 10(1), 1–28.

Morley, S. & Adams, M. (1989). Some simple statistical tests for exploring single-case time-series data. *British Journal of Clinical Psychology*, 28(1), 1–18.

Onghena, P. (1992). Randomisation tests for extensions and variations of ABAB single-case experimental designs: A rejoinder. *Behavioral Assessment*, 14(2), 153–71.

Onghena, P. & Edgington, E. S. (2005). Customisation of pain treatments: Single-case design and analysis. *Clinical Journal of Pain*, 21(1), 56–68.

Parker, R. I. & Vannest, K. (2009). An improved effect size for single-case research: non-overlap of all pairs. *Behavior Therapy*, 40(4), 357–67.

Parker, R. I., Vannest, K. J. & Davis, J. L. (2011). Effect size in single-case research: a review of nine non-overlap techniques. *Behavior Modification*, 35(4), 303–22.

Parker, R. I., Vannest, K. J., Davis, J. L. & Sauber, S. B. (2011). Combining non-overlap and trend for single-case research: Tau-U. *Behavior Therapy*, 42(2), 284–99.

Parsonson, B. S. & Baer, D. M. (1992). The visual analysis of data, and current research into the stimuli controlling it. In T. R. Kratochwill & J. R. Levin (eds), *Single-case Research Design and Analysis: New Directions for Psychology and Education* (pp. 15–40). Hillsdale, NJ: Lawrence Erlbaum.

Scruggs, T. E., Mastropieri, M. A. & Casto, G. (1987). Quantitative synthesis of single subject research: Methodology and validation. *Remedial and Special Education*, 8(2), 24–33.

Seigel, S. & Castellan, N. J. (1988). *Non-parametric Statistics for the Behavioral Sciences*. New York: Wiley.

Shadish, W. R. (2014). Analysis and meta-analysis of single-case designs: An introduction. *Journal of School Psychology*, 52(2), 109–22.

Shadish, W. R., Rindskopf, D. M., Hedges, L. V. & Sullivan, K. J. (2013). Bayesian estimates of autocorrelations in single-case designs. *Behavior Research Methods*, 45(3), 813–21.

Teasdale, J. D. & Fennell, M. J. V. (1982). Immediate effects on depression of cognitive therapy interventions. *Cognitive Therapy and Research*, 6, 343–53.

Vannest, K. J., Parker, R. I. & Gonen, O. (2011). Single Case Research: web based calculators for SCR analysis. (Version 1.0) [Web-based application] Retrieved 6 August 2015 from www.singlecaseresearch.org

Vlaeyen, J. W., de Jong, J., Geilen, M., Heuts, P. H. & van Breukelen, G. (2001). Graded exposure in vivo in the treatment of pain-related fear: a replicated single-case experimental design in four patients with chronic low back pain. *Behaviour Research and Therapy*, 39(2), 151–66.

Wampold, B. E. & Worsham, N. L. (1986). Randomisation tests for multiple baseline designs. *Behavioural Assessment*, 8, 135–43.

Wessa, P. (2015). Free Statistics Software, Office for Research Development and Education, version 1.1.23-r7. Retrieved 5 October 2015 from www.wessa.net

Chapter 7
Replication, replication, replication

In both single-case and between-group research, being able to make a statement – to generalise – beyond the individual case or trial can only be achieved by replication and subsequent exploration of the successes and failures of replication. Kazdin (2010, p. 372) comments that 'single-case designs (as a methodology) do not inherently produce more or less generalizable effects'. Although he is writing primarily in the context of applied behaviour analysis, where researchers have typically focused on 'strong' interventions that produce immediate and noticeably large changes in the dependent variable (clinical outcome), there is no reason to suspect that the methodology of single-case research *per se* is inherently less replicable when applied elsewhere.

This chapter considers some of the issues around replication in single-case research. As with other texts in this field (Barlow, Nock & Hersen, 2009; Gast, 2010; Kazdin, 2010), the basis for thinking about replication in single-case research draws heavily on the distinction between direct and systematic replication described by Sidman (1960). More recently, researchers have sought consensus on criteria for assessing the number of replications needed to establish a treatment effect (Kratochwill et al., 2010). Once replication has been established we need methods for integrating and combining this information. For the most part, single-case researchers have relied on narrative review (and this chapter will include some examples of this) but, since the 1980s, single-case researchers have sought to establish effect size measures for individual experiments and their combination using meta-analytic methods. These will be illustrated in the latter part of this chapter.

Sidman (1960) defined direct replication as a replication of a given experiment by the same investigator using either new subjects or repeated observations on the same subject under each of several experimental conditions. Direct replication could therefore, in Sidman's terms, be intra- or inter-subject. Although Sidman was specifically writing about experiments with animals in highly controlled experimental environments, the same distinction between intra- and inter-subject (or within and between subject) replication can be made in the clinical research context. Many of the experimental designs discussed in Chapter 4 (ABAB, CCD, multiple baseline-within subject and the alternating treatment design) include an element of within-subject replication. Each of these designs can therefore generate and provide information about the robustness of a possible causal relationship between the intervention and the outcome in an individual case. In the clinical context, where our participants have widely different histories and current life circumstances and where interventions may be more complex and inherently more variable in their delivery, replication across a number of participants by the same investigator perhaps provides a more compelling argument for concluding that there is something to be taken seriously and to warrant the attention of other clinicians and researchers.

For Sidman, systematic replication 'demonstrates that the findings in question can be observed under different conditions from those pertaining in the original experiment' (Sidman, 1960, p. 111). For Sidman, systematic replication meant that the investigator should attempt to replicate the basic functional relationship between a stimulus and the animal's response when conditions such as its motivational state, duration of experimental session and schedule of reinforcement were systematically manipulated. Sidman's view of systematic replication did not necessarily involve experimenters in other laboratories attempting to replicate findings. However, the term 'systematic' also may imply a planned sequence of experiments that logically determine the limits of the phenomena as bounded by different parameters; in the applied clinical context, systematic replication takes on rather different characteristics. It is relatively rare for one researcher or research group to pursue a research question in such a systematic manner, although there are exceptions. It is more likely that once the therapeutic technique has been investigated and published by one group of clinical-researchers, others will attempt to replicate it. Such replications necessarily imply the likelihood of different therapists, a different client pool and variation in the intervention being delivered (this is especially likely when the therapy is complex). Changes in the way the outcome is measured and the choice of different experimental designs are also likely to increase the variability of the conditions, which makes it difficult to understand why a replication attempt has failed. Successful replications, on the other hand, achieve Sidman's goal for systematic replication, i.e. demonstrating that the finding in question can be observed under different conditions. Whereas systematic replication in Sidman's original sense may be relatively easy to assimilate and permit conclusions to be drawn, many replications published in the clinical literature are less easy to assimilate because of the lack of a programmatic approach to replication. Thus reviewers must attempt to impose order on the data in a *post hoc* manner in order to understand sources of variation. The development of statistical methods in the field of meta-analysis provides a potentially powerful set of tools for attempting this.

HOW MANY REPLICATIONS?

Just how many replications should be obtained before one can be reasonably confident that there is a robust finding? In brief there is no hard and fast rule that can be applied. As in many instances in psychological science we must reach our conclusion by weighing the various sources of evidence, including our knowledge of the clinical problem, the likely skills of the clinician-researcher and the features of the experimental design, with consideration also of alternative explanations for the findings. These factors will all play a part in our conclusion. Attempts have and are being made to systematise the process of evaluating the evidence by setting standards for the evaluation of single-case experiments. These are discussed in more detail in Chapter 8, but here we consider one set of guidelines developed by a consensus panel. This comprised seven experts both in methodology of single-case research and in its application in the field of special education, where applied behaviour analysis has been particularly prominent (Kratochwill *et al.*, 2010). These guidelines published by the What Works Clearinghouse (WWC) include standards for assessing the quality of single-case studies and provide recommendations for the minimum number of studies necessary to establish an effect, with the proviso that each study considered meets the necessary quality standard. Although the WWC guidance does not discuss direct and systematic replication explicitly, it does emphasise replicability within a single experiment as a criterion for meeting the evidence standard. These recommendations are explicit; 'each study must include at least three attempts to demonstrate an intervention effect at three different points in time or with three different phase repetitions'. Many of the designs covered in Chapter 4 meet these criteria. The ABAB design is included in this group because there are three attempts to test the intervention: the transitions between the first AB, the BA and the second AB phases. Multiple baseline designs with at least three baselines qualify, as do changing criterion designs with three or more shifts in the criterion. The guidance offered on alternating treatments states that five repetitions of the alternating sequence are required. In essence these criteria are an attempt to codify the internal validity of the experiment. This, however, poses a problem for some designs that do not include repeated phases, the most common of which is the AB design (commonly used in clinical settings where reversal is not possible or always desirable). The WWC authors recognise this and in a footnote they indicate that there 'might be circumstances in which designs without three repetitions meet the standards'. When this happens a case must be made by the principal researcher on the basis of 'content expertise', and at least two reviewers must agree with the decision for a valid consensus to be reached. Although these conditions apply to researchers allied to WWC, they are more widely applicable and in Chapter 8 we will examine judging the quality of studies in more detail.

Many of the basic single-case experimental designs include an element of replication, but it is a matter of debate as to how far this constitutes evidence of direct replication at the study level. The ABAB design replicated over three individuals is certainly stronger evidence of the robustness of the treatment effect, and it is this replication at the individual study level that forms the basis for making a judgement. The WWC guidance recognises this and recommends three criteria as a minimum requirement for combining studies into a single summary rating, i.e. evidence for any effect. They suggest three criteria which are sometimes referred to as the 5–3–20 criteria. First, there should be a minimum of five single-case design research reports examining the intervention that meet the evidence standards. The criterion may include studies that fall short of the highest standard but partly fulfil the requirements. Second, the single-case design studies must be conducted by at least three different research teams in different geographical locations. This item guarantees that there is an element of external replicability, as it is likely that the populations from which individual participants are drawn, the therapists, the physical setting and other parameters will be different. Finally, the minimum number of experiments in the research reports must total at least 20 – in practice this means that the total number of participants may be more than 20.

EXAMPLES OF REPLICATION IN SINGLE-CASE RESEARCH

In the rest of the chapter we examine several examples of replication in single-case research which illustrate the variation in and development of approaches to summarising the data, and that highlight the application of single-case methodology in developing effective interventions. The first example is a series of studies by Vlaeyen and his colleagues (Vlaeyen, Morley, Linton, Boersma & de Jong, 2012) of an intervention for people with chronic pain in which the single-case approach is used. In the subsequent examples, uses of replication in the investigation of specific treatment procedures are illustrated, in both narrative and systematic reviews of single-case literature.

Using single-case research to develop an intervention

There is tremendous potential in the replication of single-case series, where the impact of an intervention can be replicated within and across studies, so that studies sequentially can explore the impact of treatment variables and differences in diagnostic groups. Vlaeyen and his colleagues' work represents an illuminating example of particular relevance for clinical researchers.

People suffering from chronic pain are markedly heterogeneous on almost any measure one cares to consider. They are usually offered complex multidisciplinary psychosocial treatments based on cognitive-behavioural principles. These treatments are also very variable and although there is evidence that they are effective, the overall effect size is small and there appears to be considerable room for improving treatment effectiveness (Morley, Williams & Eccleston, 2013; Williams, Eccleston & Morley, 2012). One strategy to achieve this is to try to include the heterogeneity of patients in the development of treatments that are particularly relevant for subgroups, in effect 'treatment tailoring' (Vlaeyen & Morley, 2005). Vlaeyen and Linton (Vlaeyen & Linton, 2000) summarised the available data on the relationship between pain-related fear of movement, the expectation of harm and subsequent avoidance behaviour. They argued that repeated avoidance of activities would result in the accrual of disability and negative mood so often observed in chronic pain sufferers. At the heart of this model is a belief about certain movements and the likelihood of catastrophic harm. Essentially the chronic pain patient with high fear of pain-related movement believes that if they engage in an activity then severe harm will occur. An example of this might be that the person with low back pain believes that bending and lifting a weight could result in something happening in their spine that will cause paralysis. Vlaeyen and his colleagues recognised that the resulting avoidance behaviour could be treated using well-known principles of graded exposure. An account of the therapy is given in Vlaeyen et al. (2012). Here we look at the series of seven single-case experiments performed by Vlaeyen and his colleagues to establish the efficacy of graded exposure in vivo as a treatment.

A summary of the 7 case series is shown in Table 7.1. Each case series comprised 2 or more single-case experiments. A central feature of 5 of the case series was a simple daily diary comprising 11 items drawn from validated scales that measured fear of movement and re-injury, fear of pain and catastrophising. These are primary dependent variables and each component is expected to reduce if the exposure treatment is effective. The researchers

TABLE 7.1 Summary of single-case experiments to test the validity of graded exposure treatment in chronic pain

Study Number	Year	Purpose	N	Group	Design
1	2002	Pilot	2	CLBP	AB
2	2001	Replication and comparison	4	CLBP	ABC/ACB
3	2002	Replication and comparison	6	CLBP	ABC/ABC
4	2004	Replication in another setting	6	CLBP	Multiple baseline
5	2005	Replication and decomposition	8	CLBP	ABC/D
6	2005	Replication in another diagnostic group	8	CRPS-1	ABC
7	2008	Replication in another diagnostic group	8	Whiplash	ABC

also incorporated other outcomes in some experiments. These included pain intensity (which was not necessarily expected to change) and measures of engagement in activity, which is expected to increase if the therapy is effective. With one exception, all of the case series were conducted in a rehabilitation centre in the Netherlands. The other study was carried out in Sweden by a separate group of investigators who collaborated with the Dutch group.

The first case series comprised just two patients (Vlaeyen, De Jong, Onghena, Kerckhoffs-Hanssen & Kole-Snijders, 2002) with low back pain and used an AB design. A 7-day baseline was followed by a 35-day treatment phase in which 15 treatment sessions were given. In this initial pilot study the investigators applied simple 10 cm visual analogue scales to fear of movement and pain intensity (scored between 0 and 10). Inspection of the data plots showed that reductions in the daily ratings of fear of movement occurred within a few days of starting treatment and continued thereafter, with most change happening in the first 2 weeks of treatment. The stable baseline scores changed rapidly on the introduction of the treatment and the pain intensity scores showed a similar shift. By the end of treatment daily ratings were reduced to between 0 and 1 for fear of movement and 0–3 for pain intensity. The study suggested that graded exposure might be a viable treatment for this group of patients, but the short baseline and lack of a plausible control condition limit the degree of confidence we might have in the findings.

In the second study, 4 patients were recruited to an ABC/ACB design (Vlaeyen, de Jong, Geilen, Heuts & van Breukelen, 2001). The daily diary measure was deployed in this and later studies. After a baseline period of 3 weeks (A) 2 patients received graded exposure for 3 weeks (B). This was followed by a 3-week treatment in which they engaged in a graded activity treatment (C). The important feature here is that the activities in the graded activity treatment were not threatening and the treatment is a *bona fide* treatment widely used in pain rehabilitation programmes. The other 2 patients received the treatments in the reverse order: graded activity followed by graded exposure. The expectation was that only graded exposure would result in a reduction of fear of movement, and this was borne out by the data. The dairy measures of catastrophising, fear of pain and movement were reduced to minimal levels by the end of treatment.

The third study, with 6 patients, attempted a direct replication of the second study using exactly the same ABC/ABC design (Vlaeyen, de Jong, Geilen, Heuts & Breukelen, 2002). There were three modifications to the protocol. First, the baseline was extended to 4 weeks. Second, a measure of behavioural activity (an accelerometer) was added to determine whether self-reported fear reduction was associated with increased behavioural activity. Third, there was concern that the apparent difference in the effectiveness of the two treatments might be attributable to differences in the perceived credibility of the treatments and different expectations of treatment gain. Vlaeyen et al. measured this and found the credibility of the treatments to be equally high (around 8.5 on a 10-point scale). The pattern of data in this study replicated the previous case series, i.e. fear was only reduced during the graded exposure phase and not during the graded activity phase. Behavioural activity also greatly increased during the graded exposure phase, providing the first evidence of behavioural change.

Whereas the first 3 case series established the effectiveness of graded exposure, the fourth case series demonstrated that it could be implemented in another setting by different therapists, with a different population of patients and using slightly different measures (Boersma et al., 2004). The study, conducted in Sweden, involved six participants recruited from the general population and allocated to a multiple baseline design. The baselines for the participants varied between 1 and 7 weeks. Four of the six participants showed marked reductions in the diary measures of fear and avoidance when treatment was introduced. One patient appeared to make a slow improvement during the study, but the data plot did not suggest that the change was associated with the introduction of treatment. Finally, one patient showed no changes. The Swedish study suggested that graded exposure treatment could be implemented beyond the confines of the original development site. It also documented the first cases where treatment was not successful, but the reasons for this are unknown. The Swedish team noted that the therapy required 'new skills to deal with the intricacies of exposure, especially the skill of discovering the most fear provoking activities and addressing inappropriate beliefs'. This raises one important issue with all the studies of this replication sequence: the absence of any external manipulation check. We do not know how well the Swedish team managed to replicate the protocol developed by the Dutch group or how well they adhered to it. Measuring adherence and fidelity to treatment is a problem that is not by any means unique to this particular set of studies (Gearing et al., 2011; Perepletchikova, Treat & Kazdin, 2007).

The graded exposure treatment protocol includes a substantial educational component in the first session before exposure and behavioural experiments are carried out. In the fifth case series the Dutch group sought to investigate the potential influence of this intensive educational session (de Jong, Vlaeyen, Onghena, Goossens et al., 2005). Six patients with chronic low back pain were recruited to the study. Three were allocated to an ABC design and 3 to an ABD sequence. After a baseline period of 3 weeks, all patients had a single education session followed by another period of 3 weeks when no further treatment was given (B). Three patients then received graded exposure (C) for 6 weeks while the other 3 patients received the graded activity treatment (D). In both treatment sequences the education session produced some decrease in the daily measures of fear, catastrophising and beliefs about movement-related harm. Further reductions in the dependent variable were shown in those individuals receiving graded exposure but not in those receiving the graded activity treatment. In this study patients also recorded the difficulty in engaging in several target behaviours, for example, playing table tennis and running, and they also carried an activity monitor. The data on these measures showed no change in behaviour activity during the education phase; change only occurred when graded exposure was introduced. There were some changes in behaviour associated with graded activity, but this was not marked. Results of this case series provided additional evidence for the efficacy of graded exposure. They also suggested that while an intensive education session may change fear beliefs, active graded exposure is required to produce behavioural change.

The remaining 2 case series were conducted to explore whether the fear-avoidance model and the graded exposure treatment could be generalised to 2 other diagnostic groups: patients with post-traumatic (whiplash) neck pain and patients with a disorder called chronic regional pain syndrome-type 1 (CRPS-1). In the sixth case series (de Jong, Vlaeyen, Onghena, Cuypers, et al., 2005) the investigators recruited 8 patients with CRPS-1 and they used the same ABC design that had been used to investigate the impact of the education component. After the education phase there was a 10-week treatment phase with patients receiving 2 treatment sessions per week. As well as daily recordings of fear and pain, patients also recorded their pain and the ease with which they could perform several individually nominated activities such as playing tennis and driving a car. Although graded exposure was highly successful in reducing fear of pain and increasing activity in the 8 patients, there were two features of the data that were different from previous case series. First, the education phase had no impact on the dependent variables, unlike the previous study where there was some evidence of change. Additional assessments of the patients' expectations that treatment would be successful indicated that they were highly sceptical. The second feature of the data was the pattern of change once treatment (phase C) was introduced. Whereas in the previous case series change occurred very soon after the introduction of graded exposure, there was a consistent and marked delay in the CRPS-1 patients. No changes were observed in the first 3 to 4 weeks of treatment, but thereafter change was quite rapid. The data plots suggested that fear of movement and pain intensity show reductions before changes in behavioural performance.

There are several notable differences between the CRPS-1 data and earlier case series with low back pain patients. Given the lag between the start of treatment and the onset of the treatment response, can we be sure that the gains can be attributed to the treatment? As noted earlier, the plausibility of interpreting treatment effect in single-case designs is enhanced if gains occur shortly after treatment onset. Alternative explanations such as maturation, history and measurement artefacts might be considered. These alternatives become less plausible because of the consistency in the replication of the pattern of the data. It would seem that although the treatment can be generalised to CRPS-1, there are some aspects of this disorder that are markedly different from low back pain. A similar pattern of the delayed change was also shown in the final case series in which 8 patients with neck pain arising from whiplash injury were treated (de Jong et al., 2008). This study employed the ABC/ACB design used in case series 2 and 3, with 4 patients being allocated to each sequence. Again the data show little or no change in fear of pain or behaviour during the graded activity phase (C), but marked change once fear was addressed in the graded exposure phase (B).

In summary, this series of 7 single-case studies, which included 40 chronic pain patients, illustrates how the systematic application of single-case methodology can be used both to test the efficacy of a treatment and to begin to explore competing hypotheses regarding the mechanisms of change. The outcome of treatment, at least in the short term, appears to be remarkably consistent in that participants' reports of their beliefs about the fear of the consequences of movement show marked changes in almost every case. The data also show evidence that behavioural activity changed in those cases where it was measured and that the treatment generalised across diagnostic categories to patients with similar beliefs about the functional relationship between movement and harm. The effectiveness with regard to CRPS-1 patients is notable because historically this has been a difficult group to treat. Additional evidence for the effectiveness of graded exposure is provided by a more recent small RCT conducted by the Dutch group (den Hollander et al., 2016). Small-scale RCTs have also been conducted with low back pain groups (Leeuw et al., 2008; Linton et al., 2008; Woods & Asmundson, 2008). The outcomes of these trials were less impressive than the single-case series. A major difference between the case series and the RCTs was the assessment and measurement strategy. The RCTs used standardised measures taken pre- and post-treatment and at follow-up times rather than the idiographic diary measure. Furthermore, all the trials were underpowered and suffered considerable attrition. It is not clear why this is so, but one wonders whether the intensive engagement, via daily measurement, of the patients required in the single-case series might not be a significant part of the treatment success.

Despite the apparent success of this set of single-case studies, they would fail the WWC 5–3–20 rule because the studies were conducted by two research groups. One might even argue that the close links between the two clinical research groups means that they were not truly independent. The main challenge of researchers in this field is to document the success of the treatment with a variety of therapists and at least one more independent clinical research group.

Narrative reviews of single-case research

In contrast to the systematic use of single-case research to establish evidence for an intervention, the following two examples demonstrate the use of existing single-case research to establish the efficacy of a treatment approach.

Use of replication in the investigation of time out

This second example of replication is very different from the preceding one in that it provides an historical overview, or replicative history, of the development and application of time out (Johnson & Pennypacker, 1980). Time out from reinforcement, or simply time out, refers to the removal of positive reinforcers for a period of time. Time out was first named as such in the 1950s when learning theorists were investigating schedules of reinforcement with animal subjects in the laboratory, but it is certain that parents and schoolteachers have used time out as a procedure to reduce the occurrence of undesirable behaviour for many years before that. Time out is a punishment procedure that does not use a physically aversive stimulus, e.g. a smack. Perhaps the most well-known version of time out is sending a child to the 'naughty corner' when he or she commits an undesired behaviour, e.g. hitting another child during playtime. Being isolated essentially removes the individual from access to desired activities (reinforcers).

According to Johnson and Pennypacker (1980), the scientific study of time out began with observations by Skinner in the early 1950s, in which pigeons that made an incorrect response were presented with a brief period of darkness. Several other experimenters explored the basic contingency in which a response was followed by a period where positive reinforcement was unavailable. Using different schedules of reinforcement and different species they showed that animals would respond in order to avoid periods of time out, thus suggesting that time out was in some way aversive. Time out was also examined in the laboratory with humans and it was shown that they too would make responses to avoid periods of time out.

Other work covered in the review explored different instantiations of time out. First, it was shown that physical removal of the reinforcer would effectively suppress unwanted behaviour. For example Baer (1962) showed that by removing the sight and sound of cartoons he could suppress thumb-sucking in a child who sucked his thumb almost 100% of each observation session. This procedure was extended and applied to other behaviours in educational and clinical settings, e.g. inappropriate speech, being out of seat in the classroom and eating and vomiting behaviour. A second strand of experiments investigated ignoring the problem behaviour as a time out procedure, which they noted was demonstrated to be effective for a wide range of behaviour. A third version, and perhaps the most frequently documented by Johnson and Pennypacker, is the procedure whereby the individual is physically isolated for a brief period of time. They concluded that this form of time out has been successfully used to control unacceptable, aggressive, oppositional and self-injurious behaviour.

The use of replication in investigating differential attention

Barlow et al. (2009), developing the work of Barlow and Hersen (1984), give another example of systematic replication in a narrative review of a treatment called differential attention. Whereas time out is technically a punishment procedure, because its purpose is to reduce the frequency of undesirable behaviour, differential attention is a positive reinforcement procedure aimed at increasing desirable behaviour. Differential attention is a particular form of differential reinforcement in which the therapist pays attention to appropriate behaviour by responding with positive social interaction such as smiling, giving praise, making eye contact or otherwise indicating approval. On the other hand the therapist systematically ignores behaviours that are not deemed appropriate. In theory the differential reinforcement of appropriate behaviour should increase the frequency of the desired behaviour while decreasing the frequency of unwanted behaviour. Unlike time out, differential attention does not have an extensive hinterland of experimental analysis in the laboratory. However, Barlow et al. (2009) note that the series of 'over 100 articles, has provided practitioners with a great deal of specific information on the effectiveness of this procedure' (p. 323). They tabulate 65 of the articles (Barlow et al., 2009: Table 10.1, pp. 324–9) between 1959, the year of the first publication, and 1979. They note that, by the 1980s, the treatment was well established and reports of differential attention in the literature were greatly reduced as the technique was incorporated into general parent training packages. Of the 65 articles tabulated by Barlow *et al.*, 30 reported data from a single case, 25 reported data on between two and nine individuals, six reported data on between 10 and 19 individuals and three articles reported data on between 20 and 29 cases. A single article (Hall *et al.*, 1971) reported a series of experiments with between one and 30 participants. In total the data presented by Barlow *et al.* represent 336 individual children treated with a differential attention protocol.

What is notable about this set of articles is the range of children's ages, conditions, settings and therapists represented. Most of the children were between five and 11 years, but the range extended from an 18-month-old girl with temper tantrums to a 19-year-old with severe learning difficulties. Similarly the range of target behaviours was considerable, including temper tantrums, disruptive behaviour in the classroom, crying, being socially isolated, very low frequency of talking, poor study behaviour, non-compliance and oppositional behaviour, self-injurious activity and aggressive behaviour. Likewise the settings ranged from the child's home, classrooms, nurseries and preschool settings to institutional environment. Therapists included parents, teachers, nursing staff and other health professionals. Barlow *et al.* note that most of the articles report experiment analyses of differential attention using single-case designs, i.e. ABAB and multiple baseline, to demonstrate the control of the undesired behaviour.

Although this replicated series overwhelmingly reported success, Barlow *et al.* note that there are reports where differential attention did not have the desired therapeutic effect. One included the failure of differential attention to help children who exhibited self-injurious behaviour. Wahler (1969) also showed that although differential attention was not effective for parents of children with severe oppositional behaviour, the addition of a time out procedure did reduce the oppositional behaviour. He then hypothesised that the reason why differential attention was ineffective was that the reinforcement value of parental attention for these children was extremely low and simply not sufficiently strong to be effective. Further research showed that after treating the children with a combination of time out and differential attention, oppositional behaviour remained at a low level after time out was withdrawn. He also showed that the joint package of time out and differential attention had the effect of increasing the reinforcement value of parental attention. As such, Wahler's work provides an exemplary case of the value of replication of the systematic application of single-case experimental methods to unpick and understand a phenomenon.

Reflections on the narrative reviews

The Johnson and Pennypacker (1980) and Barlow *et al.* (2009) reviews illustrate systematic replication across a significant number of individual publications. But how systematic are these examples? Neither presents a series of well-planned experiments that systematically explore every facet of generalisability, but over time evidence accrues that the procedure is effective across problems, settings and variations in treatment protocol. Thus we can have some confidence in the evidence base. Sidman's view of systematic replication follows the logic of experimentation in which control is established by isolating causal influences one step at a time. While this is ideal, it would seem that in the dispersed community of clinician-researchers all acting relatively autonomously, the prospect of such ordered exploration of various parameters is unlikely. Any appearance of order in the reviews is therefore largely the consequence of narrative reconstruction. The temptation is to focus the narrative on the success and consistency in replication in order to establish the generalisability of the procedure but, as Barlow et al. (2009, p. 334) note, 'systematic replication is essentially a search for exceptions'. As with other research it is difficult to gauge the non-success rate because the problem of publication bias (not reporting unsuccessful replications) is very real. On the other hand there is evidence, for example in Wahler's studies, that when treatment failure occurs, single-case methods can be quickly adapted to explore the reasons for failure. So, although Barlow et al. (2009) noted that published research on differential attention diminished after 20 years of research, it does not mean that replication attempts should cease. Indeed one could regard every clinical case as a potential replication. What should stimulate our interest and enquiry is not our repeated successes, but those cases where an apparently robust finding fails to replicate.

These narrative reviews illustrate the incremental building of knowledge about a procedure. Guidelines for assessing the quality of single-case studies have only appeared in the last few years (see Chapter 8). In reviews published before guidelines for conducting systematic reviews were developed, we know little about the inclusiveness or exhaustiveness of the sample of studies included within the reviews. Similarly the reviewers offer little by way of information on the quality of the studies incorporated in the review. Furthermore, we know little about how either the original authors or the reviewers made decisions about the effectiveness of the intervention in each study. It is almost certain that the analyses relied on visual inspection of the data, but little information is given about the methods that were employed. This does not mean that we should reject the findings. Given that researchers in the tradition of applied behavioural analysis tend to focus on large and clinically important changes between baseline and control conditions (Parsonson & Baer, 1992), we may have some confidence in the results.

SYSTEMATIC REVIEWS AND META-ANALYSIS OF SINGLE-CASE DATA

The development of systematic review methodology and meta-analysis overcomes two of the potential limitations of the previous examples: (1) possible bias in the selection of primary source on which the review is based; and (2) provision of a replicable metric to assess the outcome of individual case data. The possibility of applying meta-analytic methods to single-case data was first mooted in the 1980s and early 1990s (Busk & Serlin, 1992; Scruggs, Mastropieri & Casto, 1987). Meta-analysis offers a way of mathematically combining the data from a set of studies to estimate the likely true effect of a treatment. When combined with the methodology of systematic review (exhaustive searching of relevant literature and appraisal of the quality of research for potential biases), meta-analysis is a powerful tool for determining the likely impact of treatment. Its application to data from randomised controlled trials is well known. In the field of psychology the most common metric used in meta-analysis is the difference between the means of the treatment and comparator group. The difference is expressed as a ratio of the pooled standard deviation, which gives an effect-size metric. The effect-sizes then are combined and the resulting average and its confidence intervals provide an overall estimate of the effect of a given treatment. However, a significant problem facing single-case researcher is to find a suitable metric to represent the effect size within a single case, and there are debates about how best to combine single-case data. Various solutions have been suggested, and the topic is currently the focus of active research by a number of groups (see Shadish, 2014). Some of the solutions are technically complex and require a good deal of statistical sophistication. In the following two examples of meta-analyses, we consider approaches to examining the replicability of treatments in single-case experiments.

The use of replication in the investigation of Social Stories™

Children with autism spectrum disorder habitually experience social difficulties. They struggle to learn social rules and conventions and consequently fail to integrate with their peers and others. They may experience high levels of anxiety and display increased frequencies of challenging behaviour in social settings, both at school and home. Gray (1998) developed an intervention called Social Stories™, based on short stories using simple language with the aim of explaining social situations and concepts. Unlike the behavioural interventions discussed earlier in the chapter, Social Stories do not aim to change behaviour directly by altering reinforcement contingencies. The premise is that the intervention will lead to a better comprehension of the social world and this will subsequently result in improvements in social behaviour and functioning. Social Stories are very varied in their content and can be tailored to individuals, but they are structured. Gray set out 10 criteria for how stories should be constructed, e.g. the story should have a positive goal and there should be a balance of sentence types. Social Stories have been used as an intervention for a wide range of behavioural outcomes, and the many publications of these interventions primarily report single-case experiments.

Wright et al. (2016) conducted a meta-analysis of 77 studies with a total of 216 participants identified through a systematic review. The modal number of participants per study was one and the median number was three, i.e. many studies included replications. Most participants were boys under the age of 10: 58% were diagnosed with autism, 14% with Asperger syndrome and the remainder comprised a mix of diagnoses including statements that the participants were on the autistic spectrum. Wright et al. assessed the variation in the studies in two ways. First, they considered the variation in the interventions – the stories and the delivery of the stories. Two-thirds of the studies used just one story and 17% used two stories. More than half of the studies use a combination of written and comic book material or photographs. The length of stories varied considerably (4–32 sentences) as did the time over which the intervention was delivered (5–85 days). Stories were delivered by a mixture of researchers, teachers and family members, or were self-administered by the child in 19% of the studies. Wright et al. also examined the extent to which the stories met the guidelines set out for constructing stories by Gray (2009),

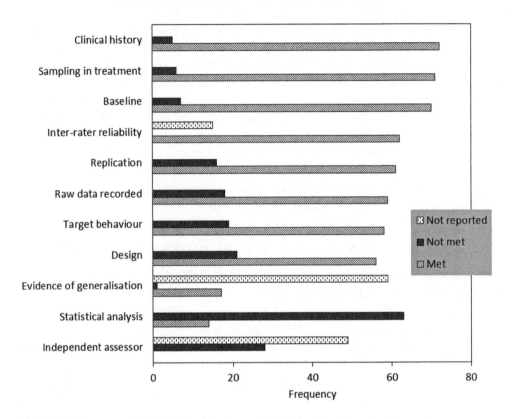

FIGURE 7.1 Assessment of quality criteria across studies

This shows the frequency with which the 77 studies in Wright et al's meta-analysis met the quality criteria in the SCED Scale (Tate *et al.*, 2008). The data are arranged from the top of the figure in decreasing order of the frequency with which the criteria were met. The figure is constructed from data reported in Table 13 (pp. 53–56) in Wright *et al.* (2016)

finding that studies met criteria for just under half of the concordance items and that some studies explicitly stated that they did not follow the Social Story criteria in developing and delivering the intervention. None of the studies met all of the 15 criteria set out by Gray.

Second, Wright *et al.* assessed the variation in the methodological quality of the studies using a scale developed by Tate and her colleagues (Tate *et al.*, 2008), the single-case experimental design (SCED) scale. More detail on this is given in Chapter 8. Figure 7.1 shows the frequency with which the 77 studies met the quality criteria specified by the SCED scale. The figure shows that a high proportion of studies met 7 of the 11 criteria, but there are three items of note where a criterion was not met (evidence of generalisation, statistical analysis and the use of an independent assessor). To a certain extent, failure to meet the generalisation criterion is not a significant problem because the data set of 77 studies is itself an assessment of the generalisation of the method, especially given the variation in implementation documented by Wright *et al.* Similarly the absence of statistical analysis is not surprising given that the dominant method of analysis in this field is visual inspection. (One might suggest that this criterion is problematic for this data set. Perhaps

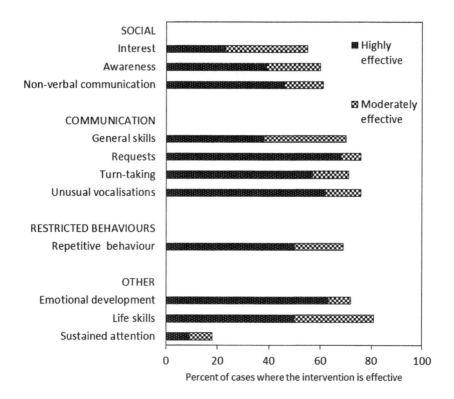

FIGURE 7.2 Assessment of outcomes across studies.

Figure drawn from data in Wright *et al.* (2016)

it should be replaced by an item to assess the quality of visual analysis of the data.) The absence of independent assessors might be considered to be more troublesome, because assessors with knowledge of the preferred outcomes may unwittingly introduce bias into their assessments. Overall the assessment of this portfolio of single-case studies might be that on balance the quality of the data is reasonable, but the application of the SCED scale does highlight where improvements in the conduct of studies could be made.

Wright *et al.* (2016) then attempted a quantitative analysis of the studies to assess the effectiveness of Social Stories. They extracted data from the published graphs and then used two of the overlap statistics discussed in Chapter 6 – PND (percentage of non-overlap data) and PEM (percentage exceeding the median). They were unable to extract usable data from five of the 77 articles because of the poor quality of graph production. There were another 23 graphs that could not be used because they did not include either baseline or intervention data. This left 307 graphs from which data could be extracted. One hundred and forty-four of these reported data on challenging behaviour. Wright *et al.* grouped the data into several categories of target behaviour, each of which had subcategories (shown in Figure 7.2). This figure also shows a summary of the data for the PEM statistic. (The PEM statistic is selected for discussion because it is less affected by a single outlying data point than is the PND statistic.) There was considerable heterogeneity between the studies with regard to the number of individuals in each study and variation in the dependent variable selected. Such heterogeneity is not uncommon in the clinical field, and Wright *et al.* simply followed a frequently used solution to the problem, which is to aggregate data into categories.

Wright *et al.* applied the qualitative descriptors of 'highly effective' when PEM ≥ 90% and 'moderately effective' when PEM ≥ 70% but < 90%. The data in Figure 7.2 suggest that social story telling is 'highly' to 'moderately' effective for a range of behavioural outcomes in between 50% and 70% of cases where it is implemented. There is one exception to this – improving sustained attention. Wright *et al.* note (2016, p. 60) that 'a surprising finding was that the majority of target behaviours were positive or pro-social in nature (53%) . . . as opposed to challenging behaviours'.

The meta-analysis provides broad support for the effectiveness of the intervention but it does not cast much light on cases where there is no treatment effect, i.e. failures to replicate. One possible source of influence is the apparent variability in the implementation of the treatment, and Wright *et al.* carefully document the extent to which the intervention used in each study was concordant with the basic protocol. Unfortunately it is not possible from the published data to determine whether variation in the protocol was related to variation in effectiveness. Other more advanced statistical procedures, such as multi-level modelling, may allow one to disentangle this influence from variations in the selection of participants, choice of dependent variable in each study, variation in therapists and the many other possible confounding variables. However, the use of the SCED scale to assess the quality of each study appears to have been successful. It is reassuring to know that most studies met the basic requirements of quality for single-case designs, but it highlighted areas where study design might be improved. Of particular note is the lack of an independent assessor. This might be difficult to achieve in behavioural studies where assessors repeatedly directly observe target behaviour throughout baseline and treatment phases. Maintaining assessor blindness to likely outcomes and treatment intentions would seem to be problematic. Careful training, calibration and inter-observer agreement may partly offset this problem.

There have been at least two other meta-analyses of studies of Social Stories (Kokina & Kern, 2010; Reynhout & Carter, 2006. Both of these analyses used the basic non-overlap statistic (percentage of non-overlap – PND), discussed in Chapter 6, to summarise the data. Reynhout and Carter (2006) obtained an average PND of 51% (range 20–95%), which falls well below the cut-off of 70% suggested by Scruggs *et al.* (1987) as the criterion for an effective intervention. Kokina and Kern's (2010) analysis, with more primary data, gave a summary statistic of 60% (range 11–100%), also below the 70% criterion. Wright *et al.* also reported an analysis using both the PND metric and the PEM metric (discussed above), but the way in which he and his colleagues reported the summary data is subtly different. Rather than reporting the average PND, Wright *et al.* report the percentage of individual experiments that exceeded the 70% criterion for PND (Wright *et al.*, 2016, Table 14, p. 58). For the PND metric, 38% of individuals exceeded the 70% criterion. This figure is somewhat less than the approximately 60% success rate (Figure 7.2) when the more robust PEM metric is used.

Use of replication in the investigation of challenging behaviours

The final example of replication in single-case research is slightly different from the previous examples in that it focuses on a range of interventions for a general class of problems, challenging behaviours, rather than a specific one. The method for examining the replicability is more complex than the meta-analysis reported by Wright *et al.* (2016). The authors (Heyvaert, Maes, Van den Noortgate, Kuppens & Onghena, 2012) used a statistical procedure, multi-level modelling, to integrate the results from the pool of available studies. This method of analysis meant that they were able to test statistically for factors that may moderate treatment effectiveness. This research illustrates the increasing sophistication of the statistical methods being used to explore the scope and generalisability of findings from single-case experiments.

In the first part of their investigation, Heyvaert *et al.* conducted a review of 137 previously published reviews and meta-analyses of research on interventions for challenging behaviours in people with learning difficulties. This review excluded reviews of single-case research and focused only on group-based research. The purpose of this review was to scope the field and to identify variables that were reported to have a moderating effect on the intervention. They categorised the potential moderators into four categories. These were: *meta-analytic*, which referred to data describing aspects of the publication (there were only two variables – year of publication and study quality); *participant variables*, e.g. type of challenging behaviour, age, gender; *context variables*, e.g. experimental design, presence of pre-treatment functional analysis; and *intervention variables*, e.g. type of psychological intervention, medication, social-contextual variables (e.g. training parents and caregivers). They then developed a coding framework to record these data in the second stage of the research.

In the second stage, a systematic search of the literature identified 285 single-case studies reporting data on 598 persons. The raw data for each individual were extracted from the published graphs and a hierarchical regression model developed. The model had three levels. At the 'top' level of the model is the studies level, which includes the 285 primary studies from the literature search. The 'middle' level is the participants' level, with 598 individuals. Each individual is nested within one of the studies and a proportion of the studies therefore had more than one individual nested within them. The 'bottom' level was the within-participant level, and this contained the individual data points for each individual. The data at the within-participant level were used to compute the effect size: the difference between the means of the baseline and intervention phases divided by the within-condition standard deviation. This is analogous to the way in which the effect size is computed in the more frequent between-group meta-analysis. By organising the data in this way the authors were able to run different analyses to answer the three questions that they had posed.

The first analysis asked the question, 'what is the overall effect of different interventions for people with challenging behaviour?' The answer to this question was that overall the interventions were highly effective. The within-participant effect size for treatment was −2.93 (SD = 0.23), although as Heyvaert *et al.* note, it is not really possible to make a direct comparison between the magnitude of this effect size and those typically found in meta-analyses that compare group data, because the comparisons made are dissimilar. Furthermore we might have some reservations about the assumptions made in computing the within-subject effect size for the within-participant data, as it does not take account of the likely correlated nature of the data (Chapter 6). Nevertheless the overall effect size is large. The second question posed by Heyvaert *et al.* was, 'which characteristics of the participants, of the context of the study and the intervention moderate this effect?' Further analyses showed that (after removing six outlier individuals) the interventions were less effective for individuals with aggressive and destructive challenging behaviours and more effective for individuals with a diagnosis of autism spectrum disorder. In addition, if the intervention included a component of manipulating antecedent factors then the outcome was better.

The final question addressed whether the conclusions of the single-case studies and the group studies reviewed in the first part of the research were equivalent. The meta-analysis showed that there was a high overall intervention effect and that there was positive evidence for the impact of psychological and contextual intervention, but 'no evidence for an overall positive effect of pharmacological interventions' (p. 776). These observations correspond to the conclusion reached from the authors' initial systematic review. Heyvaert *et al.* suggest that multi-level modelling of the single-case data provided a more detailed analysis of the moderating factors.

A CRITIQUE OF THE REPLICATION LITERATURE

This chapter began with Sidman's useful distinction between direct and systematic replication as a way of framing issues in replicating single-case research. What is important for clinical problems is that: (1) any clinical intervention should be effective across individuals, therapists and settings; and (2) obtaining knowledge of factors that indicate when the intervention is likely to fail is crucial. Systematic replication in the clinical context is actually rather difficult to accomplish, especially with regard to the second objective. Sidman's perspective on systematic replication did not necessarily mean the replication of the findings by other researchers in other laboratories, but attempts to replicate a phenomenon when contextual variables were systematically and quantitatively changed, e.g. the hours of deprivation needed to install a motivational drive state in an animal. Importantly, the manipulation of a contextual variable necessarily followed the experimental protocol of keeping all but the variable of interest constant. In clinical settings context rarely, if ever, follows this strong definition of systematic replication of a study by allowing us to change one variable at a time. Although authorities such as Barlow *et al.* (2009) recommend that investigators should 'clearly note the differences among their clients, therapists, or setting from those in the original experiment' (p. 334), there are problems with following this advice. First, the original account may not be reported in sufficient detail, and the authors may not know or be able accurately to identify the critical factors associated with change. Second, the new setting is likely to be different from the original setting in a myriad of ways that are unknown. The reasons for the failure of a replicative study are therefore unknown, and the investigator must begin a forensic search for likely explanations. Despite the problematic nature of systematic replication in what we might call the clinical research eco-system, there are many examples where replication across different clinical contexts can be demonstrated, as illustrated by the examples in this chapter.

The series of studies by Vlaeyen and his colleagues illustrate how the impact of an intervention can be replicated both within and across studies. Here the intervention was constant, but across the studies the impact of additional variables, such as education and different diagnostic groups, was explored. The critical element was probably the careful assessment of each participant to ensure that the fear-avoidance formulation was applicable in each case, i.e. the proposed functional relationship between the intervention and the outcome was present. Although we do not know why the two participants in the Swedish case series (Boersma et al., 2004) were unsuccessful, I suggest that this factor is likely to be the most important element of whether replication can be established. In the light of Wahler's experimental studies it is certainly possible to interpret Barlow et al.'s (2009) account of differential attention in this way. The key factor in these studies would appear to be the differential application of a valued reinforcer to shape desirable behaviour. The review by Heyvaert et al. (2012) also identifies the importance of functional analysis, i.e. correct identification of the controlling variables, as the factor that is most strongly associated with a larger effect size (better outcome).

The example of time out (Johnson & Pennypacker, 1980) offers a slightly different perspective on replication. Here the aim was to offer an historical narrative of the development of a therapeutic technique based on a principle derived from basic science research that removing access to positive reinforcers is punishing, i.e. it will reduce the frequency of the antecedent (target) behaviour. The history illustrated the establishment of the basic principle and then its application to a wide range of problems. However, the probable boundaries of the phenomenon, i.e. those features associated with failure of time out to control behaviour, were not documented by Johnson and Pennypacker. We do not know from the account how many studies of time out were performed where its application was unsuccessful. There may be two reasons for this: (1) Johnson and Pennypacker, for whatever reason, elected not to weave an account of failure into the narrative (we have no evidence for this) or, alternatively, (2) there is the possibility that unsuccessful applications were not reported in the literature (authors may decide not to submit accounts or editors may reject null findings). Distinguishing between these alternatives is problematic in this particular case, but the problems are not unique to single-case research. Fortunately, attempts to overcome selective reporting and the problem of unpublished studies are being addressed. First, the methodology of systematic reviews has developed subsequent to Johnson and Pennypacker's review. Second, the establishment of trial registers with published trial protocols increases the likelihood that relevant trials can be identified and unpublished trials identified. While single-case research studies may be registered on trial databases, single-case studies that arise as a consequence of clinical serendipity would not be registered.

The final two examples of replication in single-case series (Heyvaert et al., 2012; Wright et al., 2016) illustrate the application of systematic review and meta-analysis to assessing the replicability of single-case data. Both these reviews attempted to collate all the available data via systematic literature searches and to assess the quality of the studies. Quality assessment can be used in a number of ways. It can be used to screen out poor studies prior to further analysis or, alternatively, all studies can be included in the analysis and the influence of various aspects of quality on the outcome may be examined. The aggregation of the results using meta-analysis, attempts to quantify the strength of the overall effect of the intervention, and it may be possible to explore the impact of methodological variation and other study features on the outcome. This latter feature may lead to the identification of features of studies that are statistically associated with the success or failure of the intervention, but this method of unpacking sources of variance in the data requires sufficient data and power to detect the robust exceptions. The interesting issue is whether this approach to identifying sources of variation is intrinsically better than astute observation and theoretical understanding of the principles of the treatment. Would the meta-analysis of the differential attention literature have revealed Wahler's (1969) observation on the role of parental reinforcement value? Similarly, was Heyvaert *et al.*'s analysis (2012) insensitive to important variations in the data because the analyses lacked sufficient power to detect relevant effects?

Although meta-analysis for single-case data has been available for many years, its methodology is still contentious and it is currently the focus of research (Shadish, Hedges & Pustejovsky, 2014). One major challenge is the identification of an appropriate effect size statistic. Two major classes of effect size have been proposed but there are problems with both of them. The non-overlap measures attempt to provide a quantification of the extent to which two sets of data, e.g. the baseline and treatment phases in an AB design, overlap with each other and express it as a percentage. However, the resulting statistic gives no indication of the magnitude of the difference between the two data sets. To illustrate this, consider the data from an AB design from two participants (Table 7.2). For participant 1 the overall magnitude of the difference between the average of the phases is 4 points and, using the PND, the percentage of non-overlap in the data is 0%. On the other hand, the mean difference between the phases for participant 2 is 1 point but the non-overlap is 100%. So although the actual magnitude of the difference for participant 2 is much less than for participant 1, the PND statistic does not reflect this. Indeed an interpretation based on the PND would suggest that there was a maximum effect for participant 2 and no effect for participant 1. In summary, the overlap statistics cannot represent the magnitude of the difference between phases of an experiment – they merely reflect the extent of overlap.

TABLE 7.2 Illustrating the problem of non-overlap statistics as a measure of effect size

	Data	Mean	Difference	PND
Participant 1				
Phase A	10,7,1,8,9	7		
Phase B	3,4,2,4,2	3	4	0
Participant 2				
Phase A	10,10,10,10,10	10		
Phase B	9,9,9,9,9	9	1	100

PND = percentage of non-overlapping data

This critique does not invalidate the use of non-overlap statistics – these are clearly a useful way of describing the data, and in certain cases (see Chapter 6), they can form the basis for statistical tests for individual cases. However, when they are combined as in the meta-analysis reported by Wright *et al.* (2016), we need to be mindful of their possible limitations.

The second method for estimating the effect size is to use a version of Cohen's d, but this test is vulnerable to both autocorrelation and the relatively small numbers in the different phases. Shadish and his colleagues have recently proposed a version of Cohen's d for single-case data, but they note that it too has limitations. First, it assumes that there is no trend in the data and second, it assumes that the outcome metric (dependent variable) is normally distributed (Shadish *et al.*, 2013).

CONCLUSIONS

Replication is at the heart of any scientific endeavour to establish evidence of effective treatments, but it can only be accomplished if individual clinician-researchers give it due regard. Individual studies should be planned with care and, wherever possible, elements of replication should be built into the fabric of the study – for example, by selecting designs in which an element of replication is possible (e.g. ABAB and multiple baseline designs). Investigators also need to consider how they report their study so that sufficient detail is provided on the selection of participants, measurement, design features and analysis of the data. This information helps readers and reviewers who wish to synthesise and meta-analyse studies to make judgements about the quality and likely value of the study. Meta-analysis is a useful technique for examining the boundaries of replication across a range of studies. This chapter can only provide the briefest sketch of some of the issues involved, and readers interested in conducting a meta-analysis of single-case data in a quest to explore issues of replication should explore the primary sources referenced in the chapter. In recent years a number of quality standards and scales for assessing the quality of single-case data have been published; these are the subject of Chapter 8.

REFERENCES

Baer, D. M. (1962). Laboratory control of thumbsucking by withdrawal and representation of reinforcement. *Journal of the Experimental Analysis of Behavior*, 5, 525–8.

Barlow, D. H. & Hersen, M. (1984). *Single Case Experimental Designs: Strategies for Studying Behavioral Change* (2nd edn). New York: Pergamon.

Barlow, D. H., Nock, M. K. & Hersen, M. (2009). *Single Case Experimental Designs* (3rd edn). Boston: Pearson.

Boersma, K., Linton, S., Overmeer, T., Jansson, M., Vlaeyen, J. & de Jong, J. (2004). Lowering fear-avoidance and enhancing function through exposure in vivo. A multiple baseline study across six patients with back pain. *Pain*, 108(1–2), 8–16.

Busk, P. L. & Serlin, R. C. (1992). Meta-analysis for single-case research. In T. R. Kratochwill & J. R. Levin (eds), *Single-case Research Design and Analysis: New Directions for Psychology and Education* (pp. 187–212). Hillsdale, NJ: Lawrence Erlbaum.

de Jong, J. R., Vangronsveld, K., Peters, M. L., Goossens, M. E., Onghena, P., Bulte, I. & Vlaeyen, J. W. S. (2008). Reduction of pain-related fear and disability in post-traumatic neck pain: a replicated single-case experimental study of exposure in vivo. *Journal of Pain*, 9(12), 1123–34.

de Jong, J. R., Vlaeyen, J. W. S., Onghena, P., Cuypers, C., den Hollander, M. & Ruijgrok, J. (2005). Reduction of pain-related fear in complex regional pain syndrome type I: the application of graded exposure in vivo. *Pain*, 116(3), 264–75.

de Jong, J. R., Vlaeyen, J. W. S., Onghena, P., Goossens, M. E., Geilen, M. & Mulder, H. (2005). Fear of movement/(re)injury in chronic low back pain: education or exposure in vivo as mediator to fear reduction? *Clinical Journal of Pain*, 21(1), 9–17; discussion 69–72.

den Hollander, M., Goossens, M., de Jong, J., Ruijgrok, J., Oosterhof, J., Onghena, P. *et al.* (2016). Expose or protect? A randomised controlled trial of exposure in vivo vs pain-contingent treatment as usual in patients with complex regional pain syndrome type 1. *Pain*, 157(10), 2318–29.

Gast, D. L. (2010). *Single Subject Research Methodology in Behavioral Sciences*. New York: Routledge.

Gearing, R. E., El-Bassel, N., Ghesquiere, A., Baldwin, S., Gillies, J. & Ngeow, E. (2011). Major ingredients of fidelity: a review and scientific guide to improving quality of intervention research implementation. *Clinical Psychology Review*, 31(1), 79–88.

Gray, C. A. (1998). Social stories and comic strip conversations with students with Asperger syndrome and high functioning autism. In E. Schopler, G. B. Mesibov & L. J. Kunce (eds), *Asperger Syndrome or High Functioning Autism?* (pp. 167–98). New York: Plenum.

Gray, C. A. (2009). *The New Social Story™ Book* (Revised and expanded 10th anniversary edition). Arlington, TX: Future Horizons.

Hall, R. V., Fox, R., Willard, D., Goldsmith, L., Emerson, M., Owen, M. *et al.* (1971). The teacher as observer and experimenter in the modification of disputing and talking-out behaviors. *Journal of Applied Behavior Analysis*, 4, 141–9.

Heyvaert, M., Maes, B., Van den Noortgate, W., Kuppens, S. & Onghena, P. (2012). A multilevel meta-analysis of single-case and small-n research on interventions for reducing challenging behavior in persons with intellectual disabilities. *Research in Developmental Disabilities*, 33(2), 766–80.

Johnson, J. M. & Pennypacker, H. S. (1980). *Strategies and Tactics in Human Behavioural Research*. Hillsdale: Lawrence Erlbaum.

Kazdin, A. E. (2010). *Single-Case Research Designs: Methods for Clinical and Applied Settings* (2nd edn). Oxford: Oxford University Press.

Kokina, A. & Kern, L. (2010). Social Story™ interventions for students with autism spectrum disorders: A meta-analysis. *Journal of Autism and Developmental Disorders*, 40(7), 812–26.

Kratochwill, T. R., Hitchcock, J., Horner, R., Levin, J., Odom, S. L., Rindskopf, D. & Shadish, W. R. (2010). Single-case technical documentation. Retrieved from What Works Clearinghouse website: http://ies.ed.gov/ncee/wwc/pdf/wwe_scd.pdf

Leeuw, M., Goossens, M. E., van Breukelen, G. J., de Jong, J. R., Heuts, P. H., Smeets, R. J. *et al.* (2008). Exposure in vivo versus operant graded activity in chronic low back pain patients: results of a randomized controlled trial. *Pain*, 138(1), 192–207.

Linton, S. J., Boersma, K., Jansson, M., Overmeer, T., Lindblom, K. & Vlaeyen, J. W. (2008). A randomized controlled trial of exposure in vivo for patients with spinal pain reporting fear of work-related activities. *European Journal of Pain*, 12(6), 722–30.

Morley, S., Williams, A. & Eccleston, C. (2013). Examining the evidence about psychological treatments for chronic pain: time for a paradigm shift? *Pain*, 154(10), 1929–31.

Parsonson, B. S. & Baer, D. M. (1992). The visual analysis of data, and current research into the stimuli controlling it. In T. R. Kratochwill & J. R. Levin (eds), *Single-case Research Design and Analysis: New Directions for Psychology and Education* (pp. 15–40). Hillsdale, NJ: Lawrence Erlbaum.

Perepletchikova, F., Treat, T. A. & Kazdin, A. E. (2007). Treatment integrity in psychotherapy research: Analysis of the studies and examination of the associated factors. *Journal of Consulting and Clinical Psychology*, 75(6), 829–41.

Reynhout, G. & Carter, M. (2006). Social Stories for children with disabilities. *Journal of Autism and Developmental Disorders*, 36(4), 445–69.

Scruggs, T. E., Mastropieri, M. A. & Casto, G. (1987). Quantitative synthesis of single subject research: Methodology and validation. *Remedial and Special Education*, 8(2), 24–33.

Shadish, W. R. (ed.) (2014). Special issue: Analysis and meta-analysis of single-case designs. *Journal of School Psychology*, 52(2), 109–248.

Shadish, W. R., Hedges, L. V. & Pustejovsky, J. E. (2014). Analysis and meta-analysis of single-case designs with a standardised mean difference statistic: A primer and applications. *Journal of School Psychology*, 52(2), 123–47.

Shadish, W. R., Hedges, L. V., Pustejovsky, J. E., Boyajian, J. G., Sullivan, K. J., Andrade, A. & Barrientos, J. L. (2013). A d-statistic for single-case designs that is equivalent to the usual between-groups d-statistic. *Neuropsychological Rehabilitation*, 24(3–4), 528–553.

Sidman, M. (1960). *Tactics of Scientific Research: Evaluating Experimental Data in Psychology*. New York: Basic Books.

Tate, R. L., McDonald, S., Perdices, M., Togher, L., Schultz, R. & Savage, S. (2008). Rating the methodological quality of single-subject designs and n-of-1 trials: introducing the Single-Case Experimental Design (SCED) Scale. *Neuropsychological Rehabilitation*, 18(4), 385–401.

Vlaeyen, J. W. S., de Jong, J., Geilen, M., Heuts, P. H. T. G. & van Breukelen, G. (2001). Graded exposure in vivo in the treatment of pain-related fear: A replicated single-case experimental design in four patients with chronic low back pain. *Behaviour Research and Therapy*, 39(2), 151–66.

Vlaeyen, J. W. S., de Jong, J., Geilen, M., Heuts, P. H. T. G. & van Breukelen, G. (2002). The treatment of fear of movement/(re)injury in chronic low back pain: Further evidence on the effectiveness of exposure in vivo. *Clinical Journal of Pain*, 18(4), 251–61.

Vlaeyen, J. W. S., De Jong, J. R., Onghena, P., Kerckhoffs-Hanssen, M. & Kole-Snijders, A. M. (2002). Can pain-related fear be reduced? The application of cognitive-behavioural exposure in vivo. *Pain Research and Management*, 7(3), 144–53.

Vlaeyen, J. W. S. & Linton, S. J. (2000). Fear-avoidance and its consequences in chronic musculoskeletal pain: a state of the art. *Pain*, 85(3), 317–32.

Vlaeyen, J. W. S. & Morley, S. (2005). Cognitive-behavioral treatments for chronic pain: what works for whom? *The Clinical Journal of Pain*, 21(1), 1–8.

Vlaeyen, J. W. S., Morley, S., Linton, S., Boersma, K. & de Jong, J. (2012). *Pain-Related Fear: Exposure-based Treatment of Chronic Pain*. Seattle: IASP.

Wahler, R. G. (1969). Oppositional children: the quest for parental reinforcement control. *Journal of Applied Behavior Analysis*, 2, 159–70.

Williams, A. C. D. C., Eccleston, C. & Morley, S. (2012). Psychological therapies for the management of chronic pain (excluding headache) in adults. *Cochrane Database of Systematic Reviews*, CD007407. pub3(11).

Woods, M. P. & Asmundson, G. J. (2008). Evaluating the efficacy of graded in vivo exposure for the treatment of fear in patients with chronic back pain: a randomized controlled clinical trial. *Pain*, 136(3), 271–80.

Wright, B., Marshall, D., Adamson, J., Ainsworth, H., Ali, S., Allgar, V. *et al.* (2016). Social Stories™ to alleviate challenging behaviour and social difficulties exhibited by children with autism spectrum disorder in mainstream schools: Design of a manualised training toolkit and feasibility study for a cluster randomised controlled trial with nested qualitative and cost-effectiveness components. *Health Technology Assessment*, 20(6).

Chapter 8

Critical evaluation of single-case research

Stephen Morley with Ciara Masterson

Twenty years ago the American Psychological Association recognised that single-case experiments could provide evidence for an effective treatment. Chambless and Hollon (1998) suggested that 'A large series of single-case design experiments (n > 9) demonstrating efficacy' was a reasonable criterion to adopt. The inclusion of single-case data as evidence in other fields has been a little slower, but in 2011 the Oxford Centre for Evidence-Based Medicine stated that systematic reviews of certain single-case trials in medicine (namely N-of-1 trials where the ordering of drug treatment versus placebo is randomly decided) constituted 'level 1 evidence' (Howick, 2011). Synthesising the evidence for the efficacy and effectiveness of treatments is a complex process, but one essential element in forming an overall judgement about treatments is the need to assess the quality of the evidence available for synthesis. Several scales (sometimes referred to as 'tools') are available to assess the quality of the evidence provided by individual studies, and these generally focus on the internal validity of the study and the possibility of bias. In assessing randomised controlled trials the features assessed include: the possibility of selection bias; inadequate randomisation to trial arms; the blinding of patients, therapists and assessors to treatment conditions; and the use of adequate measurement tools (Higgins *et al.*, 2011). The overall aim is to assess the risk of bias, i.e. that the observed result is affected by factors other than receipt of the intended treatment.

SCALES TO ASSESS THE QUALITY OF PUBLISHED RESEARCH

The evaluation of single-case research has seen the development of scales to assess the quality of studies prior to synthesising the data and drawing general conclusions. In 2014, Heyvaert and her colleagues surveyed the status of two particular features (randomisation and data analysis) in scales measuring the quality standards of single-case research (Heyvaert *et al.*, 2015). Their search revealed 11 distinct scales for reporting and evaluating single-case studies. Of these, five were designed for particular applications, e.g. reports of young people with autism, and six were designed for more general use. Since the publication of Heyvaert *et al.*'s manuscript, one of the scales they identified has been extensively revised (Tate *et al.*, 2008, 2013), and a comprehensive set of guidelines for reporting single-case experiments has also been published (Tate *et al.*, 2016). It is not possible to review all these scales in detail here, but we have chosen to examine and contrast two approaches to assessing the quality of the evidence that may be provided by single-case research. The first is the 'Standards' document produced by the What Works Clearinghouse (WWC, Kratochwill *et al.*, 2010) and cited in Chapter 7. This was developed mainly by researchers steeped in the tradition of applied behavioural analysis and single-case methods in the field of special education. The second is the Risk of Bias in N-of-1 Trials (RoBiNT, Tate *et al.*, 2013) scale, developed by a group of neuropsychologists, in which the influence of 'traditional' thinking about the design of randomised controlled trials is discernible.

The WWC Standards

In Chapter 7 we noted the guidance provided by the WWC on standards for replication in single-case research (Kratochwill *et al.*, 2010). The WWC guidance is produced by the Institute of Educational Sciences within the United States Department of Education, which reviews the evidence for existing policies and practice within education. In certain areas of education research, the nature of some problems and their relative infrequency mean that it is difficult both to do large trials using standard randomised controlled trial methodology and to make causal judgements about the effectiveness of treatments using this methodology. However, there is an established tradition of using single-case experiments to test treatments for children with special educational needs. The question is: how should such evidence for causality be evaluated? A panel of seven individuals with expertise in single-case methodology and quantitative methods proposed a set of standards (criteria) for judging whether or not single-case research provided evidence that an intervention could be judged as effective or not (Kratochwill *et al.*, 2010, 2013). The experts first proposed a review of the design of each study to decide whether it met the criteria, i.e. establishing the internal validity of the study. Second, they proposed that reviewers trained in visual analysis examine the data to decide whether the study provides 'strong', 'moderate' or 'no' evidence for the treatment. In addition to defining the evidence standards, the documentation provided by the WWC includes other guidance on the conduct and visual analysis of single-case experiments. In passing, it also noted the possible use of statistical methods but commented that no method was sufficiently established to be recommended, and therefore the guidance is based only on visual analysis of the data.

Unlike other sets of guidelines, there is no scale in which scores from items are aggregated to provide an overall 'quality' score: the WWC documentation provides a series of statements accompanied by text that details the features to be taken into consideration when determining whether the study either (1) meets the standard, (2) does not meet the standard or, in some cases, (3) meets the standard with reservation. The basic designs covered by the evidence standards are the ABAB, multiple baseline, alternating treatments and changing criterion designs. The WWC panel explicitly stated that the commonly used AB design does not meet the required standard.

TABLE 8.1 What Works Clearinghouse standards

Criteria for designs that meet evidence standards

- The dependent variable (i.e., the intervention) must be systematically manipulated, with the researcher determining when and how the independent variable conditions change.
- Each outcome variable must be measured systematically over time by more than one assessor, and the study needs to collect inter-assessor agreement in each phase and on at least twenty per cent of the data points in each condition (e.g., baseline, intervention) and the inter-assessor agreement must meet minimal threshold.
- The study must include at least three attempts to demonstrate an intervention effect at three different points in time or with three different phase repetitions.
- For a phase to qualify as an attempt to demonstrate an effect, the phase must have a minimum of three data points.

Criteria for demonstrating evidence of a relationship between an independent variable and an outcome variable

- Documenting the consistency of level, trend and variability within each phase
- Documenting the immediacy of the effect, the proportion of overlap, the consistency of the data across phases in order to demonstrate an intervention effect, and comparing the observed and projected patterns of the outcome variable
- Examining external factors and anomalies.

Source: Kratochwill *et al.*, 2010

Assessment of quality

Table 8.1 displays the four criteria to consider when judging whether a single-case design meets the evidence standard. The first criterion addresses whether or not the intervention was systematically and deliberately manipulated by the researcher. Interventions that are serendipitous and not under the control of the researcher are therefore excluded. The item requires a dichotomous decision: i.e. either the study meets or does not meet the evidence standard.

The second criterion is concerned with the quality of measurement of the dependent variable (outcome). It stipulates that the outcome must be observed by more than one person, specifies the proportion of observations that must be taken by two or more observers, and in the supplementary text indicates the minimal levels of inter-rater agreement or Kappa values (Chapter 3) that are required for the measure. The measurement conditions in a study must meet *all* these criteria in order for the study to be judged equivocally as meeting the evidence standard. There is no provision in the document for giving partial credit so that the study can be judged as meeting the standard with reservation. However, in a footnote to this item the authors suggest that if there are exceptions then these 'will be specified in the topic area or practice protocol'. One implication of the measurement criteria is that studies in which the independent variable is self-report cannot meet the standard. This state of affairs probably arises because of the applied behaviour analytic background of research in this field, which has generally eschewed verbal report as a dependent variable. However, the intent of this criterion is to require that we are satisfied that the reliability of the measurement procedure can be established using sufficient sampling of data across the duration of the experiment. The validity of the measure is not considered within the framework of the WWC guidance, perhaps because it is assumed that what is measured has high criterion validity (Chapter 3).

The third WWC design criterion specifies the number of replications of an effect within a study that is necessary to demonstrate the effect of the intervention, as discussed in Chapter 7. The minimum acceptable number is set at three but, as the authors note, more replications increase the confidence in the experimental control of the effect and thus add weight to ruling out alternative explanations. The supplementary text provides details of the experimental designs that meet this evidence standard. These include the ABAB design, multiple baseline experiments with at least three baselines and treatment phases, changing criteria designs with at least three criteria and alternating treatment designs. As with the previous two items, assessors are required to make a dichotomous decision as to whether an individual study meets the evidence standard.

The fourth and final criterion specifies the number of data points required in each phase. The minimal number of points is set at three, but designs with three or four points per phase can only meet the standard with reservation, and in order to fully meet the standard five data points are required. Thus, importantly, experiments with fewer than three points *cannot* be used to demonstrate the presence or lack of an effect. These criteria apply to ABAB and multiple baseline designs. For an alternating treatment design, the authors suggest that five repetitions of the alternating sequence are needed to meet the standard and four repetitions would meet the standard with reservation. The authors omit specifying details for the changing criterion design, but the reader may recall from Chapter 4 that one of the essential features of the changing criterion design is that the length of each phase should vary to ensure that phase changes are not associated with other possible periodic effects. It would seem reasonable to recommend therefore that the same criteria of three and five points applied to the phases in a changing criterion design should be used to meet the standard with and without reservation, respectively.

Assessing evidence of a causal relationship

Once the design quality of a study has been assessed and found to meet the standards, the WWC document provides criteria that can be used to judge whether the study provides evidence that there is a causal relationship between the intervention and the outcome (see Table 8.1). There are three grades of evidence; strong, moderate and no evidence. The WWC document makes it clear that the demonstration of an effect is to be made on the basis of visual analysis of the data. As previously noted, statistical analysis is largely eschewed and the judgement of the presence of an effect essentially requires that the assessors visually reanalyse the data. This process is notably different from other checklists and scales used to judge the quality of studies, in which the assessor is required to determine whether the statistical analysis reported in the original articles has followed stated procedures, e.g. intention-to-treat analyses have been conducted. The WWC document provides brief guidance on visual analysis along the lines of the material given in Chapter 5. In brief, the conclusion of strong evidence can only be reached if 'two WWC reviewers certified in visual analysis conclude that a causal relationship has been identified'. This stipulation would seem to invalidate the use of the standards for anyone outside the WWC. Nevertheless, the points to be made are that judgements should be made by assessors with some expertise and that their competence needs to be corroborated by some method. In order to reach a conclusion, the WWC requires that the assessors should (1) document 'the consistency of level, trend and variability within each phase'; (2) document 'the immediacy of the effect, proportion of overlap, consistency across phases, and compare the observed and projected patterns of the outcome variable'. (This latter phrase suggests that the WWC explicitly endorses a method like the Conservative Dual Criterion method discussed in Chapter 5.) Finally (3), the assessors should explicitly examine 'external factors and anomalies such as sudden changes in level within a phase'. Later in this chapter we will consider a method for doing this, as developed by Elliott (2002).

The WWC document suggests that three demonstrations of an effect are required to establish a causal relationship. A judgement of moderate evidence can be made if there are three demonstrations of an effect and at least one demonstration of no effect. This might be the case, for example, in a multiple baseline experiment with five subjects in which three showed an effect and two did not.

The RoBiNT scale

The RoBiNT (Risk of Bias in N-of-1 Trials) scale offers a different approach to assessing single-case research (Tate et al., 2013). Whereas the WWC sets categorical criteria as to whether a study meets evidence standard, the RoBiNT scale follows the path of most other scales in that it provides an overall rating of the quality of a study. The RoBiNT was developed from the Single-Case Experimental Design (SCED) Scale (Tate et al., 2008) as discussed in Chapter 7. The further development lengthened the scale, revised the content and changed the item scoring format by replacing a dichotomous rating with a three-point rating to allow partial credit for each item. The scale was split into two parts to assess the internal and external validity of each study. This also contrasts with the WWC approach, which essentially focuses on the internal validity of each study, thereby leaving judgements of external validity to be made by those synthesising the studies. Tate et al. (2008) provide an outline of the items in the RoBiNT and a manual provides a comprehensive guide defining each item and how to allocate scores. The construction of the RoBiNT scale is clearly influenced by conventional thinking regarding the evaluation of randomised controlled trials, as reflected in the established CONSORT guidelines (Schulz et al., 2010) and extended in the CONSORT Extension of N-of-1 Trials guidelines (Vohra et al., 2016). This scale therefore highlights some of the potential problems in transferring approaches to evaluating randomised controlled trial design to single experiments, and conversely highlights some of the quality issues that advocates of single-case research must consider.

Internal validity subscale

There are seven items on this subscale:

1   *Design*. This item requires that the design of the study is sufficient to allow cause and effect to be established. ABAB and multiple baseline studies are explicitly included and the AB design is excluded. For a full two points to be awarded the three

demonstrations of the treatment effect are required, as per the WWC criteria. However, the RoBiNT criteria also give partial credit of one point if there are two demonstrations of treatment effect.

2   *Randomisation.* The RoBiNT scale introduces randomisation as a quality item, and points can be awarded for randomising the sequence of phases and/or the onset of treatment. The authors do, however, note that randomisation in single-case studies is problematic in some contexts (see the discussion below).

3   *Sampling of behaviour.* This item also follows the WWC guidelines in requiring at least 5 data points in each phase for full credit, and awards 1 point for 3 or 4 data points in a phase.

4   *Blinding of patient/therapist.* As Tate et al. (2013) note, 'this issue has not been raised previously with respect to single-case methodology in the behavioural sciences'. Indeed it seems most unlikely that in any form of psychological treatment delivered by a therapist that the recipient would be unaware that they are receiving an intervention (this will be especially true of complex interventions) or that the therapist would be unaware of what they are doing. Tate et al., whose main field of research is neuro-rehabilitation, do suggest that blinding may be feasible for some interventions in this field.

5   *Blinding of the assessor.* One point is awarded if the assessor is independent of the therapist and an additional point if the assessor is also blind to the phase of the intervention. A moment's reflection suggests that this item might prove problematic for data collection in many single-case designs. Unlike randomised controlled trials where data are usually collected at two or three discrete time points (pre-, post- and follow-up) and outside of the delivery of any intervention, data collection in single-case studies is more or less continuous and it would be very difficult for an observer to be unaware of the current experimental condition.

6   *Inter-rater reliability.* This item mirrors the WWC standard that inter-rater reliability must be established to a sufficient degree and that suitable samples of behaviour must be observed.

7   *Treatment adherence.* This item assesses whether the investigators took steps to check/ensure that the treatment had been implemented as intended, and is an essential check on the internal validity of any study.

External validity and interpretation subscale

The items in this scale begin with an item to capture:

1   *Baseline Characteristics.* In the first iteration of the scale (Tate et al., 2008) this item was named clinical history and required that information about the demographics and clinical history of the case be provided so that the reader could make a judgement as to the 'applicability of the treatment to another individual'. The revised RoBiNT scale takes an entirely different approach to this item and is influenced by the thinking of applied behaviour analysis. The item is endorsed if there is evidence that the investigators have considered the way in which the target behaviour is maintained in the baseline and that this assessment informs the subsequent intervention (i.e. there is some form of functional analysis present).

2   *Therapeutic setting.* This item requires that the report contains detailed information on the therapeutic setting.

3   *Dependent variable (target behaviour).* This item considers whether or not a sufficiently clear definition of the measurement of the dependent variable has been given.

4   *Independent variable (the intervention).* This item requires that the intervention is described in sufficient detail (i.e. the frequency, duration and number of intervention sessions that have been administered).

5   *Raw data record.* The scale requires that reports should provide a complete session-by-session record of the dependent variable across all phases of the experiment.

6   *Data analysis.* In the earlier version of the scale, the analysis item required that a statistical analysis should be performed. The revision, however, recognises that prescribing the form of analysis is controversial and perhaps given the state of development of statistical analysis it is a little premature. The current version of this item mirrors the criterion for visual analysis stipulated by the WWC Standards document. It requires that the systematic visual analysis described by the WWC (Kratochwill *et al.*, 2010) should be used, or, when a statistical method is used, the rationale for its suitability should be provided: see Chapters 5 and 6.

7   *Replication.* This item directly addresses the generalisability of the effect and requires that there should be at least three replications of the original experiment.

8   The final item, *Generalisation*, assesses whether the study included attempts to demonstrate generalisation of the effect to other behaviours or settings. The criteria state that generalisation strategies should be built into the fabric of the experiment and evaluated through all its phases.

Considerations in the use of guidelines

Both the WWC Standards and the RoBiNT scale illustrate some of the issues in arriving at a set of hard-and-fast guidelines for contemporary single-case design and methodology. The two scales are designed to assess quality from rather different perspectives: applied behavioural analysis (WWC) and the medical trial (RoBiNT). It is probably true that neither scale, nor any of the other available scales, is capable of meeting the requirements of all assessors in all circumstances. Indeed, there are several items, especially in the RoBiNT scale, that might unduly penalise high-quality studies. The obvious example of this is the specification of randomisation of treatment onset or sequence of phases as a desirable design feature in single-case experiments.

The status of randomisation as an essential design feature, and thus hallmark of quality in single-case designs is debatable. Advocates, such as Kratochwill and Levin (2010), state that it can be used to reduce or eliminate two threats to internal validity (history and maturation). Others, coming from a behavioural tradition, take issue with this. For example, Wolery (2013), while acknowledging that randomisation has its uses in some circumstances (such as the implementation of alternating treatment designs), questions its ability to enhance internal validity *per se*. Indeed it is difficult to conceive how either history or maturation is experimentally controlled by the act of randomising the start of treatment phases. What randomisation *can* do is ensure that the decision to start treatment is not influenced by events associated with history or maturation, thereby reducing the likelihood of a possible experimental confound. What randomisation *cannot* do is influence the likelihood or presence of history events and maturation processes. On the other hand, the argument for randomising the start of treatment phases can be made when the design of the study explicitly includes an analysis based on a randomisation test. In this case randomisation will impose some constraints on the design. Before any data are collected the investigator must determine the minimum and maximum number of data points in the baseline phase. In an AB design, if the investigator wants to be able to detect an effect at $p < 0.05$ then there must be at least 20 possible start points for the intervention.

Perhaps it would be wise only to include randomisation as a hallmark of quality if there is an explicit statement that a randomisation test will be used as the chosen statistical analysis. The judgement as to whether or not randomisation adds to the quality of the design therefore depends upon the particular circumstances of each experiment.

Another issue with the use of such scales is deciding what constitutes a satisfactory analysis. The WWC Standards deal with this by stating that studies should report all the data so that they are available for visual analysis by experts within the WWC, i.e. they do not make a judgement as to the adequacy of the original analysis. In contrast, the RoBiNT scale requires assessors to make such a judgement. The point being made here is that given the plurality of visual and statistical analytic methods available, judgements about the quality of the reported analysis must be made in the context of the methodology employed in the original study. Thus studies relying on visual analysis might be required to document evidence of how that analysis was conducted. Similarly, studies employing statistical techniques should demonstrate that the necessary assumptions have been met.

It could be argued that, because the tradition in single-case research is to display all primary data in graphical format, high-quality graphs for each participant in the study ought to be considered as the 'gold standard'. Readers and reviewers are therefore given access to reanalyse the original data. Many of the techniques reported in Chapters 5 and 6 can be readily applied to good-quality published graphs, and digitising software makes it possible to recover data points with a high degree of accuracy and reliability (e.g. Shadish *et al.*, 2009).

The advantage of tools such as the WWC Standards and the RoBiNT scale is that they provide an explicit framework with which to evaluate single-case research studies. One merely needs to be mindful that their blanket application should be tempered by an understanding of the context of particular studies – for example, the requirement for randomisation should perhaps be restricted to studies where the statistical analysis relies on randomisation tests. Furthermore, the scales assume target variables that are measured by direct observation where inter-observer agreement can be demonstrated; they penalise studies that use self-report measures. Nevertheless, self-report is the only way of capturing many affective and cognitive variables of interest, and the essential feature of any item assessing a dependent variable is that its validity and reliability in the study are assessed. This raises challenges for those who wish to use subjective report (see Chapter 3).

EVALUATION OF A SINGLE CASE

As yet there is no overarching scale for assessment of the quality of an individual single-case study, but the study of one individual is likely to be the norm in clinical practice or as a training assignment. The following list is suggested as the minimum requirement for considering the quality of a study of a single individual:

1   Clear specification of the experimental design and the rationale for using it.
2   Clear definition and specification of the dependent variable(s) and evidence that its validity and reliability in this study have been assessed, i.e. it is insufficient to say that measure 'X' is valid and reliable.
3   Clear definition and description of the intervention: who conducted it; the number and timing of treatment sessions; and the attempts made to verify treatment integrity.
4   Sufficient data points in the baseline and intervention phases for the intended analysis, i.e. in visual analysis the detection of trend, variation, level, and in statistical analysis, sufficient data points for the power of the test.
5   There should be a plan of the intended data analysis and a report on who conducted it and how it was carried out.
6   The full data set should be produced in a high-quality graph or table.

These guidelines are offered so that students and clinicians can evaluate the quality of their own single-case research and consider the implications of their findings. Further guidelines for the consideration of individual case research are discussed below, where the approach of Elliott (2002) is described in detail.

In order to draw conclusions about more than one individual, as is the case when a planned series of experiments is performed in a research context, additional features such as selection (inclusion and exclusion) criteria should be available so that we can begin to assess the homogeneity of participants. This is particularly important if differences between participants affect the proposed relationship between the treatment and response. This is partly suggested in the RoBiNT scale, and certainly implied in the functional analysis approach in applied behavioural analysis. A further essential consideration for judging the interpretability of a series of single-cases is the guidelines on replicability between subjects. The WWC offers clear guidelines for this, but we must remember that the numbers cited (although determined by experts) are arbitrary and yet to be validated by the development of empirical methods, such as systematic review and meta-analytic techniques (see Chapter 7).

MAXIMISING THE POTENTIAL OF THE AB DESIGN

It is clear that most authorities do not regard the AB design as a 'true' experimental design – at best it is considered 'quasi-experimental' (see Tate *et al.*, 2016 for discussion). As such, it is a step up on the simple pre–post design discussed in Chapter 2. At the start of Chapter 4 we saw how additional data points collected during baseline and treatment can help us evaluate the stability of the dependent variable (outcome) and the possible relationship between the instantiation of treatment and response.

The question is how we should think about AB designs: are they to be discarded as a tool of clinical scientific enquiry? That would be unfortunate given that they are often the only option available to the curious clinician. For clinicians in training, the AB design offers an excellent introduction to thinking about interventions, outcomes and causality in specific cases.

Whereas experiments attempt to remove confounding influences by deliberately manipulating crucial factors, opportunistic clinical studies will not be able to meet strict experimental requirements. In many services, the length of baseline will not be within the clinician's control, and for many psychological therapy cases, designs including reversal will be both impractical and ethically problematic. However, AB designs with sufficient data (particularly at baseline) do allow for the client to act as their own control. Recall that the point of evaluation is to rule out as many plausible rival hypotheses as possible. This is a process of reasoning and judgement about confounds in clinical cases so that we can make a balanced summary statement about likely probability that there is a meaningful change in outcome and that it can be attributed to the treatment given. Such judgement can be achieved by careful data collection and scrutiny of a range of data, as discussed below.

Elliott's HSCED

Elliott's 2002 article outlines an approach to the evaluation of treatment causality in N = 1 studies of psychotherapy: the hermeneutic single-case efficacy design (HSCED). Elliott's focus is on the development of a convincing case that therapeutic processes are responsible for any change observed. This requires both building a good case that change has occurred and the consideration and ruling out of other explanations for the change (see Chapter 1). As well as emphasising the need for thoughtful and thorough collection of data in order to establish clear links between the process of therapy and outcome, he outlines eight competing explanations for change that need to be considered. The first four explanations assume that the observed change does not represent a clinical improvement: (1) *trivial or negative changes* on measurement, which can be evaluated using reliable and clinical change calculations; (2) *statistical artefacts*, such as measurement error or regression to mean, which can be evaluated through the use of multiple data points, use of different measures and calculation of reliable change; (3) *relational artefacts*, in which the client acts 'improved' in order to please the therapist. Elliott suggests that this be evaluated by careful assessment of specific changes in the client's experiences, as is the case with (4) *expectancy artefacts*, where the client's expectations have led to an apparent change. The second four explanations assume change has occurred, but that the causes of that change are not related to the therapy provided: (5) *self-correction*, where the improvement is caused by self-help and which can be evaluated by considering the client's perspective; (6) *life events*, which may have an interaction with therapy to lead to positive change; (7) *psychobiological factors*, such as a change in medication or illness state; and finally (8) the *reactive effects* of participating in research.

In considering these explanations, Elliott emphasises the need for a variety of data (both quantitative and qualitative) from different sources (i.e. therapist and client). To provide qualitative data on the process and outcome of therapy, he outlines the use of a 'change interview' to establish the participant's perspective and attributions regarding any changes.

In addition to the client's retrospective attributions regarding general and specific changes, Elliott emphasises the importance of establishing a clear link between the process and content of therapy and the outcome. He recommends careful process-outcome mapping; consideration of within-therapy process-outcome correlation (e.g. of treatment adherence and change); assessment of whether change in stable problems coincides with starting therapy; and the exploration of therapy event-shift sequences. These considerations entail the careful collection of relevant data throughout the course of therapy. Elliott rejects 'mechanistic data collection and analysis' and emphasises the complex task of the single-case researcher in weighing up convergent and contradictory evidence regarding change. This complexity seems likely to relate to the multiple causal factors involved in bringing about therapeutic change. His careful and thoughtful approach to the problems of establishing causal change in single-case studies provides clinician-researchers with an excellent model for collecting and considering data.

CONCLUSIONS

This chapter has introduced and discussed two evaluation tools for assessment of the quality of single-case research. Whilst these offer helpful ways to consider the quality of a published study, their usefulness to clinician-researchers is limited: both the WWC standards and the RoBiNT scale require standards that are impossible to meet in everyday practice. We have therefore suggested a list of criteria that can be more broadly applied to assess the quality of a single-case report, and which can be used to guide the planning of a single-case study. However, it is important to remind ourselves that no study is perfect and that the merits of each investigation need to be thought about in the context of the problem addressed and the constraints of the environment in which the study is carried out. Developing our understanding of critical appraisal will help us both to read others' research more thoughtfully and to plan our own research more thoroughly. Careful appraisal of the data, taking into account design, will allow us to consider the plausibility of casual explanations.

The AB design is often the only option available to clinicians, for whom implementation of experimental manipulation may be limited by service constraints. Elliott's HSCED brought a new perspective to single-case research, developing a thoughtful strategy for considering questions of psychotherapy efficacy within a therapeutic encounter. Furthermore, given the nature of the questions that are likely to be of interest to clinicians as outlined in Chapter 1 (Did the client improve? Was the treatment effective? Why did the patient improve? Will this treatment be of use to others?), this approach is likely to be of interest to many clinician-researchers. The HSCED approach, of thorough data collection and consideration of the client's perspective via a 'change interview', is also a useful reminder of the complexity of analysis and interpretation. Elliott's emphasis on the careful weighing up of evidence may help remind us to maintain our critical appraisal and healthy scepticism about our own therapeutic work and to maintain our professional interest in the production of practice-based evidence.

REFERENCES

Chambless, D. L. & Hollon, S. D. (1998). Defining empirically supported therapies. *Journal of Consulting and Clinical Psychology*, 66(1), 7.

Elliott, R. (2002). Hermeneutic single-case efficacy design. *Psychotherapy Research*, 12(1), 1–21.

Heyvaert, M., Wendt, O., Van den Noortgate, W. & Onghena, P. (2015). Randomization and data-analysis items in quality standards for single-case experimental studies. *The Journal of Special Education*, 49(3), 146–56.

Higgins, J. P. T., Altman, D. G., Gøtzsche, P. C., Jüni, P., Moher, D., Oxman, A.D. *et al.* (2011). The Cochrane Collaboration's tool for assessing risk of bias in randomised trials. *BMJ*, 343.

Howick, J. H. (2011). *The Philosophy of Evidence-based Medicine*. Chichester: John Wiley.

Kratochwill, T. R., Hitchcock, J., Horner, R., Levin, J., Odom, S. L., Rindskopf, D. & Shadish, W. R. (2010). Single-case technical documentation. Retrieved from *What Works Clearinghouse* website: http://ies.ed.gov/ncee/wwc/pdf/wwe_scd.pdf

Kratochwill, T. R., Hitchcock, J. H., Horner, R. H., Levin, J. R., Odom, S. L., Rindskopf, D. M. & Shadish, W. R. (2013). Single-case intervention research design standards. *Remedial and Special Education*, 34(1), 26–38.

Kratochwill, T. R. & Levin, J. R. (2010). Enhancing the scientific credibility of single-case intervention research: randomization to the rescue. *Psychological Methods*, 15(2), 124.

Schulz, K. F., Altman, D. G. & Moher, D. (2010). CONSORT 2010 statement: updated guidelines for reporting parallel group randomised trials. *BMC Medicine*, 8(1), 18.

Shadish, W. R., Brasil, I. C., Illingworth, D. A., White, K. D., Galindo, R., Nagler, E. D. & Rindskopf, D. M. (2009). Using UnGraph to extract data from image files: Verification of reliability and validity. *Behavior Research Methods*, 41(1), 177–83.

Tate, R.L, Mcdonald, S., Perdices, M., Togher, L., Schultz, R. & Savage, S. (2008). Rating the methodological quality of single-subject designs and n-of-1 trials: Introducing the Single-Case Experimental Design (SCED) Scale. *Neuropsychological Rehabilitation*, 18(4), 385–401.

Tate, R. L., Perdices, M., Rosenkoetter, U., Wakim, D., Godbee, K., Togher, L. & McDonald, S. (2013). Revision of a method quality rating scale for single-case experimental designs and n-of-1 trials: The 15-item Risk of Bias in N-of-1 Trials (RoBiNT) Scale. *Neuropsychological Rehabilitation*, 23(5), 619–38.

Tate, R. L., Perdices, M., Rosenkoetter, U., Shadish, W., Vohra, S., Barlow, D. H., . . . Wilson, B. (2016). The single-case reporting guideline in Behavioural interventions (SCRIBE) 2016 statement. *Archives of Scientific Psychology*, 4(1), 1–9.

Vohra, S., Shamseer, L., Sampson, M., Bukutu, C., Schmid, C. H., Tate, R. *et al.* (2016). CONSORT extension for reporting N-of-1 trials (CENT) 2015 Statement. *Journal of Clinical Epidemiology*, 76, 9–17.

Wolery, M. (2013). A commentary: Single-case design technical document of the What Works Clearinghouse. *Remedial and Special Education*, 34(1), 39–43.

Afterword

Chris Main and Ciara Masterson

The focus of this book is on single-case designs; an approach to clinical evaluation and research that is suited particularly to investigate individual variability in response to treatment but which, to date, has received insufficient attention. The book identifies the single case as a potentially rich source of learning for curious clinicians and endeavours to promote single-case methodology, not only in the development of critical understanding and interpretation of data, but also in the design of clinical interventions.

As a precursor to a number of conclusions, we should like to summarise the content of the previous eight chapters.

Chapter 1 introduced the argument for considering single-case methods as a valid research strategy within the context of the dominance of the randomised controlled trial and 'big' data. In single-case research, quantitative data are drawn from systematic planned observations and this chapter introduced the essential concept of validity, including methods for selecting and tailoring measures and strategies for data analysis.

Chapter 2 discussed the use of standardised measures and highlights the advantages of such measures in the study of single cases. The Reliable Change Index and Clinically Significant Change criteria were introduced, and their calculation and application illustrated. The chapter ends with guidance on how to perform a meta-analysis of data sets in order to produce usable norms for a clinical setting.

Chapter 3 focused on the concept of validity in measurement and identifies criterion validity as central to the assessment of clinical problems. Several types of idiographic measures were discussed, along with the advantages of personal questionnaire methodology. The importance of reliability in idiographic measures is highlighted, and methods for obtaining reliable observations are given.

Chapter 4 reviewed the major types of single-case designs. There are particular challenges in the identification of change and attribution of causality, and therefore in considering design the critical importance of the timing of measurement is highlighted. Single-case design factors (such as establishing the stabilty of baseline) were considered in both clinical and research contexts.

Chapter 5 contained discussion of the historical origins of graphic (visual) analysis and its comparison with statistical approaches. The benefits of exploratory data analysis were discussed alongside techniques for systematic exploration. The chapter recommends the use of simple graphic techniques, complemented where appropriate by computerised programmes specifically designed for data exploration.

Chapter 6 reviewed options for statistical data analysis in single-case research, focusing on the non-overlap statistics based on semi-graphical methods and tests based on randomisation principles. Methods were illustrated with worked examples, and available resources for running the analyses were identified.

Chapter 7 tackled the differences between single-case research carried out in different contexts and how a body of single-case research can be examined using narrative or meta-analytic reviews. The essence and value of replication was discussed, particularly in treatment evaluation and development.

Chapter 8 focused on the critical evaluation of single cases. Tools to assess published research were reviewed, not only to encourage critical appraisal but also to encourage clinician-researchers to develop good quality studies. The chapter emphasised the value of Elliott's hermeneutic single-case efficacy design, which is considered to be particularly useful to students when preparing case studies.

In conclusion, the purpose of this textbook has been to re-energise interest in single-case methodology. It has been argued that single-case design offers a way of illuminating the process of change which traditional grouped analyses do not. In health care research there have been significant advances in our understanding of the interactions between personal characteristics and the nature of illness, but the nature of the underlying mechanisms of change is insufficiently understood. Only relatively recently has the importance of identifying the influence of *moderators* of treatment (concerned primarily with the influence of context and the characteristics of people who present for treatment) and *mediators* of treatment response (i.e. the determinants of change in response to our interventions). Even then, somewhat speculative inferences are sometimes drawn about influences on behaviour change or symptomatic relief, since there is insufficient knowledge about determinants of change in the particular individual with whom we are concerned.

The single-case method is first and foremost the 'science of the individual'. It is carefully grounded in the analysis of change over time, uses multiple and relevant measurement and is flexible in design and application. It harnesses the power of visual analysis which, in addition to appropriate statistical analysis, allows us to carefully explore the interface between the individual and his/her environment. This allows us to design interventions that are highly responsive to specific influences on individuals' problems and their responses to treatment. Replications and adaptations can then safely be developed in the light of increasing knowledge about the moderators and mediators of treatment response. As such, single-case methods offer an illuminating, powerful and flexible application of scientific methodology to clinical practice. Hopefully this textbook will serve as a guide to those who wish to offer the most effective psychological treatments possible and as encouragement to improve the understanding of, and effectiveness of, our interventions.

Index